Walki
Melbourne

MELBOURNE

Station Pier
PORT MELBOURNE
WEST GATE FWY
Footscra
PORT PHILLIP
Bay St
Spencer S
SOUTH MELBOURNE
CITY RD
Kerferd Rd Pier
Kerferd Rd
BEACONS FIELD PDE
MIDDLE PARK
Albert Rd
Canterbury Rd
Kings Way
Albert Park Lake
St Kilda Pier
Kings Domain
QUEENS RD
Royal Botanical Gardens
YARRA RIVER
ST KILDA
FITZROY ST
ST KILDA RD
Fawkner Park
PUNT RD
Commercial
PRAHRAN
Chapel St
Church St
DANDENONG RD
High St
Malvern Rd
Toorak Rd
Hotham St
Williams Rd
Burnley St

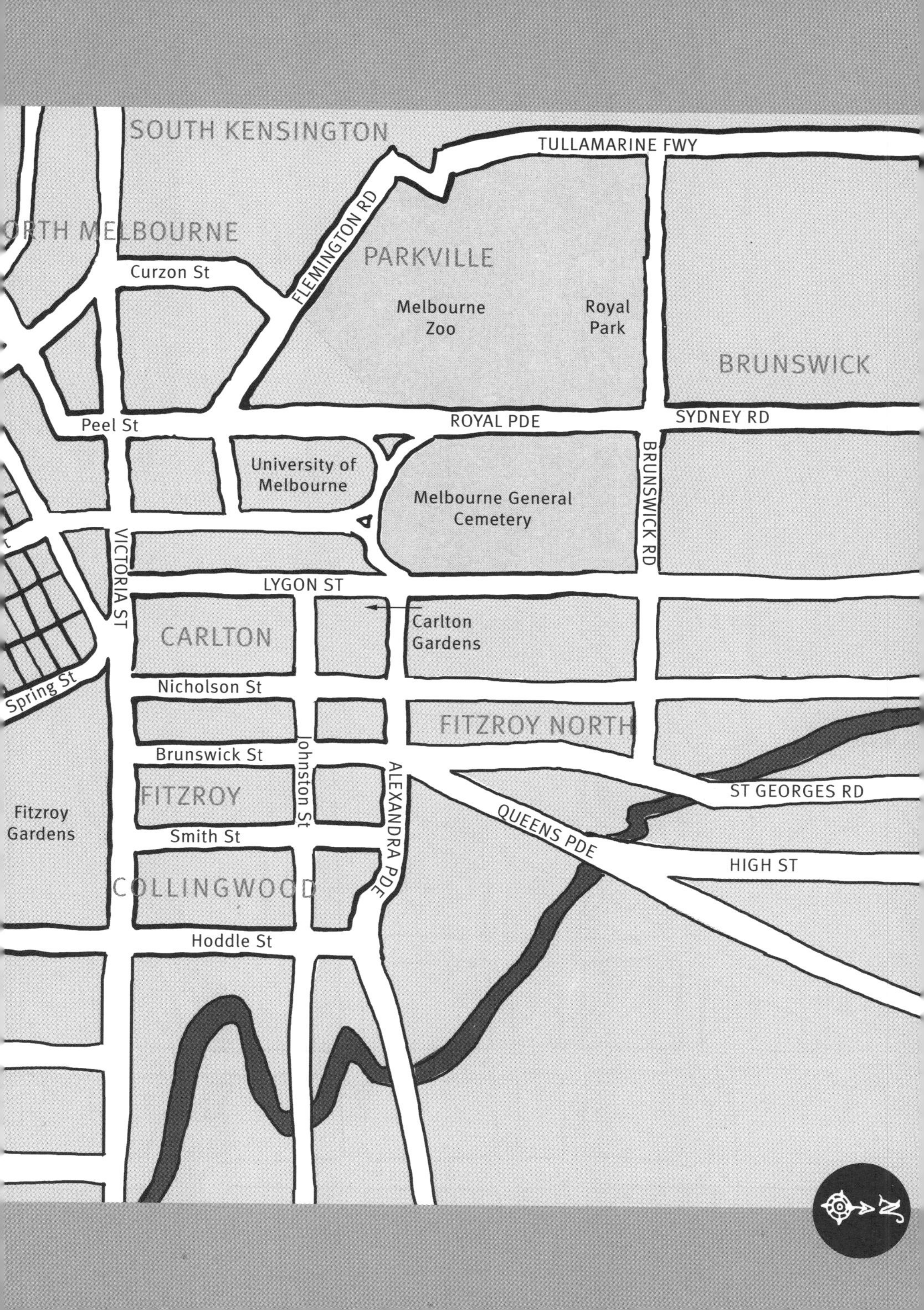
SOUTH KENSINGTON
TULLAMARINE FWY
FLEMINGTON RD
ORTH MELBOURNE
PARKVILLE
Curzon St
Melbourne
Zoo
Royal
Park
BRUNSWICK
Peel St
ROYAL PDE
SYDNEY RD
University of
Melbourne
Melbourne General
Cemetery
BRUNSWICK RD
VICTORIA ST
LYGON ST
CARLTON
Carlton
Gardens
Spring St
Nicholson St
FITZROY NORTH
Brunswick St
Johnston St
ALEXANDRA PDE
FITZROY
ST GEORGES RD
QUEENS PDE
Fitzroy
Gardens
Smith St
HIGH ST
COLLINGWOOD
Hoddle St

Walking Melbourne

HELEN DUFFY AND INGRID OHLSSON

First published in Australia in 1999 by
New Holland Publishers (Australia) Pty Ltd
Sydney • Auckland • London • Cape Town

14 Aquatic Drive Frenchs Forest NSW 2086 Australia
1A/218 Lake Road Northcote Auckland New Zealand
24 Nutford Place London W1H 6DQ United Kingdom
80 McKenzie Street Cape Town 8001 South Africa

National Library of Australia
Cataloguing-in-publication data:
Duffy, Helen.
Walking Melbourne.
Bibliography.
Includes index.
ISBN 1 86436 335 5.
1. Walking - Victoria - Melbourne - Guidebooks.
2. Melbourne (Vic.) - Guidebooks. I. Ohlsson, Ingird. II. Title.
919.45104

Designer: Peta Nugent
Project Coordinator: Julie Nekich
Editors: Neil Conning and Julie Nekich
Artwork: Mitch Vane
Layout: Stephanie Cannon and Black Dog Books
Printer: Times Offset, Malaysia

Contents

Acknowledgements

The authors wish to thank the people and institutions who provided information for this book. In addition to the historical societies (the staff and the local history publications they produce), grateful acknowledgement is given to the Local History Collection of the Port Melbourne Branch Library, the Main Catalogue Collection of the University of Ballarat and the Yarra–Melbourne Regional Library.

The following people deserve special mention: Craig Albiston of the Albert Park office of Parks Victoria; Fraser Faithfull, archivist for the Good Shepherd Provincialate, for the information on the Good Shepherd Convent (Our Lady of Mount Carmel); Nick Jensen of the Danish Club; Paul Macgregor of the Chinese Museum, for his answers to many questions on Chinatown; the staff of the Melbourne General Cemetery; Paul Osmond, Design Projects Officer for the City of Port Phillip; the staff of Pellegrinis cafe; Andrew Robertson of Hill of Content; Celestina Segazio of the National Trust of Victoria, for the provision of materials on Melbourne General Cemetery and help with innumerable queries; Noela Steward of Marchetti's Latin and the Jewel Group for information on early Melbourne restaurants; and Ron Webber of Esso Australia Limited.

Particular thanks to A.J. Ohlsson for his research on the history of Melbourne; Dianne Campbell for her research on local shire histories, and Laura Zimmerman for her help with preparation of parts of the early manuscript. Finally, special thanks to Faruk Avdi for his ideas on the best way to walk Melbourne's northern suburbs, his invaluable assistance with research and compilation of the walks in these areas, and his editorial eye.

Introduction

Melbourne is a city made for walkers. In the city centre, the wide streets create the impression of a pleasantly open, ordered and spacious place, while a busy network of back lanes and alleys provides a shadowy and slightly chaotic counterbalance. The traffic, by no means light, is generally manageable, and rules and conditions tend to favour pedestrians. Navigation, even for the most directionally challenged, should present no problems at all. This is, after all, the city of the famous grid – straight up and down and across and no arguments about it. The attractions are many and varied, ranging from the stately monoliths of the Victorian era, the famous Gothic Revival churches, state-of-the-art postmodernist giants, a grand avenue – flanked by monuments – leading into the city centre, a cosmopolitan riverside precinct, restaurants bearing international reputations, and a network of bookshops second to none. There are plenty of places to stop for coffee and lunch, and the many formal parks and gardens on the city's outskirts, gems of Victorian botanical design, offer respite from the hub of the inner metropolis.

If the city is the heart of Melbourne, then the inner suburbs are its soul. The intense, compact suburbs on the immediate outskirts offer a window into working and middle-class life of early Melbourne, and represent some of the most intact domestic Victorian streetscapes anywhere. They are also Melbourne's vital cultural pockets, full of cafes, galleries, theatres and interesting street life. You can choose Brunswick multiculturalism, the bohemianism of Fitzroy and Prahran, or the Roman Italian recreation of Lygon Street – 'Little Italy' as it is known. A quieter tone is offered by the traditionally more upmarket suburbs of East Melbourne and Parkville, the latter also the site of the historic and architecturally interesting University of Melbourne and Melbourne General Cemetery.

Further away, St Kilda is in a class of its own, a 19th-century resort atmosphere crossed with strong evidence of an upbeat modern style, and buildings and streets that could slot into any category in between. Here is the chance to explore the calm foreshores of the bay via promenades and piers, or the architecturally eclectic leafy streets of Melbourne's favourite seaside suburb.

Trams are the recommended mode of transport, and no walk included here is more than a 20-minute ride from the city. A transport information booth is at Flinders Street Station where you can pick up timetables and a map of the network. For telephone information on routes and tram numbers call Met Information on 131 638. For maps and brochures drop in to the Visitor Information Centre in the Town Hall, Swanston Street, or call 9658 9955.

Despite the negative press, Melbourne weather is really not that bad. There are a few dreadful days at the height of both summer and winter, but temperatures are generally mild, and the rain, of which there is a fair amount, tends to fall in short bursts. As long as you take an umbrella and find a good cafe for shelter, you should have no problems. Spring and autumn are the favoured seasons for viewing the city's famous gardens, riverside parklands, ornamental lakes and landscaped streets. Wear a hat against the sun at all times and carry a bottle of water in warmer weather.

These walks are suitable for all levels of fitness. Melbourne has few steep hills, and where they exist, such as the gentle rise of the city centre, the walks tend to start at the top and head down. Use the information at the beginning of each walk to judge time and distance, and remember to add time if you are going to call in to the visitor attractions mentioned on many of the walks. Most of all, enjoy your walking hours in this most walkable of cities.

Melbourne's History

The British government made two attempts to settle the Port Phillip district before 1830: at Sorrento in 1803, and near Corinella on the shores of Western Port in 1826. The idea was to stop other European powers occupying the south-east corner of New Holland, but both settlements failed because of poor soil and lack of water.

In May 1835 John Batman crossed Bass Strait from Van Diemen's Land (later Tasmania) in search of grazing country. He 'bought' 600,000 acres from the Aboriginal people and found 'the place for a village' on the banks of the Yarra River. Three months later, John Pascoe Fawkner's party arrived from Launceston and built a hut below Yarra Falls. A cluster of wattle and daub huts with earthen floors developed around it, serving as a 'head station' for the squatters occupying grazing land to the north and west of Port Phillip.

The pastoral age

The great pastoral boom of the late 1830s fuelled Melbourne's astonishing growth as a port for the wool trade. Squatters swarmed in from Van Diemen's Land and the United Kingdom, especially Scotland. Government-assisted migrants from the British Isles worked as tradesmen, servants and labourers for the growing town, and shepherds for the sheep runs.

Government at Port Phillip began in September 1836 when a police magistrate arrived from Sydney. When the governor of New South Wales visited in March 1837, he named the town of Melbourne in honour of the British prime minister. The surveyor Robert Hoddle laid out a town with wide streets on a grid, a mile long and three-quarters of a mile wide.

In 1839 the government in Sydney appointed Charles La Trobe as the district's first superintendent. Melbourne's subsequent growth overwhelmed the financial and administrative resources of the New South Wales government. In 1841 the town could not supply even basic services for its 6,000 residents. The water supply from the Yarra River became contaminated, causing many deaths, particularly among children.

Golden dreams

The campaign for separation from New South Wales culminated in the creation of the Colony of Victoria on 1 July 1851. Melbourne had a population of 39,000. The gold rush began a few weeks later. During the 1860s, Melbourne's population increased five-fold, far outstripping that of Sydney.

Public and private revenues from gold and wool transformed the city. Buildings of 'time-defying solidity', many of bluestone, replaced weatherboard and corrugated iron shanties. Parliament House, the Treasury, the Public Library, Melbourne Grammar, Victoria Barracks, a new Melbourne Club and the Wesley Church were just some of the buildings to give Melbourne its Victorian character, still evident today.

The well-to-do began moving to the rural seclusion of Kew, Richmond, South Yarra and Hawthorn. The Municipal Act of 1854 extended local government to these rapidly growing suburbs. Melbourne's first railway line, from the city to Sandridge (Port Melbourne), was completed in 1854. By 1861 trains were bringing commuters to the city from St Kilda, Richmond, Hawthorn, Prahran, Brighton and Williamstown.

'Marvellous Melbourne'

By 1880 Melbourne had become the financial and commercial centre of the Australian colonies. The city's population of 206, 780 in 1871 was concentrated in the inner suburbs. As gold petered out, private investors moved into manufacturing, commerce and real estate. Protected by tariffs, factories making clothes, footwear, machinery, coaches and furniture grew around Collingwood and Clifton Hill and by 1890 Melbourne boasted 3,000 large factories. The government raised loans in London to build railways, public buildings and port facilities for the booming rural export trade.

Chinese migrants from the goldfields crammed into the lanes off Little Bourke Street. While Chinatown's numbers were never large – about 500 in 1880 – its shops, furniture workshops, joss houses and opium and gambling dens made it the city's most exotic quarter.

The Exhibition Building, completed in 1880 to host the International Exhibition, symbolised the new decade. Pastoralists, merchants and speculators built mansions in St Kilda, Kew, Toorak, Hawthorn and Parkville in an Italianate Renaissance style, with occasional forays into Gothic and Baronial Baroque. Conservatories, ballrooms, picture galleries, square towers and flagpoles were de rigueur. The new Government House (1870s), modelled on Osborne House on the Isle of Wight, is the best example of Melbourne's grand mansions.

The middle classes, who preferred living close to the city, settled into rows of bluestone or brick terraces with filigreed cast-iron balconies in Carlton, Parkville, East Melbourne and Albert Park. Workers lived in tiny wooden or brick cottages in the old suburbs north of the river. By 1891, Melbourne's population had grown to nearly half a million.

Nightmares

Early in the 1890s, falling prices for wool, silver and other commodities, industrial unrest and the collapse of the building industry ushered in a decade of depression. One after another Melbourne's banks closed their doors. Thousands of people left the city for Western Australia or New South Wales. With no social security, many of those who remained had to depend on charity. The colonial government had little money for public works but improvements to parks and roads offered relief work at the local government level.

The new federal parliament opened in the Exhibition Building on 9 May 1901. Sittings were held from then on in the Victorian Parliament House in Spring Street and Melbourne served as the national capital until 1927. Commonwealth money contributed to economic recovery. The construction of Flinders Street Station, the National Museum and a new Melbourne Hospital were the most notable new buildings of the Edwardian era.

About 8,000 Melbourne men died in the First World War of 1914–18. On the home front, there were shortages and bitter divsions over conscription. Industry grew to fill gaps left by shortfalls of British imports and many women joined the workforce. With peace came the great influenza epidemic of 1919. Schools, theatres and churches were closed. The Exhibition Building served as an emergency hospital.

The Jazz Age of the 1920s barely touched Melbourne. Industrial strife, including a police strike in 1923, fears of Bolshevism and sectarian bitterness marred a decade of patchy prosperity. Manufacturing, helped by tariffs and the cheapest power in the country generated by the State Electricity Commission, grew steadily. Much of the city was rebuilt with multi-storey office blocks. The arrival of the motor car gave renewed impetus to the suburban sprawl.

Melbourne's population reached one million during the depressed 1930s. Unemployment in 1932 was 30 per cent. Some left the city for itinerant jobs in the bush. Many 19th-century mansions became private hospitals, boarding houses or schools. During this decade, sport and Hollywood movies flourished.

War from 1939 to 1945 solved the unemployment crisis as Melbourne's industry turned to war production. Melbourne became Allied headquarters for the south-west Pacific and a military base for American troops. American dollars sustained a flourishing black market.

Multicultural Melbourne

Melbourne in 1950, with a population of just over a million, was a city of survivors. In just over 30 years the predominantly southwest Pacific and a military base for American troops. American dollars sustained a flourishing black market.

Multicultural Melbourne

Melbourne in 1950, with a population of just over a million, was a city of survivors. In just over 30 years the predominantly Anglo-Celtic population had been through two world wars and a depression. The post-war boom brought prosperity to those with steady jobs. With the sale of alcohol severely restricted and most forms of gambling outlawed, a Saturday afternoon at the Australian Rules football matches gave meaning to many a Melburnian's life.

The arrival of hundreds of thousands of Italian, Greek and other European migrants eroded Melbourne's cultural insularity. The advent of television and the staging of the Olympic Games, both in 1956, brought the world to Melbourne. With tariff assistance, the car industry at Fishermans Bend grew rapidly. The 'new Australians' – as they were called – worked on assembly lines in footwear and clothing factories, and on the building sites that transformed the city and pushed the suburbs more than 30 kilometres from Flinders Station. The 1970s and 1980s brought new waves of immigrants from Turkey, Lebanon, South America and Asia. Many Asian immigrants were war refugees from Vietnam. A few were wealthy Chinese 'business' immigrants from Hong Kong and Singapore. Their capital transformed Chinatown, particularly its restaurants, into a tourist attraction. Middle Eastern immigrants made Brunswick their home. The Vietnamese transformed Victoria Street in Richmond.

Today Melbourne has relinquished its position as Australia's largest city and centre of commerce, but still has a third of the country's manufacturing. It may not have Sydney's harbour and glitz but its lifestyle is more gracious and affordable. The range and standard of Melbourne's restaurants are among the best in the world. The survival of many 19th-century buildings and its trams and parks give Melbourne a European aura fast disappearing elsewhere in Australia.

Key to Maps

 Hospital

 Church

 Parks and gardens

 Information

 Parking

 Post office

 Gallery

 Public toilets

 Railway station

 Train or light rail line

Route Marks

- route of walk
- 7 key numbers
- S walk start
- F walk finish

An easy-to-follow illustrative map accompanies each walk. The walk route is clearly marked in green; buildings and sites are dark blue; parks and gardens are green; and 'general' areas are shaded light blue.

On each map the walk route begins at the point S and finishes at F. Key numbers are located on the map as well as in the walk text. The Key to Maps, left, displays full details of symbols that appear on the maps in order to assist the walker.

Walks in Order of Length

Historic Collins Street | 2km
City Sights | 2km
University of Melbourne | 2km
Melbourne General Cemetery | 2km
Fitzroy | 2km
Richmond | 2.4km
Law, Learning & Labour | 2.5km
Parliament Precinct & Eastern Hill | 2.5km
Carlton | 3.5km
St Kilda Bayside Precinct | 3km
South Parkville & Melbourne Zoo | 3.5km
Brunswick | 3.5 km
Kings Domain | 3.5km
Chapel Street Precinct | 4km
Bookshops Old & New | 4.5km
Yarra River West | 4.5km
Yarra River East | 4.5km
Station Pier to St Kilda Pier | 4.6km
CBD Gourmet Tour | 5km
Fitzroy Gardens & East Melbourne | 2.5km
St Kilda Road | 5km
Albert Park Lake | 5km

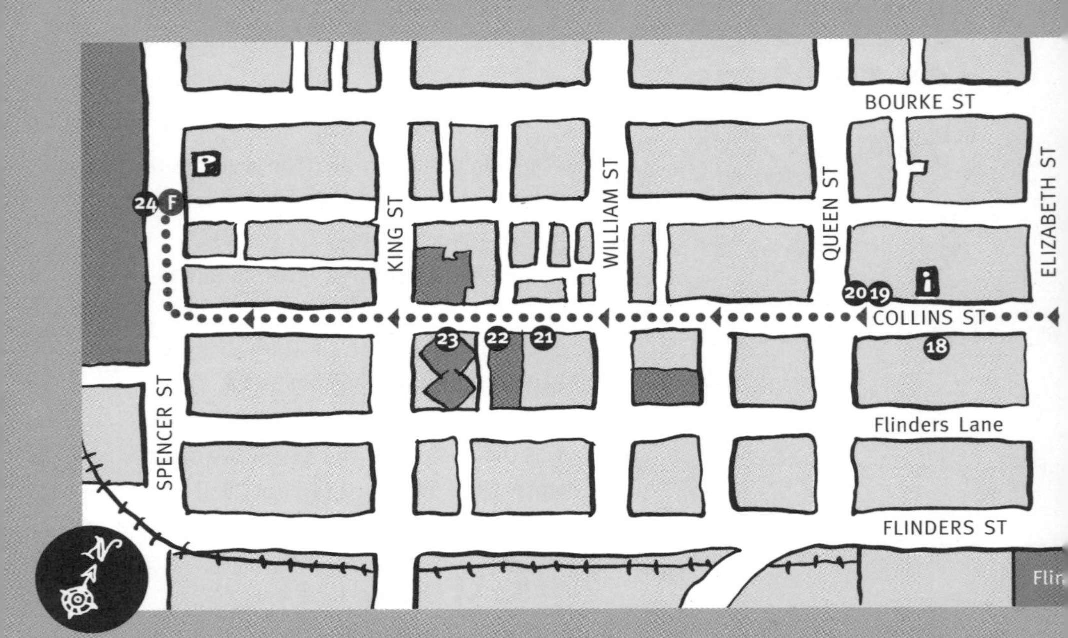

Walk key

1. 1 Collins Street | **2.** Alcaston House | **3.** Hotel Sofitel | **4.** Melbourne Club | **5.** St Michael's Uniting Church | **6.** Athenaeum Club | **7.** 101 Collins Street | **8.** Grand Hyatt | **9.** Alexandra Club | **10.** Scots Church | **11.** T&G Building | **12.** Georges | **13.** Baptist Church | **14.** Athenaeum Theatre | **15.** Regent Theatre | **16.** Burke and Wills statue | **17.** Block Arcade | **18.** 333 Collins Street | **19.** Old Stock Exchange Building | **20.** Gothic bank building | **21.** Olderfleet Buildings | **22.** Le Meridien at the Rialto | **23.** Rialto Towers | **24.** Spencer Street Station

Start

South-east corner of Collins Street. Parliament Station – trams 11, 12, 42, 86, 96, 109, City Circle tram.

Finish

Corner Collins and Spencer streets. Spencer Street Station – trams 11, 12, 42, 48, 75, 86, 96, 109, City Circle tram.

Length/Time

2 km/2.5 hours

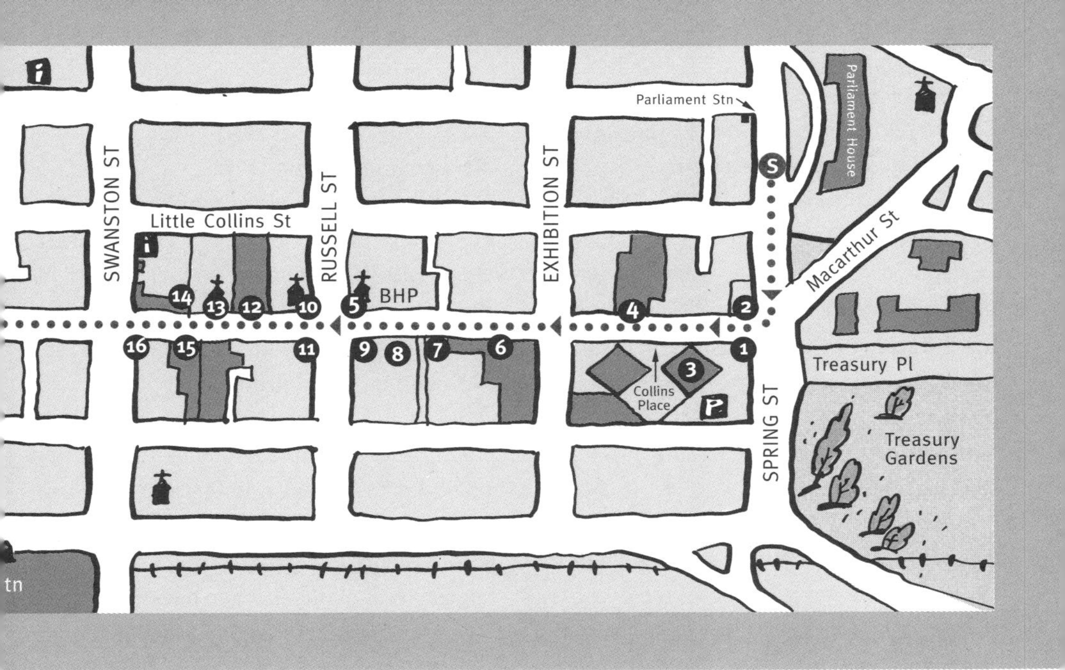

Walk No. 1

Historic Collins Street

Glorious architecture from Victorian times

No other city in Australia can equal the Victorian splendour of Melbourne's 19th-century buildings, a result of the great wealth that flowed into the capital's coffers following the gold rushes of the 1850s. And no other street in the city exemplifies the height of Victorian splendour more than Collins Street. Although many old buildings were demolished in the decades following the Second World War, a surprising number remain. This walk takes you through the leafy 'Paris end' of Collins Street with its exclusive shops and clubs, past churches, theatres and the imposing town hall, on past shopping arcades and finally to the banking and financial district.

Collins Street was named after Captain David Collins, who attempted the first settlement of the Port Phillip district in 1803. With a party of convicts he landed at Sorrento on the south-eastern rim of the bay and set up camp. Problems plagued the group from the start and Collins abandoned the site some three months later. It was to be another 20 years before prospective settlers looked favourably on these tea-tree lined shores.

In the first few decades of the colony, the west end of Collins Street was the heart of town and the most sought-after address. William Street sloped down to the turning basin and busy port area. The first land to be sold was at the corner of Collins and William streets in 1837 – here John Batman built a two-storey residence. Slightly further east in Collins Street, between William and Queen streets, was the renowned Lamb Inn. Several of Melbourne's first men's clubs – in particular the Melbourne Club – were founded within its walls. Across the road from the Inn colonists built the first gaol and unruly drunks were placed in the stocks nearby.

Elizabeth Street was at the bottom of a hill and after heavy rains the road turned into a rushing stream of water, making transport impossible. The eastern end of Collins Street rose sharply from this boggy track and early colonists complained of the inherent dangers of negotiating the steep incline in order to attend church services at the Baptist, Scots or Independent churches half-way up the hill. In 1849 part of the slope was blasted away to reduce the steepness of the gradient.

The settlement grew rapidly after the gold discoveries in 1851, and Collins Street along with it. The street was lit by gas in 1854 and in the 1860s horse-drawn trams transported citizens along its length. Electric lighting was introduced in 1882 and cable trams in 1886. The Collins Street tram line extended out to Richmond. By the 1880s Collins Street was the graceful thoroughfare depicted so often in old photographs, with the 'softly tinted shades of English trees' lining its wide pavements.

As you walk along Collins Street it is possible to imagine what it must have been like during the land boom years of the 1880s. Space does not permit a discussion of all the buildings – we have chosen the most historically significant (excluding those discussed elsewhere in this book). Keep in mind that the buildings on the south side have odd numbers while those on the north side have even numbers.

Spring Street to Exhibition Street

In the second half of the 19th century the eastern end of Collins Street became the abode of the wealthy and professional classes. Medical practitioners built fashionable town houses that incorporated consulting rooms and surgeries; the Melbourne Club commissioned architect Leonard Terry to design a suitable home for its expanding membership; and successful artists set up studios.

Among these, the talented photographer J.W. Lindt was to be found at No. 7 from 1877 to 1883, and the sculptor John MacKennal had a studio near the corner. Painters John Mather and Julian Ashton worked in premises opposite on the north side.

The house on the south-eastern corner of Collins Street, actually 61 Spring Street, was built in 1870 for pastoralist, politician and financier William Campbell (1810–96). Born in Scotland, Campbell arrived in Sydney in 1838 and worked for a time on a property in the Blue Mountains belonging to John Macarthur. In about 1845 he brought the first Camden merino sheep overland to the Port Phillip District, and in the ensuing years rose to become one of Australia's richest pastoralists. As a politician he worked to preserve the interests of the squattocracy, and even kept secret his early discovery in mid-1850 of gold at Clunes, fearful that mining would adversely affect pastoral lands. Campbell employed the Yorkshire-born architect Leonard Terry to design his town house. English flower painter Marianne North was a guest here in 1880, remarking on the 'beautiful marble staircase'. The house had 15 bedrooms, and a dining room and drawing room each 11 metres long. To help the Campbells' invalid daughter, a lift was installed, powered by water. The huge windows had double sashes for insulation against the cold of winter and the heat of summer, as well as the noisy clatter of passing carriages. William Campbell returned to England in 1882. During the First World War

Opening Times

Melbourne Town Hall: Free guided tours are available Tue, Wed & Thurs, 10.30am & 2.30pm, and on third Sat of each month, 10am–3pm hourly (9658 9658).

Regent Theatre: Tours Tue & Thurs 10am–12 noon (9820 0239).

Block Arcade: Tours Tue (9650 2777) and Thurs 1pm (9654 5244).

ANZ Banking Museum: Mon–Fri 9.30am–4pm (9273 5555).

Rialto Towers Observation Deck: Mon–Fri, 10am–10pm, Fri–Sat 10am–11pm.

Refreshments

There are numerous eateries along Collins Street. Our favourite is **Il Solito Posto** (9654 4466), which is tucked away in George Parade, a tiny lane beside the Grand Hyatt.

the house was a meeting place for the Australian War Cabinet.

The terrace houses at **1 Collins Street |1|,** adjoining the corner residence, are of later construction, dating from 1884 and 1888. The deeply recessed verandahs feature beautiful old lights, visible below the colonnaded arches. The corner house and terrace were threatened with demolition in the 1970s, but were thankfully preserved and incorporated into a new development in 1984. The resulting building that rises behind the corner facades is a successful blend of old and new. It was designed by Robert Peck YFHK and Denton Corker Marshall. The narrow three-storey Grosvenor Chambers at No. 9 was built as apartments and artist studios.

On the opposite side of the street, at No. 2, is **Alcaston House |2|,** designed in 1929 by A.&K. Henderson. Built as apartments in Renaissance Revival style, it now includes the Contemporary Aboriginal Art Gallery and Alcaston House Gallery. Next door is Anzac House, built in 1938–39 for the Victorian branch of the Returned Sailors', Soldiers' and Airmen's Imperial League of Australia. The reinforced concrete building, faced in sandstone, was designed by Stanley Parkes.

Portland House at Nos. 8–10 helps you to visualise the 19th-century residential streetscape. Designed by Lloyd Tayler as a town house and surgery, it was built in 1872 by merchant, politician and financier Henry Miller for his daughter and her husband, Dr Aubrey Brown. Miller (1809–88), an Irish immigrant, was a great opportunist and brilliant investor, so dedicated to amassing wealth that he was dubbed 'Money Miller'. The lovely three-storey facade is festooned with ivy, further preserving the memory of its once residential status. No. 12, Victor Horsley Chambers, dates from 1924 and provides an excellent example of the Georgian Revival style. It was designed by Blackett & Forster as an investment office building for Victor Horsley of Horsley & Evans Costume Manufacturers. Today doctors' brass plaques adorn the entrance.

Stretching almost the entire length of the southern side of the Spring Street to Russell Street block are the twin towers of Collins Place, incorporating the **Hotel Sofitel |3|.** Between the towers an atrium houses an array of shops on the ground level and a food court on the lower ground level.

Across the road, at No. 36, is the **Melbourne Club |4|,** the fourth home of this city institution. It was founded in 1838 by a group of officers and other prominent colonial gentlemen – 27 in number. After purchasing the site of the present-day building in 1858, the Club commissioned architect Leonard Terry, who had established a fine reputation since his arrival in Melbourne in 1853. Completed in 1859, the three-storey brick and stucco building is Italian Renaissance in style, and was based on the West End clubs of London. Additional land was purchased in 1883 and the west wing, featuring bay windows on two floors, was designed by Terry & Oakden. The new section housed the impressive dining room on the ground floor, while above was a library and an extension of bedroom accommodation to 38 rooms. At the rear of the building a verandah stretches along the length of a private garden courtyard, where huge plane trees offer shade and high walls provide seclusion. Here members could relax on a sunny day, perhaps after imbibing a bottle or two of Chateau Lafitte, their favoured wine.

Today the Melbourne Club is one of the last male strongholds, withstanding challenges to its right to accept only men as members. In mid-1998 the Club bought the adjoining property, Melville House, fearful that its purchase by others could end forever the privacy enjoyed by the Club's rear garden. This beautifully proportioned terrace pair was created in 1881 for Dr Robert Ray by extensively altering an 1850s brick house. Each terrace offered house and surgery to a single practitioner. In 1989 the front portions of these buildings were renovated and incorporated into a new and impressive office building.

Exhibition Street to Russell Street

No. 70 Collins Street, on the north-west corner of the intersection, is an elegantly proportioned three-storey building erected in 1867 for Dr John Wilkins as a residence and consulting rooms. Again you get a window into the past, offering a view of the town houses that once graced this fashionable street. Next door is one of the oldest remaining houses in Melbourne, a tiny Georgian style remnant dating from 1855 and now with distinctive copper surrounds to the door and entrance.

The square exterior of St Michael's Church belies its circular interior spaces.

A little further down, Nos. 86–88 are two surviving terrace houses occupied by exclusive shops. Once a triple-fronted terrace designed by James Gall in 1873 for Dr Robert Martin, a little of the early splendour can be seen in the fine tile work still remaining at the entrances. Cross over Alfred Place to the BHP Petroleum building, which incorporates Professional Chambers, all red brick and moulded plasterwork, built in 1908 as offices for the Independent

Church (St Michael's). The design, by architect Beverley Ussher, displays the mediaeval influences often present in the Federation style. BHP Petroleum added two modern wings at either end of the building.

On the north-eastern Collins–Russell street corner is **St Michael's Uniting Church |5|**, formerly the Independent Church and long a Melbourne landmark with its distinctive polychrome brickwork. Designed by Reed & Barnes and built in 1866–67, it is characterised by a reassuring solidity rather than the commonly displayed elegance of slender lofty spires seen in other 19th-century churches. At street level is a rambling garden and steep steps leading up to the corner entrance. The circular theatre-like interior features superb stained glass windows, designed and made by Klaus Zimmer in 1988 to celebrate Australia's Bicentenary and the 150th anniversary of the church. Melbourne's first permanent church was built on this site in 1839 for the Independents, who prior to this held services in John Pascoe Fawkner's tavern at the other end of town. It was Fawkner who called the church members to their first service in the newly established colony.

On the south side of this block is Harley House, at Nos. 71–73 on the Exhibition Street corner, now housing the National Bank. It was designed in Classical Revival style by Sidney Smith Ogg & Serpell in 1923 and built for medical practitioners. The owner was Dr Gengoult Smith, Lord Mayor of Melbourne 1931–34. The facade displays Greek, Roman and Egyptian motifs.

The five-storey cream building at Nos. 83–87, with fashionable shops at street level, has been home to the **Athenaeum Club |6|** since 1929. It displays an elegant Classical design by Cedric H. Ballantyne. Founded in 1868, the Club first met in the Athenaeum Theatre and later in Block Court (which is further down Collins Street).

In the midst of 19th-century Victoriana is the magnificent edifice of **101 Collins Street |7|**, housing the offices of some of the state's largest companies. A four-storey black marble facade fronts the street, while set back is a high-rise glass tower, competing with the copper-coloured glass of the nearby **Grand Hyatt |8|.**

On the Russell Street corner, the impressive four-storey grey building was once home to the **Alexandra Club |9|**, an association of women that was formed in 1903 'exclusively for social and non-political purposes'. Cromwell House, as the building was first called, was constructed in 1887 for Dr J.G. Beaney as a residence and surgery, to a design by William Salway. Beaney was a controversial figure, regarded by some as a charlatan and abortionist, and respected by others as a highly successful surgeon, author of the first book on surgery published in Australia, politician and generous benefactor. He was flamboyant and showy, his fingers bedecked with diamond rings and his shirts with diamond studs. He was a master at self-promotion: the cast of a huge stone was put on display in a Collins Street bookshop with an account of its successful removal by Dr Beaney (the unsuspecting public were not told that the patient had died). The death of a barmaid after an allegedly illegal operation led to a murder charge being brought against Beaney, but he was acquitted when the jury could not reach agreement.

The original Cromwell House was built in symmetrical Italian style. The corner entrance arch was framed by Doric columns of polished grey granite with bronze caps and bases, and Dr Beaney's crest was mounted within the pediment above. The character of this fine mansion was eroded during the time of its second owner, Dr Henry O'Hara, who destroyed the symmetry by extending the Russell Street facade, and by the Alexandra Club, who moved the entrance and added the fourth storey. The Alexandra Club took up residence in 1916 and remained there until 1983. The building is best viewed from the north-west corner of Collins Street – the tall crescent-shaped copper-coloured Grand Hyatt rises in stark contrast to offset the blue-grey facade.

Russell Street to Swanston Street

Opposite St Michael's is **Scots Church |10|**, dating from 1873 and designed by Joseph Reed in the Gothic Revival style. It is constructed of sandstone and limestone, affording a marked contrast to the deep red brick of St Michael's on the other corner. The interior displays rich timber fittings. The builder was David Mitchell, father of Dame Nellie Melba, and both father and daughter sang in the choir. An earlier church on the site was erected in 1841, and between 1838 and 1841 services were held by the Reverend James Forbes in temporary premises – the land was granted to the Presbyterians in 1839. Next door, now housing a bookshop, is the Assembly Hall, designed by Henry H. Kemp in 1914. The top storey was a 1935 addition. The Gothic Revival architecture belies the relatively recent construction. Between the two buildings is a fern-rimmed bluestone fountain, designed by Peter Staughton and donated by Georges in 1981 to mark its centenary.

On the opposite corner is the **T&G Building |11|**, branded in the memory of many Melburnians in the 1950s and 1960s as an enclave of dentists, a place of much dread. Somewhat incongruously in hindsight, it was proclaimed 'Melbourne's most beautiful building' in 1930. Designed by A.&K. Henderson, and built in three stages between 1928 and 1959, the building first housed the offices of the Temperance and General (T&G) Life Assurance Society.

The grand facade of **Georges |12|** is a highlight of the block. The building was designed as a warehouse by Nahum Barnet in 1884 and Georges took over the building in 1888, converting it to a store. It was reopened in 1998 after its closure earlier in the decade. Next to Georges is the oldest **Baptist Church |13|** in the state, and the oldest remaining church in Collins Street, designed by John Gill and dating from 1845. In 1861 the church was enlarged, and the fine Classical facade, modelled on a Roman temple with Corinthian columns, dates from this time, the design of Reed & Barnes.

Towards the end of the block, next to the town hall, is the **Athenaeum Theatre |14|,** its Classical facade dating from 1885 and designed by Smith & Johnson. It features a statue of Athena on the parapet. The earliest structure on the site, built in 1841, housed the Mechanics' Institute and School of Arts. A second building dated from 1857 and the third from 1872 – the Mechanics' Institute changed its name to the Melbourne Athenaeum in this year. The institute was a society formed to promote cultural activities and it helped establish libraries throughout the state. The building housed a reading room, lecture hall and was the home of a travelling library. It also offered a venue for social, charitable and political occasions and exhibitions. The theatre and verandah are 20th-century modifications, dating from 1924.

Opposite the Athenaeum is the **Regent Theatre |15|** and Plaza Ballroom. Designed for Hoyts Theatres by Cedric Ballantyne in the days of the silent movies in 1929, it was refurbished in true Hollywood style after a 1947 fire. In the 1950s and 1960s the Regent Theatre attracted thousands of moviegoers, but then fell into disuse. Restored and lavishly refurbished, it was opened as a live theatre in 1997 and is a venue for popular musicals.

On the south-eastern corner of the Collins–Swanston Street intersection is the imposing **Burke and Wills statue |16|,** towering above the pedestrians in Swanston Street Walk. Probably best known of all Australian explorers – as a consequence of failure rather than triumph – the domineering Robert O'Hara Burke and the mild-mannered William Jonathon Wills led the ill-fated Victorian Exploring Expedition on a legendary overland journey which accomplished the first south–north crossing of the continent. After leaving Melbourne in August 1860, the party camped at Menindee on the Darling River. The impetuous Burke, determined to be the first to cross the continent, made a mad 1,600-kilometre dash for the Gulf with only three companions and scant provisions. Charles Gray died in the Stony Desert on the return trip and the remaining three arrived at the base camp only to find their supply party had left the same day. Burke and Wills rejected the help of local Aboriginal people and starved to death; only John King survived due to Aboriginal assistance. Around the base of the statue bronze panels tell the story: the setting out from Melbourne amid the cheers of thousands of optimistic onlookers; the burying of a note to would-be rescuers alongside what later became known as the 'Burke and Wills tree'; the death of Burke; and the rescue of King. The statue was sculpted by Charles Summers, funded by a parliamentary grant and unveiled in 1865. It originally stood in the middle of the Collins–Russell Street intersection but was relocated in 1886 to make way for the cable tram.

At Swanston Street look south for a wonderful view of the Shrine of Remembrance (see Walk No. 17, Kings Domain).

Swanston Street to Elizabeth Street

On the north-west corner of Swanston Street is the Manchester Unity Building, completed in 1932 to a Commercial Gothic design by Marcus Barlow. Today its upper levels house a conglomeration of jewellers and associated trades. The building was constructed by the curiously named Australia Felix Lodge of the Independent Order of Oddfellows. One of its founders in 1840 was Dr Augustus Greeves (1805–74). A man of many interests, Greeves was a physician, politician and newspaper editor. In 1848 he was one of the first colonial surgeons to operate using chloroform.

A little further along, on the opposite side of the road, is a building with an intriguing Art Nouveau style facade, its deep pink colour looking slightly out of keeping with the streetscape. This makeover of the building was for the Fourth Victorian Building Society to a design by Robert Haddon in 1911. Cream tiles feature on the exterior of the ground level and green tiles adorn the entire first storey. Two green tiled 'columns' extend to the upper level, each topped by a decorative oval motif.

Halfway down the block you reach the outskirts of the banking and financial heart of the city. The Bank of Melbourne resides at No. 267, the National Bank at No. 271 and the ANZ Bank on the corner of Elizabeth Street. Back from the corner on the north side of the street, you will see the entrance to the magnificent **Block Arcade |17|**. This was named after the colonial ritual of 'doing the block', which meant promenading along this part of Collins Street to see and be seen. In the 1890s midday was the appointed time, and the fashionable place to eat was Gunsler's Vienna Cafe, on the site of the latter-day Australia-on-Collins complex. Block Court, adjacent to the arcade, as already mentioned, was the one-time home of the Athenaeum Club. At the corner take a look south down Elizabeth Street for a view of the massive Flinders Street Station, which stretches for more than one city block.

Elizabeth Street to Queen Street

In the 19th century, banks and building societies lined both sides of this block. You must take a look inside **333 Collins Street |18|**. The dome crowning the octagonal banking chamber, with its fine arches and extraordinary lighting, is one of the masterpieces of Melbourne architecture, and is part of the original building constructed in 1891 to a design by Lloyd Tayler and Alfred Dunn. The facade of the building was remodelled in 1939 to a design by A.&K. Henderson, and the present office tower was erected in 1990.

Continue towards Queen Street and on the north-eastern corner are the adjoining **Old Stock Exchange Building |19|** and the former English Scottish & Australian Bank.

The Stock Exchange, founded by Benjamin Fink, was designed by William Pitt and built between 1888 and 1891. Erected of stone the interior features fine timber detailing. The building has been substantially altered, inside and out, notably in 1923 when it merged with the bank and the banking chamber was extended into the exchange. It now houses the ANZ Banking Museum, well worth a visit.

The **Venetian Gothic bank building |20|** is one of the most outstanding of the Melbourne boom period, built largely due to the vision of politician and banker Sir George Verdon, appointed Australian manager of the bank in 1872. A great patron of the arts, Verdon was a friend of architect William Wardell, whom he commissioned to design a building that incorporated a residence and banking chamber. Erected between 1883 and 1887 at a cost of over £50,000, the cast-iron columns for the banking chamber came from England, marble for the fireplaces was imported from Italy and the timber for the panelling was blackwood from Tasmania. The floor of the banking chamber, now carpeted, was laid in marble and mosaic. Contrasting with the opulent interior is the beautifully plain facade. Built of Pyrmont sandstone, the combination of intricate window ornamentation and plain walling is unique.

Queen Street to William Street

More banks are located in this section of the walk, notably the old Bank of Australasia on the north-east corner of Collins Street. The bank first opened in Melbourne in 1838 and a two-storey building was designed in Classical Revival style by Joseph Reed and Frederick Barnes in 1875. The upper three levels were added in 1930, to a design by A.&K. Henderson.

On the opposite corner is the former National Mutual Life Association building, more widely known as Goode House. This Gothic Revival style building was built between 1891 and 1903 to a design by Wright, Reed & Beaver. On the corner of William and Collins streets is the current National Mutual building, an ugly structure that is mercifully set back from the street. In the forecourt there are two statues of the city's founders. The figure of John Batman, sculpted by Stanley Hammond in 1978, depicts Batman marking a place on a map and declaring, 'This is the place for a village'. The second figure, by Michael Meszaros in 1978, is of John Fawkner.

William Street to King Street

The highlights of this city block are the **Olderfleet Buildings |21|** and the Rialto. The Olderfleet Buildings are actually three separate edifices, designed by three different architects and built between 1887 and 1889. The first one, inscribed Olderfleet Building on the facade, is a three-storey brick structure, Gothic in style, and highly decorated, with arches, pinnacles and clock tower. It was designed by William Pitt for businessman Patrick McCaughlan. The second building, Record Chambers, was designed by J.A.B. Koch for the printers McCarron Bird & Co. A sign on the facade proclaims 'The Olderfleet Buildings'.

Classical in design, it is constructed of brick and stucco. The third is the South Australian Insurance Building, designed by Oakden Addison & Kemp in Gothic Revival style. It has Gothic arcaded windows and polychrome brickwork on the facade.

At 495 Collins Street is the five-star hotel, **Le Meridien at the Rialto |22|.** The hotel has been cleverly incorporated within two historic buildings once separated by a laneway. The facade of the eastern section originally belonged to the Federation style Winfield Building, once the Melbourne Wool Exchange, designed by Charles D'Ebro and Richard Speight in 1891. The Rialto, on the other side of the lane, was designed by William Pitt for Patrick McCaughlan in 1890. The name and Gothic facade were symbolic of Venice. The area was known as the state's wool and wheat headquarters, housing stock and station agents and stores of primary produce, alongside Melbourne's original mercantile enterprises, law firms and government offices. The cobbled bluestone laneway, retained within the building today, once rang with the clatter of horses and carts conveying wool and wheat to Melbourne's wharves. The hotel incorporates the original Rialto linked by a nine-storey glass-roofed atrium to the Winfield building. There is a pleasant bar, Franc's, right on the street, if your thirst needs quenching, or you can have a coffee inside on the historic cobblestone terrace.

At No. 525 is the **Rialto Towers |23|,** a glass structure built in the mid-1980s. It is the tallest building in the southern hemisphere, rising 242 metres above street level. Take the lift to the 55th floor and savour the 360-degree views from the observation deck.

After King Street, there is little of interest in the final block before Spencer Street. When you reach Spencer Street, cast your eyes left and note the huge grey building along from **Spencer Street Station |24|.** This is the former Victorian Railways Administration Office, the largest 19th-century office building in Melbourne. Designed by the Victorian Railways Engineering department, it was built of brick and stone in 1893. The upper floor was added in 1912 and the attic level in 1922. The interiors have been renovated and the northern section has been converted to apartments, while the southern end has become the All Seasons Premier Grand Hotel.

Walk key

1. Trades Hall | **2.** Eight-Hour Day Memorial | **3.** Old Melbourne Gaol | **4.** Old Magistrates Court | **5.** Storey Hall | **6.** Building 8 RMIT | **7.** City Baths | **8.** Queen Victoria Market | **9.** Flagstaff Gardens | **10.** St James Old Cathedral

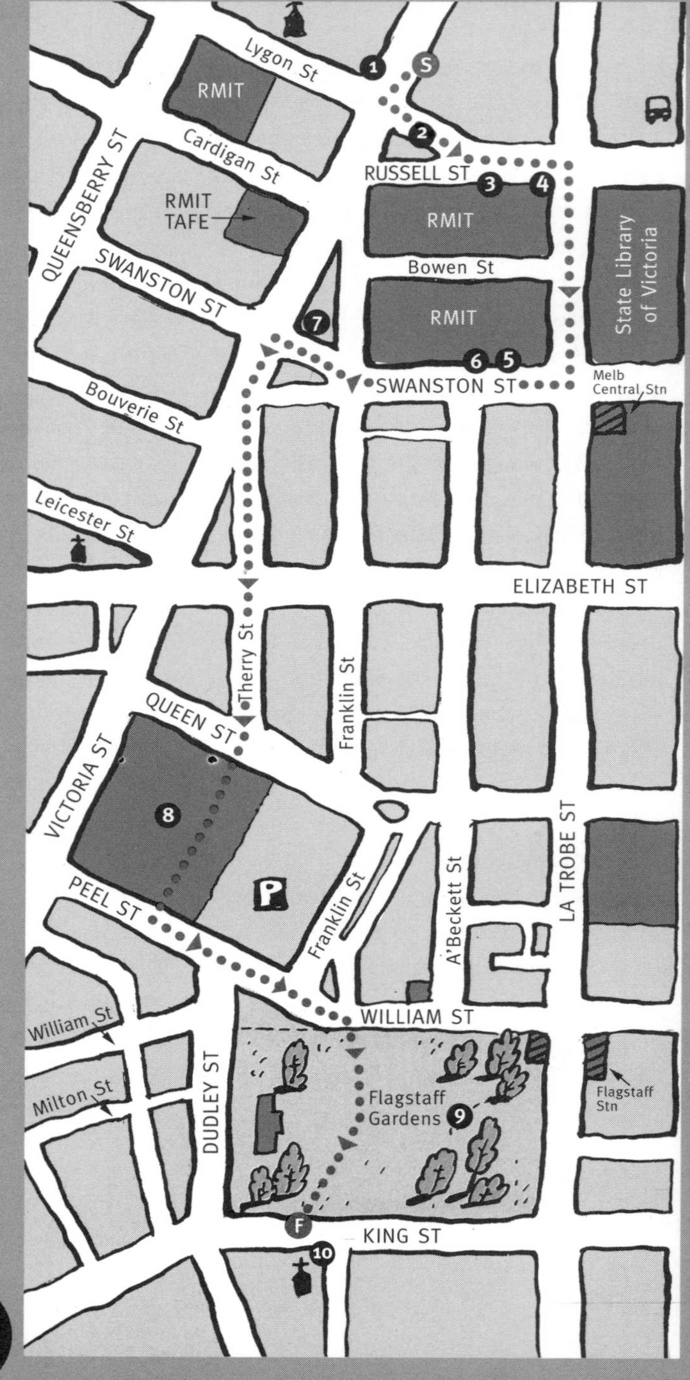

Walk No. 2

Law, Learning & Labour

The best of old Melbourne

Start

Trades Hall, corner of Victoria and Lygon streets, Carlton. Short walk from the centre of the city, or any bus from Russell Street. Any tram heading north along Swanston Street may also be taken to the City Baths, and Trades Hall is just a short stroll up the hill in Victoria Street.

Finish

St James Old Cathedral, corner of Batman and King streets. A train from Flagstaff Station and trams along La Trobe Street will take you to other parts of the city and suburbs.

Length/Time

2.5 km/2 hours

Packed into a small pocket is some of the city's most innovative architecture, several of its best social institutions, and the history of a number of its worst brutalities and crimes. Where late 20th-century Melbourne, like so much of the world, is marked by the turbulence of technological change, the turbulence in the Melbourne of last century was borne of social change. The fight for universal education and rights, the railing against wealthy landlords for the establishment of public systems of sewerage and hygiene and the struggles to attain universal suffrage – all are in some part preserved by the buildings that remain in this section of the city.

Of unions, bushrangers and suffragettes

Start this walk at **Trades Hall |1|.** In the times of rampant and unrestrained exploitation of working people in Western nations, the push for an eight-hour working day was won by Victorian workers and artisans in 1856 – the first win for the eight-hour movement in the world. The Trades Hall, Melbourne's temple to the labour movement and success of the Eight-Hour Day movement, was erected on the current site in 1859. Initially built of timber in the Carpenter Gothic style, the original establishment was built on land allocated by the Crown for a 'Trades Hall and Literary Institute'. The current building was commenced in 1874, with substantial extensions added in the 1880s and 1890s. Between 1917 and 1922, the Academic Classical facade was constructed to incorporate a portico of large-scale Corinthian columns, and designed to make the building look as if it had all been made in the same period. This incorporated a Regency style two-storey structure that faced Victoria Street, designed by Joseph Reed.

The Trades Hall has been the venue for some of Victoria's most significant political debates and identities since its establishment, including those involved in the formation of the Australian Labor Party. It has and continues to be the venue of support for a whole range of union and related social causes and organisations. As well as housing unions and the Victorian Trades Hall Council, the Trades Hall is also home to the executive of the ACTU, the Centre for Union Research and Education, a Library and Information Service, the International Bookshop and houses a small cafe.

Diagonally opposite the Trades Hall is the 'Eight-Hour Reserve'. This reserve is home to the **Eight-Hour Day Memorial |2|,** which celebrates the achievement of 'Eight hours work, eight hours play, eight hours sleep, and eight "bob" of pay'. This monument stood outside the Victorian Parliament between 1891 and 1902.

Just past the Eight–Hour Reserve, on the west side of Russell Street, is the **Old Melbourne Gaol |3|.** The gaol was used as a remand centre and execution chamber, and its grim history is preserved in macabre detail in the interior of the building, which has been transformed from a place of pain and suffering into one of curiosity, education and black entertainment. Built between 1841 and 1864, the structure and interiors are a blend of Old Colonial Georgian and Regency penal architecture. Only one cell block of the original gaol remains, with the chapel and original entrance absorbed into the layout and architecture of Emily McPherson College (next door, to the north, built in 1926). Inside the gaol one hundred and thirty-five men and women met their end on the gallows, which are preserved. Legendary bushranger Ned Kelly, just before taking the big swing in 1880, is reported to have intoned the words 'Such is life'. The woman convicted of systematically poisoning her entire family with arsenic, Martha Needle, was also despatched here in 1894. Such were the times in the Old Melbourne Gaol.

Further along Russell Street and opposite the former Victoria Police Headquarters is Melbourne's best architectural regurgitation of mediaeval Europe, the sturdy sandstone **Old Magistrates Court |4|**. Cross over to the south-east corner of the intersection to appreciate fully the detailed ornamentation, turret forms, parapets, octagonal dome with lantern, and rock-faced masonry. Designed by G.H.B. Austin, the court was built in 1911 in the Federation Romanesque style. The building was active as a court until the early 1990s, before being taken over by RMIT University. At the time of writing, the Old Magistrates Court is being used as a venue for the Melbourne Festival of the Arts.

Turn right at La Trobe Street and move west down the hill to Swanston Street. Turn right at Swanston Walk to the entrance to the recently refurbished Storey Hall, a part of the Royal Melbourne Institute of Technology, now RMIT University. The university started off as the Working Man's College in the early 1880s, in the same spirit and with similar social and educational objectives as Trades Hall and the Mechanics' Institutes. The Victorian Academic Classical style **Storey Hall |5|** was built in 1887 by the Irish Catholic community. The cost of the building led the developers into financial strife, and it was later taken over by a series of left-wing groups that included the early suffragettes. This social history is now borne in the remarkable cave-like

Opening Times

Trades Hall: Mon–Fri 9am–5pm; tours of the building available, bookings essential.

Old Melbourne Gaol: Seven days a week 9.30am–4.30pm; closed Christmas Day and Good Friday. Entry fees apply and tours are available for groups of 10 or more, bookings essential (9663 7228).

Melbourne City Baths: Mon–Fri 6am–10pm, Sat–Sun 6am–8pm (9663 5888).

Queen Victoria Market:
Tue & Thur 6am–2pm; Fri 6am–4pm; Sat 6am–3pm; Sun 6am–4pm (9320 5822). Tours available, departing from 69 Victoria Street, bookings essential.

St James Old Cathedral: Mon–Fri 10am–4pm, Thur 10am–3pm (9329 6133). Services Tue 12.30pm & Sun 10am.

Refreshments

There are numerous cafes and pubs along the way, particularly in and around the Queen Victoria Market. On days when the market is open, inexpensive gourmet snacks and non-alcoholic beverages are available in the stalls at the deli section.

The City Baths have provided Melburnians with ornate swimming facilities since the turn of the century.

building erected next to the original Storey Hall. The extremely contemporary design, by Ashton, Raggatt & McDougall, defies easy classification although the works of Walter and Marion Griffin (architects of Canberra) are cited as an influence. It incorporates the Irish and suffragette histories of Storey Hall's occupants with its use of a green and purple colour scheme, and it refers to the original building in terms of its scale and detail.

Further north along Swanston Street is **Building 8 |6|,** designed by Edmond & Corrigan. It is best appreciated from the opposite side of the street or even by sauntering a brief way down A'Beckett Street and looking back. The ultra contemporary exterior of Building 8 is a lively and vivid play of colour and vernacular materials, such as corrugated iron, combined with geometrical forms. The architect, Peter Carrigan, has been known to cite the suburban Australian Chinese take-away as an influence on his work. Continue north along Swanston Street to the City Baths at the corner of Franklin Street.

Feeding the great unwashed

The **City Baths |7|** were first established in 1858 and redeveloped to their current Federation Free Classical form in 1904. For decades, Melburnians and visitors have enjoyed the use of this cheerful and friendly facility. The main pool is 33 metres long and sports a delightful upper-level balcony that provides a very pleasant place to sit and enjoy the aquatic sounds and light atmosphere. Bathing, sauna, massage, gym, a cafe and a whole range of other physical and sporting services are on offer. Before taking a dip, however, you may be interested to continue to the Queen Victoria Market. Head west along Victoria Street, then angle left, still heading roughly west, along Therry Street until you reach the corner of Therry and Elizabeth streets.

The **Queen Victoria Market |8|** occupies 6.5 hectares of land. It possesses a most convivial and multicultural atmosphere, particularly on busy Friday and Saturday mornings, and is Australia's largest multiple goods market, trading since 1878. The market has four main sections: the meat market, the deli section, the fruit and vegetable market, and aisles with stalls selling clothing and other goods. The meat market at the north-east corner is on the site of former cattle and wholesale vegetable markets dating back to 1842. Most of the rest of the market sits on the site of Melbourne's first formal general cemetery, which commenced burials in 1837 and was quickly filled to capacity by 1854. We recommend a cafe latte and a spicy bratwurst sausage with hot mustard from the deli section, before moving west to the Flagstaff Gardens and Flagstaff Hill (wend your way through the various aisles of produce until you reach Peel Street). Turn left at Peel Street and continue south until you come to the gardens on the right.

Signs of early mourning

The **Flagstaff Gardens |9|,** incorporating Flagstaff Hill, is an important location in the early history of Melbourne. Some of the first European settlers were buried here – the first a boy by the name of James Goodwin in 1836 – and the Hill was Melbourne's main platform for communication from 1840 until the arrival of electric telegraph communications in 1854. Lookouts would spy and signal the arrivals of ships entering the nearby harbours, and the early community's chronometers were set by the falling of a black 'time ball' from the flagstaff at noon each day. When Victoria was granted the right to a separate representative assembly in 1850, the proclamation from the British parliament was read from here. Geological and magnetic surveys were conducted from the Hill, and the prison hulks and shipping movements at Williamstown could be easily monitored from this vantage point. A memorial was built on the rise opposite Batman Street in 1870 to commemorate the grave sites of the early pioneers. The gardens today provide a leafy retreat for office workers and city dwellers.

Just across the road from the Pioneer Memorial, on the corner of King and Batman streets, is Victoria's oldest church, **St James Old Cathedral |10|,** one of Victoria's few examples of the Old Colonial Georgian style of architecture. Its construction was prompted by the death of the previously mentioned James Goodwin; the community had no adequate place to mourn the tragic loss of this young soul. Building of St James commenced in 1838 and the stone structure was completed by 1842. It was initially situated near the corner of Little Collins and Williams streets and moved to its present location in 1913. It was designed by Robert Russell, who was said to be influenced by the famous Sydney convict architect, Francis Greenway. After a decree making it unidenominational, it became the first permanent home of the Anglican Church in Victoria. The first Anglican bishop's throne and the original cedar pews and panelling are preserved, with the interior remaining much as it was when built.

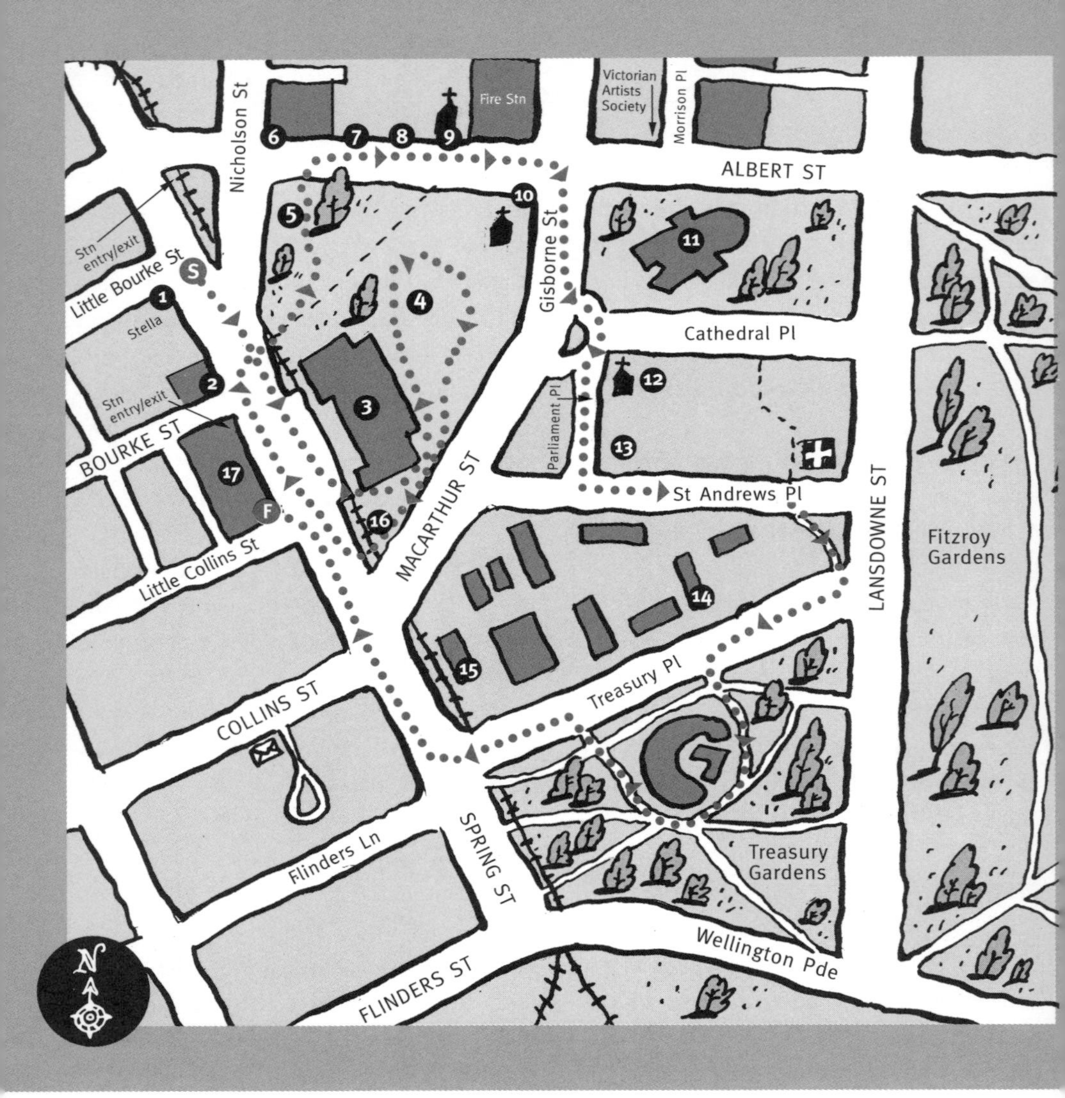

Walk key

1. Princess Theatre | **2.** Imperial Hotel | **3.** Parliament House | **4.** Parliament Gardens | **5.** Coles Fountain | **6.** ICI Building | **7.** Salvation Army printing works | **8.** East Melbourne Synagogue | **9.** Baptist Church | **10.** St Peter's, Eastern Hill | **11.** St Patrick's Cathedral | **12.** Lutheran Church | **13.** Tasma Terrace | **14.** Commonwealth Building | **15.** Old Treasury Building | **16.** Gordon Reserve | **17.** Windsor Hotel

Walk No. 3

Parliament Precinct & Eastern Hill

Victoriana, gardens and streetscapes

Start

Princess Theatre, Spring Street (just a minute along from the top of Bourke Street). An easy walk from the city centre. City loop trains to Parliament Station from all city stations; free City Circle tram from anywhere on the network; tram 96 along Bourke Street.

Finish

Windsor Hotel, Spring Street (transport as above).

Length/Time

2.5 km/1.5 hours

The area straddling the low slopes of Eastern Hill, at the north-east end of the city centre, is one of Melbourne's most significant precincts in terms of its history and architecture. The first governor of Victoria, Charles La Trobe, saw the value of the district's elevated position and decreed that it be set aside for the city's most important institutions. The wide streets were laid out in the 1840s and have a genteel, orderly feel. The buildings, many constructed during the gold rush and land boom years (1850–90), reflect the grandiose imaginings of those who lived through a period of unparalleled wealth in Victoria. This circular walk takes in the magnificent public buildings of Spring Street, ecclesiastical buildings and a peaceful 19th-century garden landscape.

The **Princess Theatre |1|,** our starting point, was built in 1887 by William Pitt, and underwent a major refurbishment in the late 1980s in time for the blockbuster musicals for which it has become known, including *Phantom of the Opera* and *Les Miserables*. The theatre comes with its own ghost – the spirit of the 19th-century actor Frederick Baker (stage name Frederici), who died during a performance of *Faust* and who now, apparently, sits in the balcony and watches performances. Architectural features include elegant French style mansard domes and a gold-detailed facade replete with allegorical figures. From the Princess Theatre, head south to Bourke Street. On the corner is the **Imperial Hotel |2|,** which began trading in 1864 and is one of the city's favourite Friday afternoon watering holes. Cross Spring Street to Parliament House on the opposite corner.

Standford Fountain, dating from the 1860s, is a splendidly detailed example of Victorian-era craftsmanship.

Parliament House and surrounds

With views that fan out across the treetops of surrounding parkland and straight down the central arterial of Bourke Street, **Parliament House |3|** occupies the city's most commanding position. Its design was conceived by local architects Peter Kerr and J.G. Knight. Construction began in 1856 and continued in stages. The original plans specified a cladding of Italian Carrara marble (quickly abandoned), and a giant dome (recently revived as an idea, but discarded because the electorate was baulking at the extravagance). Despite these omissions, the building, with its design in the idiom of Roman Classicism, and its references to the great public buildings of Europe and America, is among the most elaborate Victorian structures in the country.

On the south side of Parliament House there is a discreet entrance to what is known as the private section of the **Parliament Gardens |4|,** although it is open to the public. Designed by Melbourne's most prominent landscaper and director of the Royal Botanic Gardens, William Guilfoyle, the gardens were laid out in 1879 and feature elements typical of the period, including curving paths, flowering borders, and expansive lawns. Exit the garden at the same place and cross back in front of the Parliament building to the official public area of Parliament Gardens on the north side. Of interest here is the geometric shower-like **Coles Fountain |5|,** designed by Robert Woodward in 1981, standing in pleasing contrast to the 19th-century style of the gardens' layout.

Ecclesiastical corner

Halfway along the Parliament Gardens there is an exit to Albert Street. Directly in front lies the **ICI Building |6|** (now bearing the Orica name). Designed by Osborn McCutcheon and constructed in 1956, this was Melbourne's first 'skyscraper'.

Just beyond the ICI Building are three historic religious buildings: the **Salvation Army printing works |7|** (1901); the **East Melbourne Synagogue |8|** (1877); and the **Baptist Church |9|** (1855–65), now an office block. The granting of prime land to these 'unconventional' religious organisations originated from the desire on the part of Governor La Trobe to foster religious diversity and tolerance within the colony. On the south side of the street lies what, at one time, would have been the bastion of religious conservatism in Melbourne, **St Peter's, Eastern Hill |10|.** Built between 1846 and 1848, St Peter's was the colony's second Anglican church, and is today the oldest Anglican church still on its original site. The old section of the church was simply designed in a Gothic idiom by

Opening Times

Parliament House: Mon–Fri tours 10am, 11am, 12pm, 2pm, 3pm & 3.45pm; tours limited when Parliament is sitting (9651 9811).

St Patrick's Cathedral: 6.45am–5.30pm daily (9662 2332)

National Trust Office: Mon–Fri 9am–5pm (9654 4711)

Old Treasury Building: Mon–Fri 9am–5pm, Sat–Sun 10am–4pm (9651 2233)

Refreshments

Afternoon tea in the lounge at the **Windsor Hotel** is one of Melbourne's essential experiences (9663 6000); **Stella** in Spring Street, for those who want a seriously good meal (9639 1555); just around the corner from Spring Street the Bourke Street cafe strip includes two of Melbourne's cafe institutions, **Pellegrini's** (9662 1885) and the **Florentino Cellar Bar** (9662 1811), both known for their coffee and quick Italian lunches; the **Imperial Hotel** is a great place for a late afternoon beer (9662 1007).

Charles Laing. Stone and timber salvaged from shipwrecks was used in the original construction. The later bluestone addition is remarkable for the crooked brickwork laid when the skilled tradesmen were away on the goldfields. Directly across Albert Street from St Peter's is the Metropolitan Fire Station. The Albert Street section is an austere modern building bearing the mural *The Legend of Fire*, while the old section (it is worth taking a stroll into Gisborne Street to have a look) was constructed in 1891 and is an exuberant amalgam of Elizabethan and Italianate architectural detail.

Back down the hill, on the corner of Gisborne and Albert streets, is **St Patrick's Cathedral |11|.** Construction of a temporary wooden structure began in the late 1840s, before the foundation stone was laid in 1850 for the permanent church. By then the gold rush had started, and Melbourne's population swelled (with no small number of Irish Catholics among the ranks), so it was decided that what was needed here was a grand cathedral. The first stage of the building was completed in 1858 to a design by William Wardell, and construction continued in bursts until 1939. Take the time to wander inside to see the finest church interior in Australia.

Directly across Albert Street at No. 430 is the Victoria Artists' Society building, completed in 1893 to a design by Richard Speight. Walk down the hill and cross Cathedral Place. On the corner of this street and Parliament Place is the **Lutheran Church |12|,** built to a design by Charles Blackmann in 1874 for the German community, on a site that was part of a land grant in 1852. In Parliament Place is **Tasma Terrace |13|** (1878–79), a row of six terrace houses designed by Charles Webb and considered an exceptional example of late 19th-century residential design. The building lies at the heart of what was, 100 years ago, a very exclusive area and one of the residences now houses the Victorian headquarters of the National Trust.

Treasury precinct

Turn left into St Andrews Place. This pretty tree-lined street contains government offices and, on the corner of Lansdowne Street, one of Melbourne's best-known medical centres, the Peter MacCallum Cancer Institute housed since 1994 in this modern building designed by Melbourne firm Castles, Stephenson and Turner.

Turn right into Lansdowne Street and then right again into Treasury Place. The first building on the right is the **Commonwealth Building |14|,** constructed in 1913 for use as offices by the federal parliament while the nation's capital, Canberra, was under construction. The elaborate white 'wedding-cake' detail on the facade is typical of the style used for official buildings before the Second World War. The next building houses state government offices. Directly in front of these buildings lies the Treasury Gardens, created in the 1860s on the quarry from which the stone came for many of the nearby buildings. The garden is noted for its flowing, informal design and

William Wardell and the Victorian Gothic style

William Wardell (1823–99) was one of the greatest exponents of Gothic Revival style in the world. Born in England, Wardell converted to Catholicism as an adult, and became known as the designer of some 30 Catholic churches in that country. Ill health prompted him to migrate to Australia, where he designed many buildings, including the country's two most important Catholic cathedrals, St Mary's in Sydney and St Patrick's in Melbourne – the latter one of the finest Gothic Revival churches anywhere.

Wardell's favoured style had as much to do with ideas as it did building materials and design features. The Gothic Revival form, based on careful studies of mediaeval Gothic architecture, was seen by its exponents as being able to contain and express the truest and most moral of the aspirations of mankind.

its overhanging fig trees and exotic palms. Take one of the paths that lead down the small escarpment into the gardens and walk downhill to the John F. Kennedy Memorial. Created in 1965, this pristine little garden with its pools, fountains, waterfall and slate terrace is a rare example in Melbourne of public-space art from the 1960s. The sculptor Raymond Ewers was asked to create something sympathetic to the style of Kennedy's grave at Arlington.

Head north-west up the hill towards the city centre. On the corner of Treasury Place and Spring Street is the **Old Treasury Building |15|**, now housing a museum displaying the history of Melbourne. The building was constructed between 1857 and 1862. A 19-year-old draughtsman, John James Clark, fresh from an inspiring trip to Italy, drew up the sophisticated Renaissance Revival design and the building is one of the best of the Victorian era in Melbourne. The gold vaults in the basement are worth a look.

Cross over Macarthur Street to **Gordon Reserve |16|**. The reserve is named for the statues of two namesakes, the robust General Charles Gordon and the fine-featured poet Adam Lindsay Gordon. The Stanford Fountain, made of basalt, was designed in the 1860s by a prisoner of Pentridge, William Stanford.

Cross Spring Street, turn to the right and walk along to the **Windsor Hotel |17|**. Designed by Charles Webb and built between 1883 and 1884, this is one of the few surviving grand hotels in Australia. Note the ornate detailing of its facade and the width of its street frontage. Inside, the huge staircase, the expansive, beautifully tiled reception area and the intricately decorated public rooms show the manner in which the wealthy of the Victorian age indulged their love of luxury. Have afternoon tea here at the walk's end. Parliament Station is nearby, and there is a city circle tram stop in front of the building.

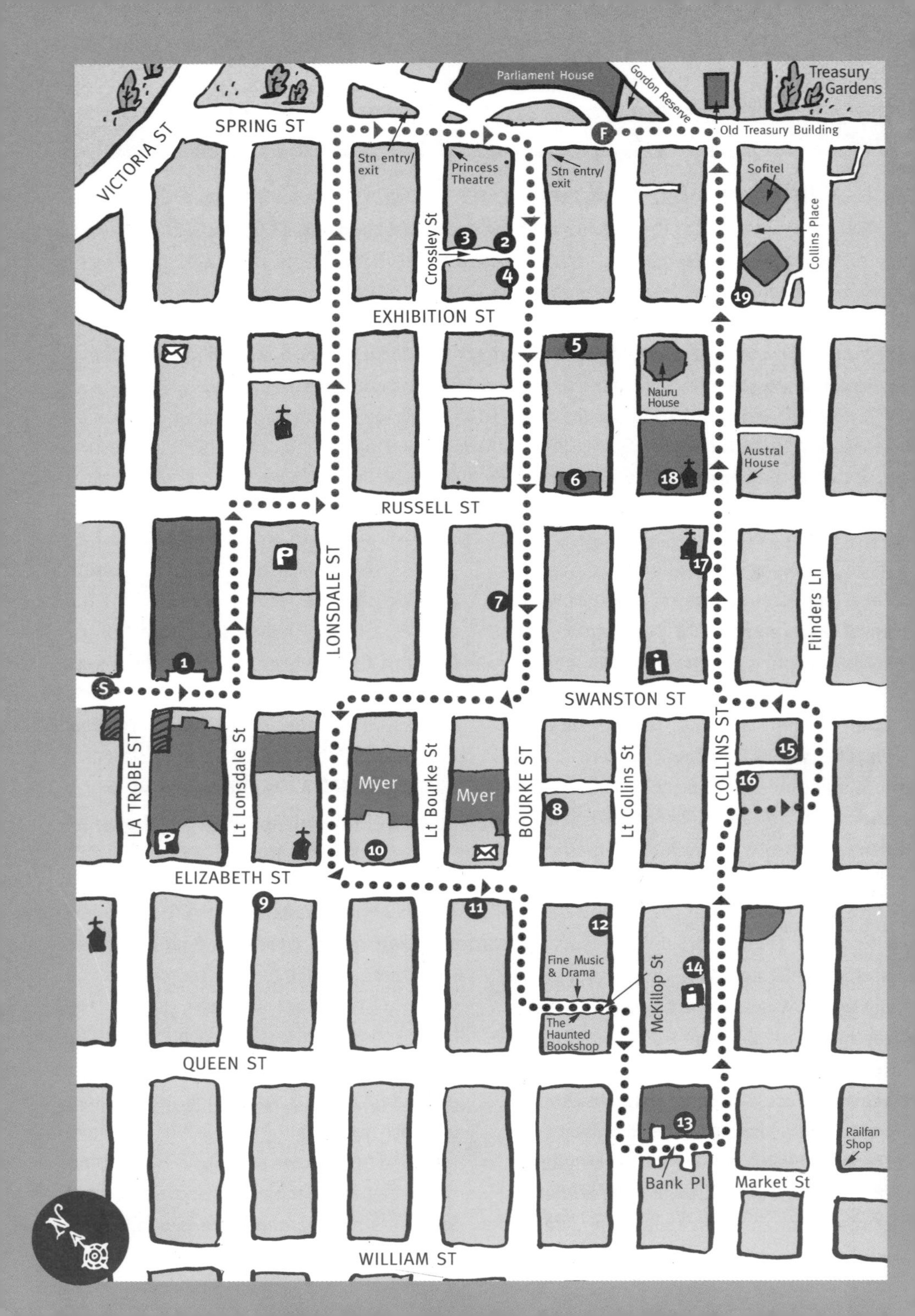

Parliament House
Gordon Reserve
Treasury Gardens
Old Treasury Building
SPRING ST
VICTORIA ST
Stn entry/ exit
Princess Theatre
Stn entry/ exit
Sofitel
Collins Place
Crossley St
EXHIBITION ST
Nauru House
Austral House
RUSSELL ST
LONSDALE ST
Flinders Ln
SWANSTON ST
LA TROBE ST
Lt Lonsdale St
Myer
Lt Bourke St
Myer
BOURKE ST
Lt Collins St
COLLINS ST
ELIZABETH ST
Fine Music & Drama
McKillop St
The Haunted Bookshop
QUEEN ST
Railfan Shop
Bank Pl
Market St
WILLIAM ST

Walk No. 4

Bookshops Old & New

Literary luminaries and lodgings

Start

Corner Swanston and La Trobe streets – trams 23, 24, 30, 34, City Circle tram; bus 684.

Finish

Parliament Station – trams 11, 12, 42, 86, 96, 109, City Circle tram.

Length/Time

4.5 km/3.5 hours

Walk key

1. State Library | **2.** Paperback Bookshop | **3.** Art Salon Bookshop | **4.** Hill of Content | **5.** Site of Cole's second-hand bookstall | **6.** Theosophical Society Bookshop | **7.** Site of Tolman Dwight's second-hand bookshop | **8.** Site of Edward Cole's Book Arcade | **9.** Napoleon's Military Bookshop | **10.** Back Copies | **11.** Little Bookroom | **12.** Australian Geographic Shop | **13.** Site of Troedel & Cooper | **14.** Information Victoria | **15.** Hylands Book Shop | **16.** Foreign Language Bookshop | **17.** Kay Craddock Antiquarian Bookshop | **18.** Site of George Robertson's bookshop | **19.** Site of Samuel Mullen's shop and library

Melbourne, apparently, has more literary readings per capita than any other city in the world. Its spiritual sister city, San Francisco, has the most bookshops. Interestingly, the places share very similar climates, and you have to wonder if their rather bleak winters, and drizzly weather generally, have contributed just a little to the well-known cultural passions of the residents. The following walk takes you on an introductory tour of the inner-city network of bookshops, representing just a fraction of what is available in Melbourne at large. Not only will you find booksellers in good number, you will also find a wide and exciting range of interests catered for by some of the most comprehensive specialist collections anywhere in Australia. And on the way you will meet some of the characters who have helped form the reputation of the literary landscape.

State Library of Victoria

The massive State Library building fronts Swanston Street and runs the entire block to Russell Street. Begun in 1853 under the direction of Sir Redmond Barry, its first president of trustees, it has grown to its present size through a process of renovation, addition and changes in function. In its early days it housed three public utilities: the **State Library |1|**; the National Gallery of Victoria until the 1960s; and the National Museum of Victoria until that institution's closure in the late 1990s pending the completion of its new building adjacent to the Exhibition Building in nearby Carlton. The portico and first floor reading rooms fronting Swanston Street were completed in 1870 to a design by Joseph Reed (for an example of grand Victoriana it is worth a look at these, and they are all that remain of the 1870s interior). It was in the domed reading room, designed by the architectural firm of Bates, Peebles and Smart and not completed until 1913, that Marcus Clarke wrote his convict classic, *For the Term of His Natural Life*, beneath the glow of the green-shaded reading lights. And many years later, in the 1970s another scribbler, Helen Garner, retreated here to produce her contemporary classic, *Monkey Grip*, a drama of sex, drugs and art set in inner-city Melbourne. It is a room beloved of generations of students and writers.

Walk south along Swanston Street to the end of the library building. Turn left into Little Lonsdale Street and continue to Russell Street. Turn right. At Lonsdale Street turn left. Cross over Exhibition Street and at Spring Street turn right. Continue on past the Princess Theatre and then turn right into Bourke Street. On the corner of Crossley and Bourke streets is the small but fascinating **Paperback Bookshop |2|**, first established in the late 1950s. The **Art Salon Bookshop |3|** is located at 5 Crossley Street. Its interest is modern art, architecture and design, and its tiny, pristine interior is a perfect setting for the sleek, beautifully produced books on display.

Further along Bourke Street, at No. 86, is the **Hill of Content |4|**. The building went up in 1840. By 1922, when A.H. Spencer moved in, the premises were in a state of disrepair. It is testament to the passion and talent of Spencer that what was little more than a shell in the city's 'foreign' corner, a place where, in Spencer's words, 'worshippers of the Bacchus sang or moaned their melodies, making midnight and a.m. eerily mysterious', became the literary epicentre of Melbourne. The customer list reads like a who's who of the city's arts community at the time. Dame Nellie Melba stopped by, as did the painters Tom Roberts and Arthur Streeton. The Poet Laureate John Masefield could be seen from time to time, and one or other member of the famous Lindsay clan seemed always to be on the premises. Spencer became an acknowledged authority of Australiana (in the days when the Australian literary product was always going to be considered second-rate to what was produced overseas), and is still revered as one of the 'greats' in Australian

'Hill of Content is to Melbourne what Rizzoli is to New York – a great bookshop.'

bookselling history. In 1952 Collins Booksellers acquired the business, preserved the name and vowed to remain true to the vision of its founder. The store stocks a wide range of books, including fiction – both modern and classics – non-fiction and literary magazines from around the world. A favourite Melbourne practice is to buy from the Hill and then pop next door to Florentino to enjoy the latest edition over a glass of wine or a coffee.

The south-west corner of Exhibition and Bourke streets was the **site of Edward William Cole's second-hand bookstall |5|**, established here at the Eastern Market in

Opening Times

State Library of Victoria: Mon 1pm–9pm, Tue 10am–6pm, Wed 10am–9pm, Thur–Sun 10am–6pm; tours available (9669 9816).
Bookshops: Open normal trading hours. Most open on Sat & some on Sun.

Refreshments

There are lots of cafes in Bourke Street and Collins Street (see Walk No.6, CBD Gourmet Tour).

1865 (now the old Southern Cross Hotel, currently undergoing an extensive makeover). Continue along Bourke Street. At Russell Street you can make a short detour to the left. At 128 Russell Street (second floor) is the **Theosophical Society Bookshop |6|.** This has been in its present location for a couple of decades, and before that was housed in the old Theosophical building next to the Regent Theatre. It was established to serve the interests of Melbourne's Theosophical Society, formed around the turn of the century. Theosophy is a spiritual movement with social interests, which was founded in the 19th century to look at those large themes of life such as the 'brotherhood of man' and the 'search for truth'. Today the bookshop is said to be the largest of its kind in the world. In addition to the many texts related to this subject, it has some 55,000 titles dealing with all aspects of religion, health, meditation and psychology. This is the place to discover that the 'new age' is actually far older than many of its proponents would care to believe.

Back in Bourke Street, continue on down to No. 234, which was the **site of Tolman Dwight's second-hand bookshop |7|.** Henry Tolman Dwight arrived in Melbourne in 1855 with a large stock of second-hand books and plans to expand the literary landscape of his new colonial home. He set up a bookshop that became a magnet for Melbourne's literati. The likes of Adam Lindsay Gordon, Henry Kendall, Marcus Clarke and Richard Henry 'Orion' Horne could be seen combing the shelves, or partaking of a bit of literary gossip. The second catalogue Dwight published advertised a stock of around 10,000 volumes. The next catalogue (1862) showed that his collection had grown six-fold. Suitably, he died at his bookshop in June 1871 and made a large bequest to the University of Melbourne.

At Swanston Street, Bourke Street becomes a pedestrian mall. Halfway along, opposite Myer and David Jones department stores, is the **site of Edward Cole's Book Arcade |8|.** Established in 1873, not far from his Eastern Market bookstall, Cole's Book Arcade moved to these premises in 1883. Cole was an innovative bookseller who used a sign of the rainbow to attract children to his famous book arcade, which ran through from Bourke Street to Collins Street. His best-selling *Cole's Funny Picture Book* series enjoyed a wide popularity despite the rather grim Dickensian view on its readers' proneness to perpetual disobedience. The brightly coloured rainbow on the front of these books, which were printed on the premises, became something of a symbol of children's publishing in Australia.

Cole, who coined the name 'the palace of intellect' for his enterprise, was a master marketer, and if such things had existed then, he would have found himself the subject of countless articles in business magazines and courses in business schools. He dressed his staff in red, employed a band to entertain family groups, and allowed people to read for hours without being disturbed or asked to buy. Customers who

Melbourne through the eyes of its writers

Those with a further interest in Melbourne's literary scene, or more precisely in the way the city of Melbourne has been imagined and re-imagined by successive generations of writers, might like to dip into a few of the following. Henry Handel Richardson (or Ethel as her family knew her) set many of her novels in Melbourne, which mostly describe the turn-of-the-century, middle-class life of their author. Martin Boyd, a member of the Boyd family that has produced more distinguished artists in Australia than any other, wrote of life in Melbourne's upper classes, setting his novels between the 1830s and 1930s. His novel *The Monforts* is worth reading for the extent to which it encompasses the broad sweep of Melbourne's history (re-imagined for the purposes of fiction, of course). George Johnston, in a series of semi-autobiographical novels, deals with the small world of the intellectual of Melbourne in the 1940s, while Judah Waten deals with a subject that would come to represent one of the city's greatest social upheavals – post-Second World War migration. Frank Hardy, a committed communist, blows the lid off class divisions in Melbourne in the 1950s with his searing, semi-real account of the life of a local business man, *Power Without Glory*.

On the contemporary scene, there are David Williamson's early plays to look at, Kerry Greenwood's detective stories set in the back alleys of the city, Helen Garner's stories of life on the radical edge of middle-class Melbourne in the 1970s and 1980s, and Peter Carey's award-winning *Illywhacker*, a look at Melbourne, and other places, from a reasonably bent but highly poetic perspective. And for the very new, try *Loaded* by Christos Tsiolkas, an account of a night in the life of a young Greek gay man, or *Three Dollars* by Elliot Perlman, which follows the fortunes or otherwise of a man and his family in a rather grimly drawn Melbourne, a city held hostage by the economic rationalism of the 1990s.

came in to peruse the bookstands would also be confronted with an enticing range of crockery, glassware, toys and music.

Head north along Swanston Street to Lonsdale Street and turn left. On the north-west corner of Elizabeth Street (No. 309) is **Napoleon's Military Bookshop |9|**. This shop should come with a warning for walking partners of military history aficionados: once you hit these premises you may as well call it a day. Napoleon's imports titles covering the full gamut of military history from ancient to modern times. Famous customers include Labor Party leader Kim Beazley, a passionate amateur military historian, who from time to time sends a wish list to this great Melbourne bookshop.

Turn left into Elizabeth Street, and a little

way along at No. 250 is a bookshop called **Back Copies |10|,** which provides a great service for prolific readers with no shelf space: a buy-back scheme, whereby you purchase the latest bestseller, then sell it back to the store and buy another one. At No. 185, between Little Bourke and Bourke streets, is the **Little Bookroom |11|,** established in 1960 and serving the literary interests of Melbourne's children ever since. Along this section of Elizabeth Street there are a number of general and technical bookshops including Angus & Robertson, Collins and McGills.

Turn right into Bourke Street. Walk up the hill and turn into McKillop Street. At No. 15, until recently the site of Webbers Booksellers established by the legendary Margareta Webber, lies the Haunted Bookshop. Opened on Halloween 1997, this shop is easily identified by its Gothic interiors with vampire overtones, and boasts a solid collection of books on the occult. If you drop in during the week, you may be able to secure yourself an appointment with the resident clairvoyant, whose advice is regularly sought by members of the legal fraternity based at this end of town. Across the lane at No. 20 is Fine Music and Drama, established in 1979. The music section of this shop specialises in classical and show music. The drama section, once the Showbusiness Bookshop, is Melbourne's only book store dedicated to the performing arts. Here you will find scripts, plays, biographies and a wide range of publications on theatre technique and theory.

Walk to the end of McKillop Street and on your left, near the corner of Elizabeth Street, on the ground floor of the Galleria Shopping Plaza, is the **Australian Geographic Shop |12|.** Here you will find some excellent Australia-based travel and adventure publications. Above this is the ABC Shop which, with its large children's section and ABC TV and radio tie-ins, is a great place for gift shopping. Turn right into Little Collins Street. Cross over Queen Street and at Bank Place turn left.

Bank Place

It was to this lane that printmaker Charles Troedel moved in 1905 to premises opposite the Mitre Tavern. Troedel came to Melbourne in 1860, and quickly set about establishing himself as the city's best printer. With the press he brought from Europe he produced the popular publication *The Melbourne Album*, and established himself as Australia's father of lithography. A first edition, with its beautiful lithographs, can be seen in the State Library's Rare Books Reading Room. Troedel was not your average 19th-century tradesman. The artistry of his work was evident and his advice was regularly sought by the arts community. Troedel formed a partnership in 1891, and the firm traded under the name of **Troedel & Cooper |13|,** until after his death in 1906. One of Troedel's descendants still carries on the fine printing tradition in a firm of that name in Melbourne's eastern suburbs.

At 12–16 Bank Place is a three-storey brick building occupied by the Savage Club since 1923. Dating from about 1884, the original building was constructed as a town house for Australia's only baronet, Sir William Clarke. It was partially demolished in 1905 and further alterations were carried out in 1927. The Classical design has some unusual characteristics such as the rusticated columns to the portico. An interesting feature of the interior are the punkahs (large fans) hanging in the dining room, used to cool the air in summer. The club has long been frequented by artists, something of a rarity in a city where the established clubs are more likely to represent deeply conservative interests.

At 1–3 Bank Place is the Mitre Tavern. Little remains of the original 1868 building; the mock Tudor features, for example, were applied in the 1920s. In its early years it was a popular meeting place for hunt clubs, and later it became the haunt of bohemians and lawyers. Walk to the end of Bank Place.

Collins Street

When you come to Collins Street, cross the road and have a look at No. 425, slightly to your right, on the corner of Market Street. A plaque near the entrance declares that this is the site of the first newspaper and printing office in Melbourne. It was here that John Pascoe Fawkner on 1 January 1838 issued a handwritten newspaper of four pages entitled *The Melbourne Advertiser.* On 5 March 1838 the tenth issue, produced on a hand-operated press, was Melbourne's first printed newspaper. Just near here, at the corner of Market Street and Flinders Lane, is the Railfan Shop, for lovers of books about trains.

Walk east along Collins Street. At the south end of Queen Street, at No. 9, is Mitty's World of Sport, which has a collection of racing books and memorabilia. At 356 Collins Street is **Information Victoria |14|**. Run by the Victorian government, this shop is well worth a look for its comprehensive coverage of the state – everything from official reports to guide books on national parks and local history. The Australia-wide map collection is excellent.

Continue along, over Elizabeth Street. On your right you come to Centreway. Walk through here to Flinders Lane and turn left. At No. 247 is Green's, a great shop for its books on all aspects of the environment and its comprehensive collection of Australian natural history. At No. 238 is **Hylands Book Shop |15|** (on the first floor of Flinders Arcade). Can a town have too many military bookshops? Not in Melbourne, it seems. Hylands (established 1965) claims, as does Napoleon's, the largest collection of military history in the state. It also boasts a preeminent collection of transport history.

Opposite Hylands is Collected Works, known as the poet's bookshop. Established in 1985, it offers for sale the largest collection of local and international poetry in Australia. So broad is its focus that Britain has not one section but several, in order to cover Welsh, Scottish and Irish poets. In addition, it has a collection of fine novels, and hard-to-get tomes on literary theory and criticism.

At Swanston Street turn left and walk back to Collins Street. In the section of Collins Street that you have by-passed is the **Foreign Language Bookshop |16|** at No. 259 and Newspaper House at No. 247. The bookshop, which has been trading for over 60 years, stocks publications in 90 languages. The collection includes learning texts and aids, but there is a substantial foreign fiction section, and magazines and newspapers from abroad. No. 247 was known previously as the W.H. Rocke building, until it was taken over in 1933 by The Herald & Weekly Times. Dominating the first-floor facade is a glass mosaic by Napier Waller incorporating the words, 'I'll put a girdle around the earth'. (The Herald & Weekly Times was for many years based at the corner of Flinders and Exhibition streets before it moved in the 1990s to a new building at Southbank.)

Qantas House is a few doors along from Newspaper House. The Melbourne *Age* (established in 1854) was published in this building until the move to its current home at the north-western end of town, on the corner of Spencer and Lonsdale streets.

Near the south-eastern corner of Collins and Swanston streets is the Regent Theatre. In the 1850s a lane (later Regent Place) ran off Collins Street, alongside the building. On the west side of the lane was the first site of the *Argus* newspaper, established on 2 June 1846. The newspaper offices were moved in the 1920s to the *Argus* building on the corner of Elizabeth and Lonsdale streets. The *Argus* used *The Times* of London as its prototype of what a respectable city daily should be. To this end the *Argus* used the same paper and type; it borrowed substantially in terms of arrangement of contents and overall style; and even ran the same kind of content including reports of English parliamentary proceedings and theatre and literary news from 'home'. The published price for this virtual news experience of London was threepence, and its circulation was estimated at between ten and fifteen thousand.

Walk up the hill. At No. 156, housed in the Assembly Hall, is **Kay Craddock Antiquarian Bookshop |17|**. Established in 1965, the store moved seven times before settling down at this Collins Street address in 1990. The range of interests represented is eclectic and draws on local and overseas publications. To say this is a second-hand bookshop misses the point. You may stumble across the odd bargain, but what most of the books have in common here is their value as rare collectable objects. Walk up to Russell Street. Just to your left is 84 Russell Street, the site of **George Robertson's bookshop |18|**. This first Melbourne bookshop was opened in 1853 by bookseller and publisher George Robertson. In 1921 it amalgamated to form Robertson & Mullen (see below), for many years known as Melbourne's leading bookshop.

At 115–119 Collins Street, just up from the corner of Russell Street, the Austral Building has interesting literary associations. The publishers of *Melbourne Punch*, Alex McKinley & Co., employed Nahum Barnet in

1890 to design the Queen Anne Revival style building, which features red brick and cream plasterwork on the facade. In its infancy the photographer J.W. Lindt, the Lyric Club and the Austral Dramatic Club tenanted the building.

ANZ Towers, on the corner of Collins and Exhibition streets, was once the **site of Samuel Mullen's shop and library |19|**, opened after Mullen returned from a visit to Europe in 1859 with a great pile of stock drawn mainly from Mudie's of London. The collection was determinedly highbrow, containing serious works as well as a better-class fiction than was, at the time, engaging the interests of the colonists. Vice-regal patronage meant that the business became an immediate success, not to mention a popular meeting place for intellectuals. Mullen was later appointed a bookseller to the University of Melbourne. In 1889 he sold out to his brother William, A.G. Melville and L. Slade. Melville and Mullen merged with George Robertson & Co. to form Robertson & Mullen in 1921.

At the top of Collins Street turn left. A short distance along on your right, between Parliament House and the Treasury Building, is Gordon Reserve, dominated by two statues: one of Australian poet Adam Lindsay Gordon and a second of General Gordon, a soldier who died at the fall of Khartoum. The figure of the scribe faces Spring Street. He is remembered as one of the first Australian poets to write about the bush, and as a reckless and daring horseman. Paul Montford sculpted the statue in the early 1930s.

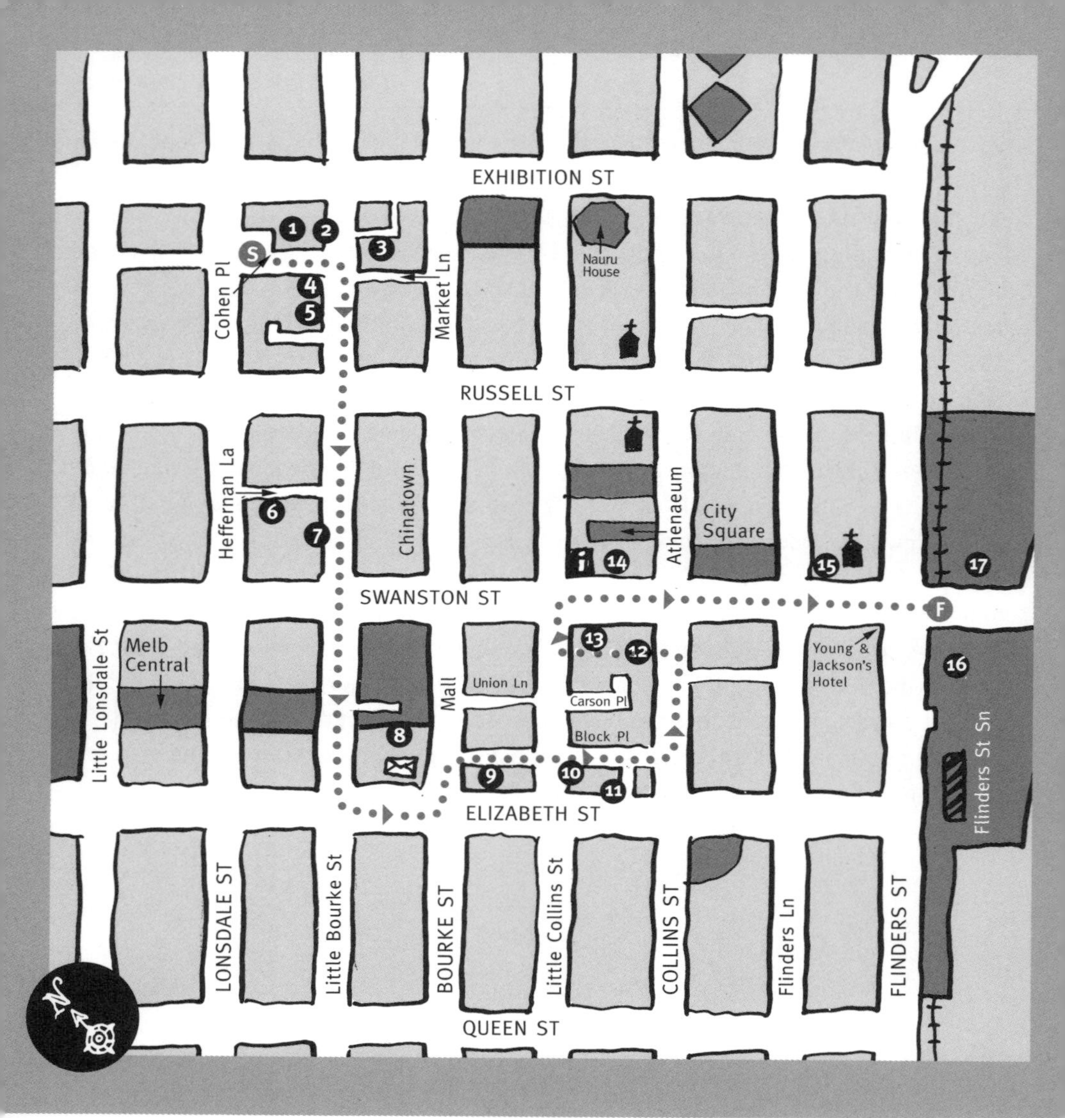

Walk key

1. Chinese Museum | **2.** Facing Heaven Archway | **3.** Kuo Min Tang building | **4.** Oriental Gourmet Restaurant | **5.** Ancient Times House | **6.** Chung Wah Cafe | **7.** Num Pon Soon building | **8.** General Post Office | **9.** Royal Arcade | **10.** Block Arcade | **11.** Block Court | **12.** Sportsgirl complex | **13.** Capitol Theatre | **14.** Melbourne Town Hall | **15.** St Paul's Cathedral | **16.** Flinders Street Station | **17.** Federation Square

Walk No. 5

City Sights

From Chinatown to Melbourne's heart

Start

Chinese Museum,
Cohen Place – any tram along Bourke Street to the corner of Exhibition Street, and then a short walk down Exhibition, left into Little Bourke Street, and along to Cohen Place.

Finish

Corner of Flinders and Swanston streets.
A train from Flinders Street Station and trams along Swanston Street travel to other parts of the city and suburbs

Length/Time

2 km/1.5 hours

The buildings and thoroughfares encountered in the city bear the history of various chapters of Melbourne's young existence, from the immigrations and social and economic impact of the city's Chinese community through to Victorian and contemporary shopping culture. The grandeur and optimism of the federation and early inter-war periods are also represented, nestled among the vibrant bustle of present-day design and activity.

Clans of Gold

Begin at the **Chinese Museum |1|** in Cohen Place. Chinatown was established during the gold rush in 1854 and is the oldest continuously occupied Chinatown in the world. It is also one of Melbourne's most popular attractions. Its story is one of immigration and entrepreneurs, combined with community cohesion. The Chinese Museum was established in 1985 and presents a rich cache of art works, cultural items and information about the history of Chinese Victorians. The museum is home to Australia's largest dragon and provides an audiovisual display, photographic exhibition, and a quite eerie mock-up of life as it may have appeared on the goldfields – claustrophobics beware.

The bulk of Chinese immigrants to Australia before the 1970s were from the See Yup district in south China, near Hong Kong. In the 1850s several hundred arrived in Melbourne every day, using the facilities of the budding Chinatown as a place to rest, stock up on supplies, and move on to the goldfields. Chinatown never had a large population of permanent residents but was more the portal and the base for successive waves of Chinese immigration.

The existing precinct of Chinatown roughly matches that of early years, which was near the Little Lonsdale Street brothels. This fact, combined with the well-known provision of opium in numerous Chinese clubs and boarding houses (the likes of which Melbourne poet C.J. Dennis used to frequent), and illegal gambling like the immensely popular Chinese lottery, made the community an easy target for innuendo. By the time the rivers of gold turned to a trickle in the 1880s, industry had diversified to market gardening and furniture-making. By the turn of the century, most of the fruit and vegetables grown in south-east Australia were produced and sold by the Chinese, and this industry created some envy. Various attempts were made by government and unions to scotch their impressive progress.

An important part of the success of the community was its entrepreneurial innovation on one hand, and its traditional social structures on the other. Chinese stores tended to be owned by different clans. The members of the clans would work in an extended chain of businesses that would use the services of the other clan businesses, thus establishing a constant and reasonably guaranteed flow of trade. During the depressions, the clans retained their customer bases by extending lines of credit and acted as philanthropic houses for their own members. They also acted as social clubs, where members could read the papers, receive interpreting and writing services, and send their earnings home to family through the stores' banking services. After a decline in numbers brought on by the White Australia Policy (1901), Chinatown almost vanished but survived due to the influx of refugees from various wars between the late 1930s and the late 1980s.

The precinct was given a new lease of life in 1974 when retail king David Wang rallied the Melbourne City Council and others to develop the area's tourist potential. The four Chinese archways that define the precinct down Little Bourke Street were built (some elements, such as the tiles, were imported from China), and a schedule of festivals and other community activities devised. The Chinese New Year Festival in February of each year is now a huge hit with Melburnians, as is the entire stretch of restaurants and cafes.

Mannerist snapshots of the Epiphany

Move to the **Facing Heaven Archway |2|** on the south edge of Cohen Square. This archway is a replica of the Ling Xing gate to the Facing Heaven Palace in Nanjing. It was provided to Victoria as a gift in 1985 by her sister province, Jiangsu, in China, and possesses a power and a sense of antiquity. From the Archway you can see the **Kuo Min Tang building |3|** at the eastern corner of Market Lane. This is the Chinese Nationalist Club Building, initially used as a meeting place for members of the Baptist Church, now housing the Guomindang who support the government in Taiwan. The facade was designed by Walter Burley Griffin in 1921.

Further west down Little Bourke Street, the building at Nos. 108–110 was designed by Charles Webb in 1894 and is a former mission hall and training centre for Chinese evangelists. It was established by social reformer Cheong Cheok Hong, who raised the funds to build this and another church down the road. Nos. 112–14 is the home of

Opening Times

Chinese Museum: Sun–Fri 10am–4.30pm; Sat 12 noon–4.30pm (9662 2888). Entry fees apply.

Ancient Times House: Collection open to public 3–5pm Fri; library Mon–Fri 9.30am–4pm (9650 3477). Entry fees apply.

Capitol Theatre: See daily newspapers for cinema screening times or telephone 9662 3722. Permission to view the interior between screening times needs to be gained from ticket desk. However, the best view of the ceiling is just as the lights are dimming for a film.

Refreshments

There are excellent cafes, yum cha places, restaurants, and pubs along the walk (See Walk No. 6, CBD Gourmet Tour). A good half-way stop is the beautiful little Italian cafe, **Porta Via** (9654 3100), just behind the Sportsgirl Complex off Collins Street.

the **Oriental Gourmet Restaurant |4|**, established in 1888. This Mannerist building was commissioned by Lowe Kong Meng, one of Melbourne's wealthiest businessmen at the time, and designed by George de Lacy Evans, a key practitioner in the Victorian Mannerist style. You will find relatively few facades quite like this in Australia. Its outrageously playful, even ostentatious design must have made quite a statement in its day. Just beyond this at Nos. 116–18 is **Ancient Times House |5|**. This was built in 1916 and converted in 1936 to a Gospel Hall, then converted once more to the current archaeological museum in 1954. It houses the Australian Institute of Archaeology, as well as the largest archaeological display in Melbourne. A mummified child, pottery shards, and gold relics from the Tombs of Ur are all on display, as are collections from Mesopotamia and ancient Syria. Opposite, at Nos. 119–125 on the corner of Paynes Place, is the Anglican Chinese Mission of the Epiphany (ACME), which stands as yet another record of the significant move towards Christianity by the Chinese community from the earliest days. Built in a warehouse-like form in 1872 and designed by Crouch & Wilson, its simple use of elegant polychrome brickwork, combined with its age and history, gives it an unusual and exotic presence. Continue west down Little Bourke Street and cross Russell Street to Heffernan Lane.

The former **Chung Wah Cafe |6|** was established on the site of the current Thai Shanghai restaurant at 11 Heffernan Lane in the 1890s and was the first Chinese restaurant to be frequented by non-Chinese, in particular by the bohemian set. Just down Little Bourke Street from here is the **Num Pon Soon building |7|** at Nos. 200–202, the oldest extant building in Chinatown and Australia's oldest Chinese Temple. This is quite a superb example of early Victorian Academic Classical architecture, constructed in 1860 to the design of Peter Kerr, who also designed Parliament House. The Sam Yup Society provided support here for migrants from the Nanhai, Punyu and Shute districts during the gold-rush years. Head down to Elizabeth Street across Swanston Street to reach the General Post Office on the corner of the Bourke Street Mall.

Arcades past and present

The General Post Office |8|, built in three stages between 1859 and 1907, stands on the site of Melbourne's first post office, which was a small cottage erected in 1841. The design for the current building was coordinated by A.E. Johnson and moves through the classical orders of Doric, Ionic and Corinthian columns before reaching the clock tower.

The Bourke Street Mall, opened in 1983, was designed by Yuncken Freeman. Slow to win acceptance, the Mall is now a very lively place, often full of street performers, crowds of shoppers and city workers. It contains some superb buildings and facades, particularly from the inter-war period. Move along the Mall and turn right into the Royal Arcade.

Royal Arcade |9|, designed by Charles Webb and built in 1869, is Melbourne's oldest and most ornate thoroughfare. Some of its more bizarre elements were modelled on precedents from England, such as the Gog and Magog characters over the south end, representing ancient Britons and Trojan invaders that echo similar figures from the London Guildhall of 1708. After enjoying a thriving patronage in the interwar period, Melbourne's arcades gradually declined until a resurgence of interest prompted by efforts of the Melbourne City Council in the 1980s. The arcades and similar thoroughfares provide pleasant connections between the major streets as well as constant surprises in their architectural diversity, and their businesses, cafes, and eating establishments. Stroll through to the connecting Hub Arcade and cross Little Collins Street to Block Place, located a little way towards Elizabeth Street.

The cafes and little restaurants in the covered Block Place provide delightful meeting spots. Block Arcade, and Block Court just beyond, were built in 1891 and the 1920s, respectively. The **Block Arcade |10|** was designed by David Askew on the model of the Galleria Vittorio Emmanuelle in Milan, Italy, and contains some impressive features, including the large-scale dome with ornate supports and the etched-glass roof. Also of interest are the Hopetoun Tea Rooms, serving the brew since 1892, and the Phillip Goatcher ceiling mural in the shop on the left side as you reach Collins Street. The nearby **Block Court |11|**, towards Elizabeth Street, is a glorious Art Deco arcade, well worth a look for its beautiful mosaic floors and other numerous decorative features. Turn left at Collins Street and enter the Sportsgirl complex for some respite shopping.

The **Sportsgirl complex |12|** was completed in the early 1990s and is a modern blend of arcade and shopping mall principles, liberally treated with light, depth and asymmetrical inclines. Its cavernous interior provides a place to eat, to shop, or simply to escape the elements. It is one of Melbourne's modern cathedrals to late 20th-century consumerism. Move through the complex and adjoining laneway (look out for the excellent cafe Porta Via) to Little Collins Street and turn right. Turn right again at Swanston Walk and find the entrance of the Capitol Theatre via the arcade of Capitol House.

Tales of Federation

Capitol House was designed by Walter Burley Griffin and built between 1925 and 1927. The building is a fine, if standard rendition from the Chicago School from which the Griffins, Walter and Marion Mahoney, hailed. The star attraction, however, is the **Capitol Theatre |13|**. The geometric ceiling and lighting scheme were Marion's work, based in large part upon the Griffins' unique form of architectural expression. Until its lower section was destroyed by a shopping development in 1965, the theatre had been described as the finest in the world.

Flinders Street Station, with its distinctive row of clocks, has long been a Melbourne landmark.

The Melbourne Town Hall |14|, opposite Capitol House, was erected in 1870. The Swanston Street portico of Ionic columns was added in 1887, just before the Centennial Exhibition. Designed by important Melbourne architect Joseph Reed (with colleague Frederick Barnes), the building incorporates a great hall, clock tower, large organ and furnishings made from Queensland maple. It provides venues for all manner of activities, including performances during Melbourne's festivals, political and fundraising meetings and council activities. Just across the road is the City Square, never the popular gathering place planned by a succession of architects. At the time of writing a major redevelopment, due to be completed in 1999, is to include shops, cafes and cinemas that will hopefully restore some life to this forlorn corner.

Continue along to the corner of Swanston and Flinders streets to **St Paul's Cathdral |15|,** standing on the site of Melbourne's first official church service, conducted in 1836. This section of the city was the premier end of town right until the 1930s when the ships were still pulling up at Queen's Wharf. The Cathedral, designed by English architect William Butterfield, who never set foot in Australia, was built in 1880–91 under the supervision of Joseph Reed. The current spires were tacked on by Sydney architect James Barr. Features of the Cathedral include horizontal striping in the interior based on that of the Cathedral in Siena; the largest team of bells in Australia (13 in all, and it is said that it would take 36 years of continuous ringing to exhaust all the possible combinations of tone); an impressive mosaic; and a wonderful sense of peace and quiet in the middle of the city.

Young & Jackson's Hotel on the north-west corner was first known as the Bridge Hotel before being taken over by Henry Young and Thomas Jackson in 1870. Since then the hotel has been an institution for successive generations of Melbourne guzzlers. The hotel attracted a great deal of notoriety (and excellent free publicity) from its 1908 purchase and display of the Jules Lefebre nude *Chloe*, which hangs in the saloon bar to this day.

Flinders Street Station |16| across the road was designed by J.W. Fawcett and

H.P.C. Ashworth and built between 1901 and 1911 in the Federation Free Classical style with strong French influences. Australia's first steam train ran from this site to Sandridge (Port Melbourne) in 1854 and the station is the centre of Melbourne's rail system. It is one of the busiest in the world with the longest platform in Australia (platform number 1 is 707.1 metres long). The distinctive clocks under the enormous round arch have been a popular and traditional meeting place for many years. The best view of the station is from one of the cafes at Southbank, across the Yarra.

Federation Square |17| at this crossroads is in the development phase and will cover the railway lines leading from Flinders Street to the eastern suburbs, allowing direct access to more sections of the Yarra and to some of Melbourne's premier sporting and concert venues. It will be designed by architects Donald Bates and Peter Davidson, and is to incorporate a massive civic plaza, a new museum of Australian art, a screen and national multimedia centre, restaurants and cafes, and an outdoor auditorium. It will also be the home of national television broadcaster SBS.

The combined effect of this development will be to extend and consolidate Melbourne's Southbank arts complex by creating an entirely new city precinct, while at the same time humanising a section of the city that for decades has been inhospitable to the general community due to earlier bad planning. It is due for completion in December 2000, in time for the centenary of Australian federation.

Walk key

1. Marchetti's Latin | **2.** Greek precinct | **3.** Entrance to Chinatown | **4.** Mask of China | **5.** Flower Drum | **6.** Madam Fang | **7.** Becco | **8.** Stella | **9.** Windsor Hotel | **10.** Site of the former Society Restaurant | **11.** Pellegrinis | **12.** Florentino | **13.** Quists Coffee Shop | **14.** Il Bacaro | **15.** Georges | **16.** Porta Via | **17.** David Jones Food Hall | **18.** Campari | **19.** Marchetti's Tuscan Grill

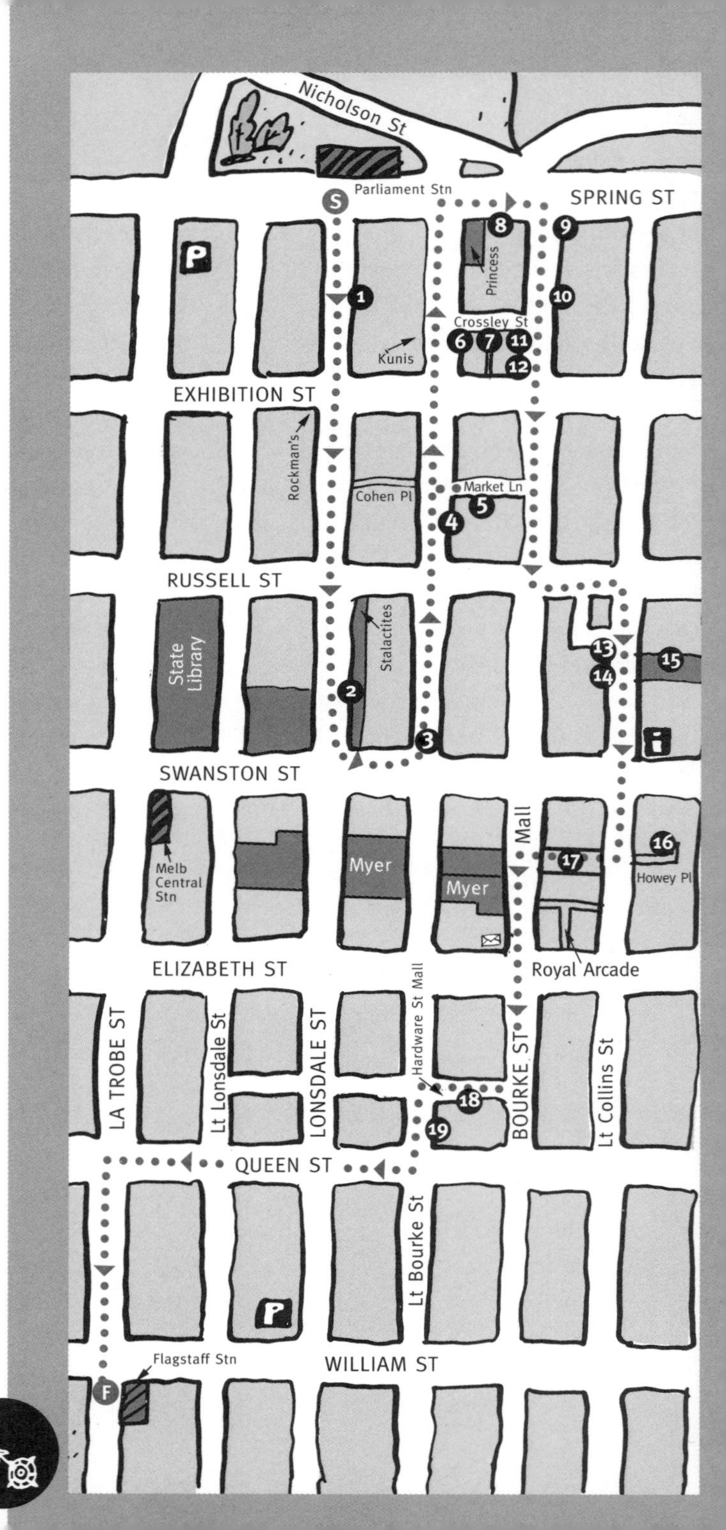

Walk No. 6

CBD Gourmet Tour

European and Asian culinary traditions

Start

Corner of Spring and Lonsdale streets. Parliament Station – trams 11, 12, 42, 86, 96, 109, City Circle tram.

Finish

Flagstaff Station – trams 23, 24, 30, 34, 55, City Circle tram; bus 684.

Length/Time

5 km/2.5 hours

Melbourne is one of the great food capitals of the world, with an eclectic range of cuisines. Although this culinary diversity is largely a phenomenon of the 1980s and 1990s, the city was not completely devoid of culinary sophistication before the Second World War. Melbourne's gourmet love affair began in the 1850s, when locals found relief from standard Anglo-colonial fare in a number of French restaurants. The Italians took over in the 20th century, dominating the scene for more than half a century with the establishment of some of the city's most revered dining institutions. In the 1970s immigrants from South-East Asia left their mark. The merging of these disparate cuisines has culminated in a magnificent home-grown style dubbed Modern Australian.

In the gold-rush era of the 1850s a Bourke Street restaurant with a French chef was the fashionable place to eat. Other French restaurants followed. When French cuisine was the rage in London in the 1890s, the colonies followed suit, and by the turn of the century French restaurants in Melbourne were numerous. In the first half of the 20th century it was the Italians who left their mark on Melbourne restaurant style, in particular a number of great restaurant families. Italian restaurants were linked to Melbourne intellectual life. Molina's, the Latin, the Society, Mario's and Florentino were meeting places for artists, writers and actors. The personalities who ran them introduced Melbourne to the joys of Italian food and wine long before the culinary resurgence of the last few decades.

The ubiquitous Chinese takeaway in many a city street and outlying suburb in the 1960s and 1970s was the product of a long history of Asian cooking in Melbourne – the Chinese were, after all, some of our earliest immigrants – but it was the influx of people from countries such as India, Thailand, Malaysia and Vietnam that finally loosened the culinary grip of the Europeans.

The restaurants of the city, in their range and number, prove that this is a place with some serious gourmet qualifications, while some individual restaurants, such as the inexpensive Nudel Bar at the top of Bourke Street or the exceptional Stella in Spring Street, combine the best of both East and West, offering the kind of potted history of the major influences on the development of a unique and exciting national cuisine.

This walk is not a cook's tour of the best of Melbourne restaurants, although some of those are definitely included. Rather, it is a culinary ramble that hopefully provides an insight into the diversity of the city's restaurant and cafe scene. En route you will be introduced to some of Melbourne's oldest eating establishments, some of its best dining institutions and some of its trend-setting newcomers and fine cafes.

Lonsdale Street

Walk down the hill in Lonsdale Street. This end of town is somewhat of an architectural mish-mash; a mix of old and new, renovated and made-over. At No. 55, **Marchetti's Latin |1|,** occupies a triple-fronted two-storey Victorian building dating from around 1881. Large windows at ground level have replaced the original facade, but the first floor retains its Victorian windows, with cast-iron balconies supporting attractive window boxes brimming with flowers. There has always been something old-world about this place, a club-like atmosphere that gives, in Leo Schofield's words, 'tradition, order, stability, purpose'. It has been serving exquisite Italian food for generations. In the days of the David Triaca ownership the walls were adorned with Australian works of art, including a huge portrait by Clifton Pugh of controversial governor-general Sir John Kerr. Today the art is less political but acclaimed owner chef Bill Marchetti has continued the tradition of the restaurant's Italian forebears: that of providing surroundings for good conversation, good food and good wine.

Cross Exhibition Street. Rockman's Regency stands on the north-west corner. On the left-hand side before Russell Street are a few Chinese restaurants, stragglers from nearby Chinatown only one block away to the south. As you cross Russell Street the huge building to your right is the State Library of Victoria.

Russell Street marks the start of the city's **Greek precinct |2|.** Stretching for a city block to Swanston Street, there are restaurants, pastry shops and travel agencies. The time to experience the ambience of the place is lunchtime during the week, when footpath tables resound with conversation and Greek music fills the air. On Greek festival days, in particular, it is easy to appreciate that Melbourne has the largest Greek population of any city outside Greece.

On the south-west corner is Stalactites, established in the late 1970s. It is open seven days a week, 24 hours a day – one of the first places to keep such hours. People from all walks of life come to eat here, either at the footpath tables or by the blazing fire inside if the weather is cold. Food is basic and cheap.

A relatively new addition to the precinct, opened in 1988, Antipodes at No. 195 is not your average Greek taverna. The concrete floor is about the only concession to rusticity; the rest is elegant and stylish, with exposed bluestone walls, white tablecloths and simple wooden furniture. The

Opening Times

Try a leisurely lunch, or coffee and snack at one of the following: **Becco**, 11–25 Crossley Street (9663 3000), lunch, snacks and dinner Sun–Fri; **Campari**, 25 Hardware Lane (9670 3813), lunch Mon–Sat, breakfast and dinner Mon–Fri; **Florentino**, 80 Bourke Street (9662 1811), lunch Mon–Fri, snacks and dinner Mon–Sat; **Flower Drum**, 17 Market Lane (9662 3655), lunch Mon–Sat, dinner daily; **Il Bacaro**, 168–170 Little Collins Street (9654 6778), breakfast Mon–Fri, lunch and dinner Mon–Sat; **Madam Fang**, 27–29 Crossley Street (9663 3199), lunch Mon–Fri, dinner Mon–Sat; **Marchetti's Latin**, 55 Little Lonsdale Street (9662 1985), lunch Mon–Fri and Sun, dinner daily; **Marchetti's Tuscan Grill**, 401 Little Bourke Street (9670 6612), lunch Mon–Fri, dinner Tue–Sat; **Mask of China**, 115–117 Little Bourke Street (9662 2116), lunch and dinner daily; **Pellegrinis**, 66 Bourke Street (9662 1885), daily; **Republique**, 25 Bourke Street (9654 6699), lunch and dinner Mon–Sat; **Stella**, 159 Spring Street (9639 1555), lunch, snacks and dinner Mon–Sat.

food is contemporary Greek and includes such delights as a single ravioli stuffed with wild mushrooms and topped with grilled quail. Other dishes include calamari, pan-fried veal and grilled calves' liver. Food is reasonably priced. Tsindos is next door on the eastern corner of Heffernan Lane. With ochre-coloured walls, terracotta tiles on the floor and some check cloths in among the white napery, this is less stylish but still smarter that most in the strip. Turn left into the Mall and head for Little Bourke Street.

Little Bourke Street

A tall Chinese archway over the street heralds the **entrance to Chinatown |3|.** Turn left and you find yourself in a street bedecked with attractive lanterns, Chinese signage, and Asian grocery stores between the restaurant frontages. The Chinese first came to Victoria in the 1850s, hoping to make their fortunes on the goldfields, and Little Bourke Street became a community to service the needs of Chinese diggers. When the gold ran out, the city enclave grew. The White Australia Policy accompanied federation and the area experienced a decline in numbers, but after the Second World War Little Bourke Street took on an exciting new vibrancy.

Melburnians were slow to accept Chinese cuisine. In the 1950s a few restaurants in the city and suburbs offered diners a choice of chop suey, chow mein, chicken and almonds, sweet and sour pork and 'special' fried rice. A Sunday night ritual involved taking a collection of saucepans to the local Chinese eatery and having them filled with takeaway versions of these dishes.

Chinese cuisine has been a significant part of the Melbourne culinary renaissance and the city now has Chinese restaurants that are world standard. The Chinese community in Little Bourke Street claims to have been adversely affected by the establishment of Crown Casino at Southbank, and these days there are fewer eating houses and less activity than a decade or so ago. You pass the Dragon Boat Restaurant, and some old buildings such as the 1873 Chinese Methodist Church on the left at No. 196, its polychrome brickwork badly in need of a clean. A further two arches stand on the Russell Street corners. Cross over and continue up the hill.

Opposite the end of Corrs Lane, at 131 Little Bourke Street, is Shark Fin House, a popular yum cha venue, and next door is the Chinese Mission Church dating from 1902, constructed of plain brick with some decorative moulding around the arched doorway. At No. 117 is the renowned **Mask of China |4|,** which specialises in Chiu Chow cuisine, rather than the more common Cantonese. Established in 1987, this elegant place vies with the Flower Drum for the accolade of Melbourne's best Chinese restaurant. Unlike some of its neighbours with their huge busy floor spaces, the interior is divided into small rooms that provide an intimate atmosphere. The varied menu offers finely prepared regional specialties.

Opposite is the Empress of China, a large friendly place of long standing. Nearby, the

Oriental Gourmet (Nos. 112–114) is housed in one of the few remaining boom period buildings in the street. Lowe Kong Meng, a 19th-century leader of the Chinese community and a wealthy merchant, erected this building as business premises, warehouse and residence in 1888. It was designed by George de Lacy Evans and has been classified by the National Trust. The current restaurant was opened in 1964 and it is worth a visit just to see the historic interior.

If you take a short detour along Market Lane you come to what many consider to be Melbourne's finest Chinese restaurant, **Flower Drum |5|**. It is owned by Gilbert Lau, who has been serving a devoted clientele for decades. The Cantonese style food is expensive and superb, with popular choices including mud crab, crayfish, abalone, squab and Peking duck. The ambience is exceptional, with antique furnishings and masses of fresh flowers.

Walk back to Little Bourke Street. At Nos. 107–109, on the eastern corner of Market Lane, is the Kuo Min Tang building, a double-fronted facade designed by Nahum Barnet. Successful merchant C.H. Cheong commissioned Barnet in 1903 to design a pair of shops, which were occupied by cafes and importers until 1921 when the Kuo Min Tang (Chinese Nationalist Club) commissioned Walter Burley Griffin to redesign one of the pair for their clubhouse. A small square opens up on the left. This is Cohen Place and you will see signs to the entrance of the Chinese Museum (see Walk No. 5, City Sights).

Cross over Exhibition Street. Just up from the corner is Kuni's at No. 56, an excellent value-for-money place, which has been one of the best Japanese restaurants in town since it first opened in Crossley Street in the early 1980s.

Take a walk up Crossley Street to see **Madam Fang |6|** at Nos. 27–29, housed within a deep red-coloured three-storey building. The menu features beautifully crafted Asian-inspired modern Australian cuisine. Inside the entrance is a bar, with oriental rugs on the floor. The sumptuous decor of rich colours and original antiques is matched by the innovative food.

The contemporary Italian restaurant and bar **Becco |7|** next door (11–25 Crossley Street) was once part of Pellegrinis (see below). Large windows display an interior that is casually stylish and bright, and in true Italian family tradition, exudes conviviality and warmth.

Back in Little Bourke Street, continue east. Two other well-patronised Chinese restaurants are located at this top end of town: Shark Fin Inn at No. 50 has been going since 1962, and on the opposite side of the street is Bamboo House.

Spring and Bourke streets

Turn right into Spring Street, passing the Princess Theatre on your right (see page 34). Just along from the theatre is **Stella |8|**, highly regarded by food critics for its skilful blend of Mediterranean and Asian flavours.

On the north corner of Spring and Bourke streets is the Imperial Hotel and, opposite, the **Windsor Hotel |9|.** When the Windsor was built in 1883 it was called the Grand Hotel, and it survives as a magnificent luxury hotel upholding the very best of 19th-century opulence with 20th-century comforts. It was renamed the Windsor in 1920. You can drop in for lunch (they offer a wonderful two-course deal for around $20) or morning or afternoon tea.

Down Bourke Street from the Windsor is the **site of the former Society Restaurant |10|,** and a generation of Melburnians will mourn its passing. Refurbished and reopened as the Republique in July 1998, some of the old atmosphere remains, created by the timber detailing and the Society appellation accorded one of the private rooms.

Cross Liverpool Street and then Crossley Street, where you will find **Pellegrinis |11|,** a Melbourne institution virtually unchanged since it opened in 1954. This is the place that introduced a generation of post-war Melburnians to authentic Italian food. Parents brought their children here for a gelati in the 1950s, and those same children dined here on minestrone and pasta in the 1960s. It was the first restaurant to own an espresso machine and, even today, invariably wins a prize in most coffee-making competitions. The black-and-white marble floor and well-worn red leather seated stools, which line the long bar on one side and long bench on the other, have stood the test of time. Pellegrinis occupies the corner half of an historically significant two-storey brick building erected by William Crossley as a pair of shops in 1848. Crossley lived in the western half above his butcher's shop and slaughter house. The celebrated artist Eugène von Guérard had a studio in the corner shop between 1857 and 1858, after coming to Australia to try his luck on the Ballarat goldfields.

A few doors down, at 80 Bourke Street, is the triple-fronted **Florentino |12|.** The building dates from the 1850s. In the upstairs restaurant an atmosphere of old-world elegance is created by wood-panelling and Italian murals painted by students of Napier Waller in 1934. The traditional Italian food draws a loyal clientele. Many older-generation Melburnians have fond memories of dining here in the 1950s and 1960s. Meals are cheaper in the bistro and cellar bar downstairs.

Little Collins Street

Cross Exhibition Street and continue down the hill to Russell Street. Turn left here and make your way to Little Collins Street. Occupying No. 166 is **Quists Coffee Shop |13|.** Delicious aromas waft out from the entrance of this haunt of caffeine lovers. Every conceivable variety of coffee percolator, plunger and pot is also on sale. Next door at Nos. 168–170 is **Il Bacaro |14|,** an award-winning Italian restaurant in Venetian bar style. Like its sister restaurant, Caffe e Cucina in South Yarra, this place, opened in 1996, has an irresistible quality.

On the left is the back of **Georges |15|,** the old store name retained for a 1998 venture by London's Sir Terence Conran. Its three eateries became an instant success,

Florentino, opened in 1929 by Rinaldo Massoni, offers old-world elegance and formal dining.

but the store failed and was forced to close its doors in early 1999.

Walk down the hill to Swanston Street – the imposing edifice on the corner is the side of the Melbourne Town Hall. Cross over and walk along to Howey Place. Turn down here, past the fashion boutiques, to a tiny lane on the left, Presgrave Place. This is the location of **Porta Via |16|**, one of the new breed of Italian espresso bars that will make you think you are in the heart of Rome or Florence. You can snack on legendary pastries and cakes on any day of the week (7am–6pm) and Sat (8am–5pm), and everything is made in the tiny kitchen.

Return to Little Collins Street and almost opposite the end of Howey Place is the rear entrance to David Jones. Take the stairs down to the **David Jones Food Hall |17|**. Marvel at the array of exotic fruits, cheeses, cold meats, fresh pasta, pies, cakes, pastries, and more. Shelves are lined with all sorts of delicacies. Exit the store in Bourke Street and turn left. Walk along the Bourke Street Mall, past the Royal Arcade on the left and the General Post Office on your right. Cross Elizabeth Street and walk up the hill.

Hardware and Little Bourke streets

Hardware Street, a brick-paved walkway, is an eclectic mix of cafes, restaurants and ski shops. **Campari |18|** at No. 25 opened in the 1960s and has retained its popularity in an area that is something of a culinary desert. Its red brick floor and distinctive central bar, where patrons can prop for a quick coffee fix or a fresh pasta, remains unchanged, and the place is still packed during weekday lunch after all these years.

At Little Bourke Street, turn left and on the corner of Kirks Lane is **Marchetti's Tuscan Grill |19|**, a subterranean eatery popular with the business crowd. It offers a sophisticated mix of Italian dishes.

Head to Flagstaff Station on the corner of William and La Trobe streets for a train or the City Circle tram, or go back to Elizabeth or Swanston streets.

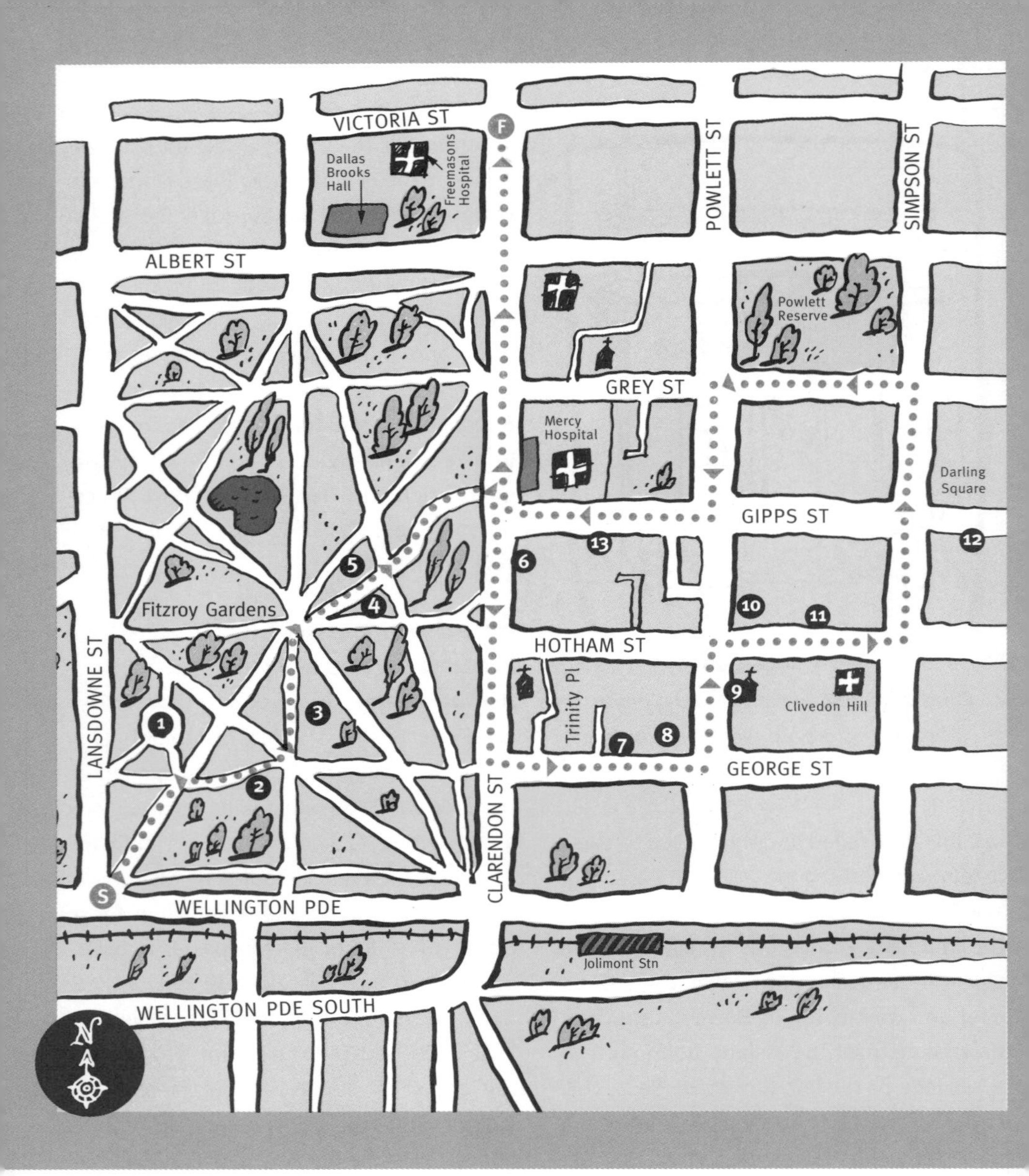

Walk key

1. Conservatory | **2.** Cooks' Cottage | **3.** Sinclair's Cottage | **4.** Fairy Tree | **5.** Tudor village | **6.** Home of the first Bishop of Melbourne | **7.** Braemar | **8.** Koorine | **9.** Cairns Memorial Presbyterian Church | **10.** Janet Terrace | **11.** Sydenham House | **12.** House and studio of Ola Cohn | **13.** Little Parndon

Walk No. 7

Fitzroy Gardens & East Melbourne

Grand gardens and historic residences

Start

Corner of Lansdowne and Wellington streets – a short walk from the city centre up Flinders Street (becomes Wellington Street); or trams 48 or 75 in Flinders Street.

Finish

Corner of Clarendon and Victoria streets – cross to the tram island in Victoria Street to board trams 23, 24 (running down La Trobe Street to Spencer Street); or 42, 109 (running down Collins Street to Spencer Street).

Length/Time

2.5 km/2.5 hours

Fitzroy Gardens is an acclaimed example of 19th-century landscape design, featuring a range of popular attractions, including Cooks' Cottage and the Fairy Tree. As well as visiting the best-known attractions, visitors should take some time to wander casually up the avenues and across the lawns to get some appreciation of what the National Trust said was one of the city's most 'magnificent and historic gardens, with outstanding landscape qualities and botanical importance,' when it classified the area in 1974. Leaving the park, the walk continues through the tiny but elegant suburb of East Melbourne, one of the city's earliest residential districts, and the place to which some of its most prominent forebears flocked to build their residences in the new colony.

Fitzroy Gardens attractions

Enter the gardens on the east side of Lansdowne Street. On the west side of the street lies the Treasury Gardens (see Walk No. 3, Parliament Precinct and Eastern Hill). The development of the Fitzroy Gardens coincided happily with a time in Melbourne's history when fashion dictated that urban environments be not only furnished with parks and gardens to facilitate the physical well-being of the residents, but that these places, in their beauty, should provide a spiritual salve for the soul of the inner-city dweller. As it is today, the Fitzroy Gardens, along with other of Melbourne's gardens, represents some of the best of what public planning and social ideals in the Victorian era gave the city.

Take the main path that leads off in a diagonal direction away from the corner of Lansdowne and Wellington streets. To the left lies the **Conservatory |1|.** Opened in 1930, the design follows the popular 'Spanish Mission' style of the period. There are five seasonal flower displays each year. On the right lies **Cooks' Cottage |2|,** the home of the parents of Captain Cook, which was shipped out to Australia from Yorkshire in 1934 in a cargo of 253 boxes, and then reassembled. The cottage was occupied by the Cooks in 1755, some time after the Captain had left home, although he certainly visited the cottage and probably spent the odd night there. The surrounding English country garden is probably a luxury the Cooks could not have afforded.

The elegant structures of the Fitzroy Gardens complement gracious European style landscaping.

To the left, behind the cottage, there are splendid avenues of towering European species. To the right is a small grove with a bridge over the little creek, secluded except for weekends when bridal parties line up to conduct their ceremonies. Walk through the grove and emerge in front of **Sinclair's Cottage |3|,** once home to the gardens' designer and director and now a gallery and craft shop. Head up the hill in a northerly direction and follow the signs to the **Fairy Tree |4|.** This landmark, described as the most 'seen' sculpture in Melbourne, was crafted in the early 1930s by artist Ola Cohn, who spent about four years carving an assortment of local and European folkloric figures into the trunk of a massive blue gum. Opposite the tree lies the **Tudor Village |5|**, another favourite with generations of young Melburnians. The tiny fenced village, with its bonsaied trees and shrubs, and its miniature roads, streams and houses, was presented to the people of Melbourne by the citizens of Lambeth, England, in appreciation of the parcels of food sent from Australia to Britain after the Second World War. Further up the hill, in a north-easterly direction, are two Classical rotundas, popular with brides for their wedding portraits.

Residential East Melbourne

Exit the gardens, just beyond the rotundas, into Clarendon Street, opposite the Mercy Hospital. Public sales of land for the suburb of East Melbourne began in 1852, more than a decade after the neighbouring suburbs of Fitzroy, Collingwood and Richmond were first developed. Because of its proximity to the city and its hilltop vantage point, and because its development coincided with the first hints of the immense prosperity that the gold rush would bring to Victoria, East Melbourne began life as a well-heeled suburb and a desirable address. Grand mansions and gracious terrace housing spread quickly down the attractive royally named streets and around the grassy reserves. Just about every prominent professional, businessman, politician and official called East Melbourne home at some stage between the boom years of 1850 and 1890. Around the mid-20th

Opening Times

Fitzroy Gardens Conservatory: Mon–Fri 9am–5pm (9am–5.30pm daylight saving)
Cooks' Cottage: Mon–Fri 9am–5pm (9am–5.30pm daylight saving)
Telephone 9419 4677 for both places.

Refreshments

If the weather is good, pack a picnic to enjoy in the Fitzroy Gardens. Or try the **Pavilion**, located at the heart of the gardens, which serves light snacks and lunches (9417 2544). The **George Street Cafe** on the corner of George and Simpson streets is open seven days a week (9419 5805). **The Hilton**, corner of Wellington and Clarendon streets (9419 2000), has a variety of eating areas including the Cliveden Room, which incorporates some of the internal features from Cliveden Mansion, a massive private residence that once occupied the site.

century the suburb suffered the fate of being unfashionable – along with its other inner-city counterparts – as the wealthy moved further east towards the larger blocks of land. Some of the old mansions were pulled down and some were turned into boarding houses. Now in favour again, East Melbourne has regained something of its former grace and still preserves some examples of domestic architecture from the Victorian period. This section of the walk can only cover some of the more interesting examples of the architecture and points of social history; further exploration will reveal more sites of interest.

Walk a little way down the Clarendon Street hill to the corner of Gipps Street and cross the road. The imposing bluestone residence here was the home of the first **Bishop of Melbourne |6|,** Bishop Perry. Continue down the hill and turn left into George Street. **Braemar |7|** at 178 George Street is classified by the National Trust and is recognised for its Regency character and elegantly shaped windows. Further along on the corner of Powlett Street lies a house called **Koorine |8|,** which was built in 1869 and was home to Sir Benjamin Benjamin, member of a prominent Jewish family, a merchant, a philanthropist, and eventually a knight of the British Empire.

Turn left into Powlett Street. On the corner of Powlett and Hotham streets is the facade of the **Cairns Memorial Presbyterian Church |9|.** The church was opened in 1884 and was much admired for its fine stone work. A planned tower and spire were never built. The building was nearly destroyed by fire and lay derelict for years. Recently, its ruins have been restored and a starkly modern, but largely sympathetic structure rises up behind the facade.

Turn right into Hotham Street. On the north side of the street is a row of grand terrace houses. Nos. 92–94 are known collectively as the **Janet Terrace |10|** (1881); at one stage the Premier of Victoria, Graham Berry, lived in one of the houses. **Sydenham House |11|,** at 80 Hotham Street, was a Ladies Academy. The grand pile of Victoriana on the corner of Hotham and Simpson streets was built in 1888 at the height of the land boom period, and was known as the Royal East Melbourne Coffee Palace. Across the road the houses are more modest affairs, providing further architectural variety. Of note is No. 125 Hotham Street, a simple and very pretty bluestone cottage, which a local builder constructed for himself in the early 1860s.

Turn left into Simpson Street, cross the road and walk around the corner into Gipps Street. Nos. 41–43 was the house and studio of **Ola Cohn |12|,** the aforementioned sculptor and long-time resident of East Melbourne. The dwelling was built in 1881 and is noted for its arched doorway that leads through to a courtyard at the front of the house. Opposite is Darling Square, representing the European tradition of building residences around a public reserve, a tradition that only a few Melbourne suburbs were fortunate to inherit. Stroll through Darling Square and head back to

Simpson Street, where you turn left into Grey Street. Opposite is Powlett Reserve, once a swampland and now another pleasant public square. Further west along Grey Street there are two interesting pairs of houses (Nos. 43–45 and 83–85), both sets noted by the National Trust for their fine styling and original features.

Turn left into Powlett Street. At No. 138 is a house built around 1868, which is classified by the National Trust, and which boasts an unusual 'opera box' balcony. Continue south to Canterbury Terrace, Nos. 82–112, the largest terrace in East Melbourne and considered to be an exceptional example of terrace architecture with its beautifully balanced design. Across the road is No. 64, a house once occupied by Peter Lalor, leader of the only armed insurrection on Australian soil, the Eureka Stockade. Lalor, a folk hero, gained respectability when he was elected to the Victorian parliament.

Double-back along Powlett Street and turn left into Gipps Street. No. 159 Gipps Street was built in 1862 and was occupied by one of Australia's most famous landscape artists, Eugène von Guérard, who was also curator at the National Gallery. In terms of its architecture the house, known as **Little Parndon |13|**, is distinguished by the elegant simplicity of its design, in an era characterised more by excess than restraint. No. 173 Gipps Street was built in 1860 and is one of the suburb's earlier residences. No. 179 also dates from the early 1860s and is noted by the National Trust for its Italianate style and its stucco detailing.

Turn right into Clarendon Street, walk past the Mercy and Freemasons hospitals and cross Albert Street. No. 206 Albert Street is classified by the National Trust and was built in 1863. In the late 1860s it was taken over by tea merchant Kong Meng, within the Chinese community, and the only one among his countrymen to set up home in the heartland of the Melbourne Establishment. Other worthy residents of this imposing manor included Sir Redmond Barry who, although a person of prominent deeds, has nothing like the fame of his nemesis bushranger Ned Kelly, sentenced to death in 1880 by Barry in his role as a judge of the Supreme Court. Nos. 208–212 Clarendon Street combine three terraced houses. The colonnaded portico is one of East Melbourne's most ambitious architectural projects: it aims for a grand classical style and more or less gets away with it.

Stroll up to Victoria Street, cross to the tram island, and take any tram heading west to get into the city.

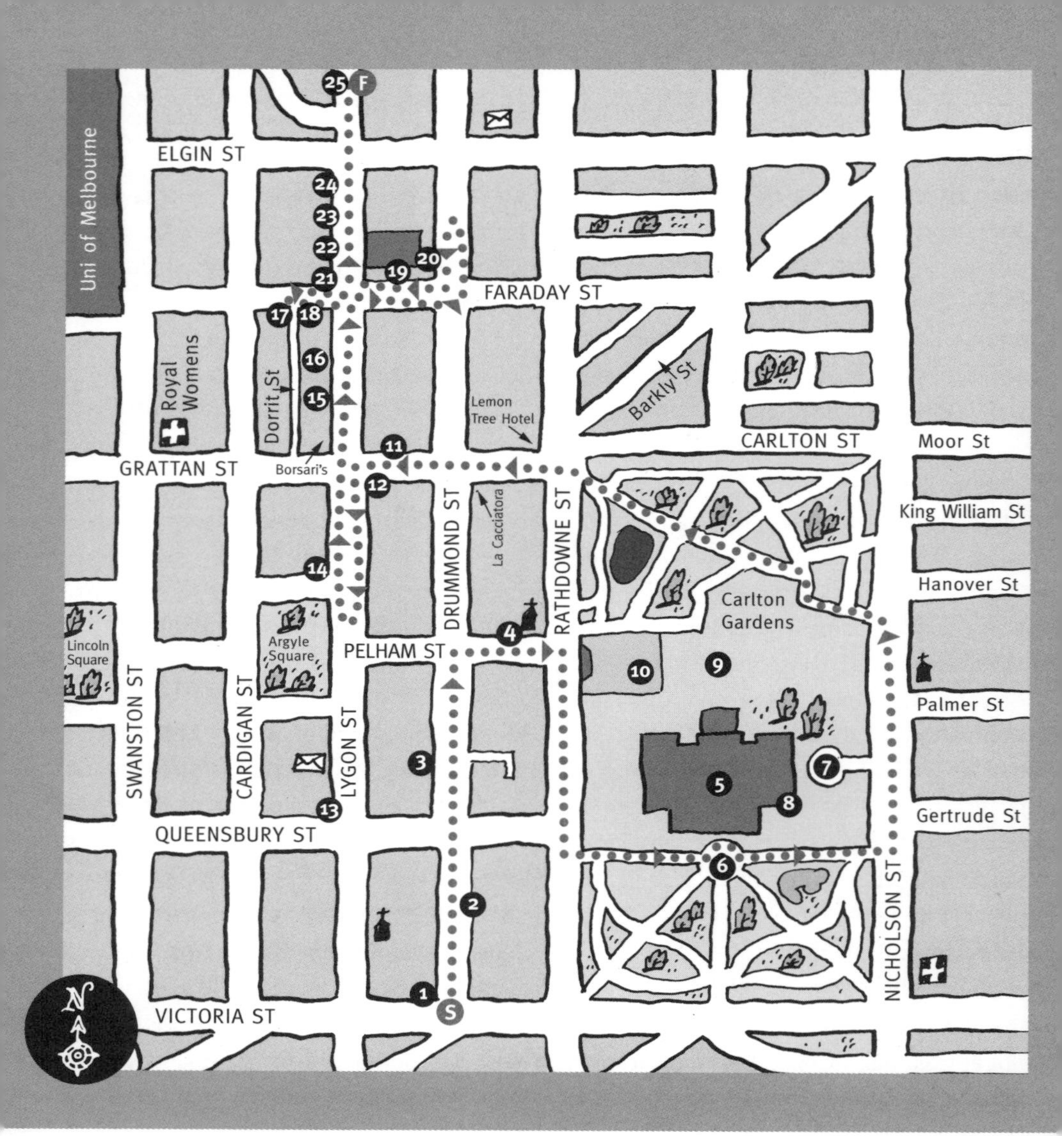

Walk key

1. Melbournia Terrace | **2.** Benvenuta | **3.** Old Carlton Weather Bureau | **4.** Sacred Heart Roman Catholic Church | **5.** Exhibition Building | **6.** Hochgurtel Fountain | **7.** French Fountain | **8.** Protest Pillar | **9.** Museum of Victoria | **10.** Imax Theatre | **11.** Comparin's House | **12.** Caffe Sport | **13.** Totos | **14.** Casa del Gelato | **15.** University Cafe | **16.** Lygon Food Store | **17.** Carlton Movie House | **18.** Genevieve Restaurant | **19.** Brunetti | **20.** Masanis | **21.** King & Godfree | **22.** Tiamo I & II | **23.** Readings Bookshop | **24.** Jimmy Watsons | **25.** St Jude's Church

Walk No. 8

Carlton

Old Melbourne meets Little Italy

Start

Corner of Victoria and Drummond streets – buses from the city to the corner of Victoria and Russell streets, including 200, 201 and 207. Get off at Victoria Street and walk east 60 metres to Drummond Street. Alternatively, catch buses 235, 236, 237 or 250 from the city to the corner of Exhibition and Victoria streets. Get off at Victoria Street and walk about 100 metres west to Drummond Street.

Finish

St Jude's Church – tram to city from north-east corner of Lygon and Elgin streets (any number), or any bus from the south-east corner of Elgin and Lygon streets.

Length/Time

3.5 km/2 hours

Carlton was laid out in 1852 according to the precepts of Regency planning, and endowed with generous allocations of parklands, boulevards and thoroughfares. It was for wealthy middle-class people in its early years, drawn to its elevation and proximity to the City of Melbourne. Pockets of contemporary Carlton have a tranquil, inner-city residential ambience. Carlton was once a densely forested area, but was denuded after establishment. The Aboriginal owners of the area were members of the Wurrundjeri Willum, whose elder Billibellary had 'signed' the treaty with John Batman on the banks of the Yarra in 1835. In the 1840s many of the visiting tribes from the western districts used to camp around the areas now occupied by the General Cemetery and the University of Melbourne.

Between the 1860s and 1880s an acute shortage of housing and accommodation created by the gold rush saw much of South Carlton become a shantytown. As gaslight graced her streets for the first time, Carlton slipped into the darkness of the 1890s depression and became a slum. Land prices tumbled, the money moved on, and the grand homes of the wealthy were sold or rented out as cheap boarding houses. Meanwhile, there was the parallel development of two of Melbourne's most outstanding institutions, the University of Melbourne and, later, the Exhibition Building. There were also waves of immigration. By 1960 every fourth person on a Carlton street was Italian born or first generation Italian. Large numbers of the Italian community left the suburb in the early 1970s, as a new interest in the area from middle class and professional families arose. They renovated the area's ageing but beautiful homes making Carlton once again one of the Melbourne's more expensive and desirable suburbs.

From tents to terrazza

Start the walk at the south end of Drummond Street. This broad and well-proportioned street, which retains some of Carlton's original land allotments, began as a crowded muddle of tents and shanties from 1854 to 1860, when the housing, most of which stands to this day, was commenced. Around the time that it became clear Melbourne was to host the 1880 International Exhibition, Drummond and Rathdowne streets became fashionable and highly sought after. Move north along Drummond Street.

Melbournia Terrace offers a glimpse of Victorian residential design at its most exuberant.

Melbournia Terrace |1| at 1–13 Drummond Street was built in 1876 for a Jewish warehouse proprietor, Woolf Davis. The grapevine design in the ironwork was No. 97 in the catalogue of Jenkins & Law, foundry providers of iron lattice and other bits, located in Exhibition Street at the time. No. 7 housed Alberto Zelman, an Italian composer and professor of music for two years in 1879–80. His eldest son, Alberto Victor, went on to found the Melbourne Symphony Orchestra. Note the Victorian Georgian style residences at Nos. 37 and 39 – these are fairly rare representatives of this style in inner-city Melbourne – before encountering Benvenuta, Italian for 'welcome', at No. 48. **Benvenuta |2|** was built in 1892 for Mrs Leah Abrahams, the widow of a small arms manufacturer. It was designed by W.S. Law in the Victorian Mannerist style with more than 15 tonnes of Italian marble in the interior, much of it in the staircase. In the 1930s it was home to the Italian Club, which hosted ballroom orchestras and boxing matches on Sundays. The vice squad raided every now and then to ensure the guests were not indulging in too much unlicensed pleasure. Benvenuta's multi-tiered cornices, lashings of mahogany, delicately cast ironwork and leaded windows also briefly served as residence to the Italian Consul from early 1940 until Italy entered the war, when the consulate was closed down. It is now Medley Hall, a residential hall of the University of Melbourne.

The National Trust-listed **Old Carlton Weather Bureau |3|** at 117 Drummond Street is an architectural oddity in bluestone. Quite eccentric, it was built for a James Matthias in 1865 and gets its name from the weathervane on the tower. Another notable home is to be found at No. 125, just before the corner of Pelham Street, where the mix of Doric columns and fretted woodworked balcony is quite unusual. Turn right at Pelham and head east to the church on the corner of Pelham and Rathdowne streets.

The **Sacred Heart Roman Catholic Church |4|** was designed by Joseph Reed and partners Smart & Tappin. It is seen as a radical departure from Gothic into a Baroque

Opening Times

Carlton Gardens: Open all hours.
Imax Theatre: Open every day 9am–late (9663 5454) – check newspapers for screening times
Museum of Victoria: Check 'what's on' section of newspapers for exhibit details (9651 6777).
Royal Exhibition Building: Open at times of exhibits or events (9270 5000). Historic tours are offered by the Museum of Victoria for 10 or more people at any time by appointment (9669 9864). These tours can be tailor-made to the interests of your party and visitors are treated to a slide show.
Sacred Heart Catholic Church: Open Mon–Fri 6.30pm, Sat 6.30pm, Sun 9am–5pm (at service times). Gates always open to see the Lourdes Grotto (9663 7877).
St Jude's Church: weekdays 9am–3pm, Sun 9.30am–9pm during service times (9347 7993).

Refreshments

There are many places to dine in Lygon Street, some open from very early to very late every day of the week. Try **Brunetti** (9347 2801), the **Universita** (9347 2142), **Tiamo** (9347 0911) or **Jimmy Watson's** (9347 3985).

variation on the Federation Academic Classical style. Built in 1897, it was meant to have a dome to match that of the Exhibition Building, but it is unlikely this will ever be completed. The church became an important location for Carlton's Italian community after the big waves of immigration in the 1950s and 1960s. The Lourdes Grotto in the church grounds was built by Italians, and this has long been a popular focal point for private worship, festas and religious processions.

St George's Gothic style Church and School, also in the Sacred Heart Church grounds, was built in 1855, and was designed by the favoured Roman Catholic architects of the time, George & Schneider. It is one of Carlton's oldest standing buildings, now an archbishop's residence.

On the opposite corner to the Sacred Heart is the location of the former residence of Sir Redmond Barry. This eminent Melbourne identity is, unfortunately, most remembered as 'the hanging judge' (the man who sentenced Ned Kelly). Chief Justice of the Supreme Court, and one of the first landowners to build his residence here, Barry used to ride his horse down Rathdowne Street to work at the Supreme Court in La Trobe Street. He was one of the founding fathers of the city, influential in establishing many of the significant social and cultural developments of the time. He set up numerous institutions and associations, including the Carlton Bowling Club and the University of Melbourne. Cross Rathdowne Street to the Carlton Gardens.

Federation of flowers

The Carlton Gardens are home to the Exhibition Building, the Museum of Victoria and the Imax Theatre. Make your way around to the large, ornate fountain at the south side of the Exhibition Building. The Carlton Gardens were established in 1857 and cover a total area of 15.9 hectares. They represent the best example in Australia of 19th-century, classically designed public gardens, with mature trees lining formal avenues that radiate from the central fountain and the Exhibition Building to the perimeter. The initial concept was designed by Edward La Trobe Bateman in 1857 and extended by the architects Reed & Barnes to accommodate their design of the Exhibition Building in 1879. Reed & Barnes established the five main paths leading to the building, including the double avenue from Victoria Parade to the Hochgurtel fountain, in the vein of the European Baroque style palace gardens.

Sweet pittosporum, cypress, plane and willow trees were among the earliest plantings, as well as flowering trees and shrubs from Asia and Africa, araucarias, Mediterranean oaks and pines, Queensland figs and English elms. Flowerbeds to the immediate south of the building are indicative of those of the earlier period.

The **Exhibition Building |5|** is a potent source of memories for Melburnians. Architect Joseph Reed, who emigrated from Cornwall in 1853, also designed the Public Library, Trades Hall, Melbourne Town Hall, and other important buildings and churches in Melbourne. The Exhibition Building (dubbed 'Royal' by Queen Elizabeth II at its centenary celebrations in 1980) is made of brick and timber with plaster finish, and modelled on a Renaissance cathedral in Florence. It was constructed by David Mitchell, the father of Dame Nellie Melba, for the Melbourne International Exhibition of 1880. Its Classical stylistic traits are obscured by the sheer scale of the adventure, with cathedralesque interiors that have housed the most diverse range of objects, events and exhibits over the years, including the world's second largest pipe organ, built by George Fincham (the massive 19 x 13.7 metre structure with 4,726 pipes was removed in the 1960s), and a 450,000-litre aquarium. The original building was almost 10 times the size of the one remaining.

The Exhibition Building is one of the most significant historic public buildings in Australia. It was home to the first federal parliament in 1901. The opening ceremony was performed in front of 12,000 people. Afterwards, it became the home of the Victorian parliament from 1901 to 1927 while the new federal parliament occupied the current Victorian Parliament House. A look inside is an absolute must. The combined balcony and ground level provides 11,500 square metres of floor space. The Florentine dome is 67 metres tall and the murals around its interior depict Justice, Truth, Morning and Evening, and the four seasons. Just below (on the pendentives) are Mercury, Venus, Hercules and Mars as well as allegorical images of War, Peace, Government and Federation.

The opening for the Melbourne International Exhibition in 1880 was a greenkeeper's worst nightmare, with 70,000 people, or one third of Victoria's population of the time, packed into the Carlton Gardens. They were treated to an hour-long cantata of 800 voices and 100 instruments, among other events, and there were 32,000 exhibits from 29 countries and Australian colonies on display. A painting of a nude woman, Chloe, shown by the French Court, caused a great sensation. It now occupies pride of place in Young and Jackson's Hotel. There was also a second international exhibition in 1888, the Centennial International Exhibition, that still rates as the largest event ever staged in Melbourne – larger than the 1956 Olympic Games. The first sightings of chewing gum and the Edison Phonograph were two items amid one million square feet of displays.

Promenading was an extremely popular pastime in the era in which the Exhibition Building was built. Hence the wide promenades on the southern and eastern perimeters of the building. The two ornamental lakes at the south end of the gardens were established not only for scenic purposes but also to store water for firefighting. The large **Hochgurtel Fountain |6|** at the south entrance was built by Joseph Hochgurtel in Cologne, using Portland cement. It was made expressly for the original exhibition and is located near what used to be the main entrance to the building. Its details include representations of the trade between nations, Victorian flora and fauna, and the concepts of Commerce, Industry, Science and Arts in the form of four naked boys dancing hand in hand.

The little **French Fountain |7|** at the eastern entrance (Nicholson Street side) has been reset in its original garden design from 1880. Just before this, on the south-east corner of the building, is the **Protest Pillar |8|**, a rather unattractive block of stone from Stawell erected by John Woods MP in protest of the choice of New South Wales stone for Victoria's Parliament House.

Head north and then east around the new **Museum of Victoria |9|**. This extraordinary structure was designed by Melbourne architects Denton Corker Marshall, who also designed the Melbourne Exhibition Centre by the Yarra. Among a host of features, this ultra-modern building (incomplete at the time of writing) will comprise a unique Aboriginal Cultural Centre, four exhibition galleries and outdoor exhibition spaces. It will house Melbourne's rich collection of local and international cultural artefacts, and will also coordinate, in a curatorial fashion, the utilisation of the Exhibition Building for the staging of cultural and ethnic events. These will include the centenary of federation in Australia and regular celebrations, festas and other activities conducted by Melbourne's diverse ethnic groups. In this way, the new Museum will reunite the Carlton Gardens and the Exhibition Building with their past role as the sophisticated leisure centre of Melbourne. Next door is the popular **Imax Theatre |10|** cinema with a screen eight storeys high (six of them underground). Amble towards the north-west corner of Carlton Gardens.

Sicilian flower-power

From the north-west corner of the gardens, note the pleasant curving facade of the Lemon Tree Hotel on the north corner of Grattan and Rathdowne streets. Cross Rathdowne and travel west down Grattan Street. On the south-east corner of Grattan and Drummond streets is La Cacciatora. Established in 1959, this is one of Carlton's oldest restaurants, established by the Sartori family whose head, Attilio, had a passion for hunting. This is reflected in the 'hunting lodge' decor and 'la cacciagione' cuisine comprised of game. At 60 Grattan Street is **Comparin's House |11|**, an example of the 'Mediterraneanisation' of a Victorian-era dwelling. This was achieved by an Italian immigrant, Giovanni Comparin, who arrived in 1920 and started one of Melbourne's earliest bus services. Continue to the south-east corner of Lygon Street.

Lygon Street developed as a commercial centre in the 1860s, and most of the Victorian-era structures were built in the boom of the 1880s. It later became famous for its Italian culture, and particularly for its coffee and food. Described as the first successful Little Italy in Australia after the major Italian migrations (mainly from Sicily and Calabria) in the 1950s and 1960s, Lygon Street was a place where very little English was spoken for quite some time. Apart from catering to the cultural and gastronomic needs of single young and lonely men, it quickly became one of the favoured playgrounds and meeting places for Melbourne's bohemian, artistic and intellectual elites. In the late 1960s and 1970s, the flower-power cultural renaissance peaked and Carlton's university and its cosmopolitan population, Italian food and lively pubs were supplemented by an explosion of political, theatrical and other cultural activity not seen in Australia since. Add the annual festa, and the Street shines as a successful multicultural strip. Turn left into Lygon Street from Grattan Street.

Caffe Sport |12| at No. 262 was converted from a milk bar in the 1950s, and became a popular meeting place for members of the Italian community to talk, play cards, and pass the time. Later, during the 1970s, it was open all night, serving the bohemian and night-owl set. It now trades as a restaurant at nights and a cafe during the days. To get a feeling for the contemporary Italian influence on Lygon Street, you could head south all the way down to **Totos |13|**, the first Australian pizza restaurant, near the corner of Queensberry and Lygon streets. But if this is too much of a hike, then travel just a couple of hundred metres south to experience the vibe from a strip of Italian restaurants that provide a quintessentially Mediterranean ambience (replete with outdoor restaurant 'touts'). Across the street on the corner of Argyle Place North, is **Casa del Gelato |14|** the first gelato shop in Lygon Street. Walk back to the south-west corner of Grattan Street. On this corner is Borsari's Ristorante. This was initially a bicycle repair shop set up by Olympic gold medallist Nino Borsari in 1941. While on a tour of Australia, he was prevented from going home due to the outbreak of the Second World War. Businessman and philanthropist Sidney Myer helped establish the business and Borsari, in turn, became known as a friend and benefactor to the local Italian community. The neon sign on the corner was installed in 1948 and is one of the oldest in Australia. Continue across Grattan Street to the University Cafe at 257 Lygon Street.

The **University Cafe |15|** was established in 1951 and, like other establishments in Carlton at the time, provided wine and billiards illegally (no doubt a substantial drawcard in a time of strict licensing and gaming laws). It has since seen successive waves of intellectuals, academics and artists, along with its Italian clientele. The old Gaggia coffee machine mounted on the back wall was one of the first in Melbourne.

Just beyond the University Cafe at No. 263 is the **Lygon Food Store |16|.** You should be able to smell the cheeses before you get there. It was the first store in Melbourne to specialise in the importation of fine and often very large rounds of cheese. Follow your nose for another strong aroma at Grinders coffee shop before coming to the corner of Lygon and Faraday streets.

From the mid-1960s to the early 1980s this corner was, for many people, the cultural centre of Melbourne. It was through here that people would pass on their way to the **Carlton Movie House |17|** (west along Faraday Street). This theatre has screened flicks since the silent movie days. In the 1970s, it came to be known as the Bug-House, and when its (then) rickety projector used to lose the soundtrack, more often than not the wags in the audience would continue the dialogue 'extempore'. Next door, on the corner of Dorrit Street (which in the 1920s contained one of a series of 'bolt-holes' for gangster Squizzy Taylor) is **Genevieve Restaurant |18|,** another Italian institution. Across the road, near King & Godfree, stood Johnny's Green Room until the late 1980s, a favoured haunt of just about everyone who liked a game of pool and some contraband smoking material on the side. And further east, on the north-east corner (now Sportsgirl) was one of the most vibrant hotels in Melbourne. The Albion used to serve drinks to, among others, the emerging cream of Australian theatre in the 1960s and 1970s. More than one actor on his or her way to La Mama Theatre, which is still hoofing it across the road at 205 Faraday Street, used to get a bit too warmed-up for their performances here. La Mama was set up in 1967 as a theatrical rebellion against the established theatres of the day. Along with the now defunct Pram Factory, La Mama housed new works, often with political overtones.

Brunetti |19|, at 198 Faraday Street, is a family business that produces delicious Italian cakes and sweets and serves arguably the best cup of coffee in Melbourne. Right next door is the new Johnny's Green Room, where you can eat pasta and play pool into the very wee hours. A little detour from here (down to Drummond Street and left for 20 metres) takes you to **Masanis |20|,** a fine Italian restaurant housed in the National Trust-listed premises of 313 Drummond Street. Note the kangaroo-like chimeras on the top of the building. Built by Sir Redmond Barry in 1856, this place housed the Carlton Gentlemen's Club in 1888, where the gents would play a game of billiards or lounge about debating such topics as to whether they were old colonists or new Australians.

Move back to Lygon Street to **King & Godfree |21|** on the north-west corner. This licensed grocery is one of the oldest in Australia and has a very fine cellar, which includes a broad selection of Italian wines. The quality of its produce and service are such that many in Melbourne would collapse at the thought of it ever closing down. Head north to **Tiamo I & II |22|.** Formerly known as Tamani, this location has been serving the most delicious, low-cost Italian food to generations of students and other low-budget shoppers for more than 30 years. Just past Tiamo is **Readings Bookshop |23|** at 309 Lygon Street. This is the third and largest location of Readings in Lygon Street. Its first shop was set among those clustered around the Holdsworth Building (across the road, with the cast-iron centre arch, behind which now stands the Nova Cinema, a supermarket and an arcade of food stores and boutiques). Where the first Readings offered

The Exhibition Building

In its prime, the Exhibition Building housed a Cyclorama with a 360-degree panoramic pencil-and-wash sketch of Melbourne in 1841 (now held in storage in the State Library), a Maze, and an aquarium with crocodiles, penguins, seals and fish from all over the world. Moving pictures were shown every afternoon from 1909, two years after Dame Nellie Melba graced an audience of 9,000 fellow Victorians with a gala performance in the Great Hall.

The Grand National Baby Show of 1893 attracted 700 entrants and an audience of 30,000. During the 1919 influenza epidemic that killed 2,319 people in the Melbourne metropolitan area and 23 million people world-wide, the building became a hospital, and the sight of ambulances arriving at one end and hearses departing from the other was common.

In 1939 the building housed the largest skating rink in the world, with 4,500 square metres of its floor resurfaced to accommodate 5,000 roller-skaters. Later that same year, one of the largest events in Australian theatrical history took place with the performance of *Hiawatha*, boasting 1,000 performers, put on as a benefit in aid of soldiers and families affected by the war. During the war the Building was used as a training school for mechanics and technicians, and was nearly demolished. The military theme continued through to the early 1970s, when the navy used the north-east annex as an R&R centre.

fine books set among raw floorboards and pockmarked plaster, the new home is modern, with the latest consumer technology. Still with heaps of character, it remains one of Melbourne's finest bookshops.

Jimmy Watsons |24|, at No. 333, has long been the home of university intelligentsia, actors and lovers of contemporary culture and a glass of wine. It was established by Jim Watson in 1935. Just before his death in 1962, plans were made to renovate the premises using a design drawn up by architect Robin Boyd. The renovation stands to this day and the business continues in Watson hands, with Jim's son Allan, a former lord mayor of Melbourne, at the helm. Move further north and cross Elgin Street, to the opposite corner.

St Jude's Church |25|, built in 1866, was designed by Reed & Barnes and was the first fully polychromatic brick church to be built in Australia. The intended tower and spire never eventuated but the building was remarkable for its time in its use of cutting edge design and deployment of materials. A look at the Fincham organ inside, from 1868, is a must for organ enthusiasts.

Retire for a pasta and a glass of wine!

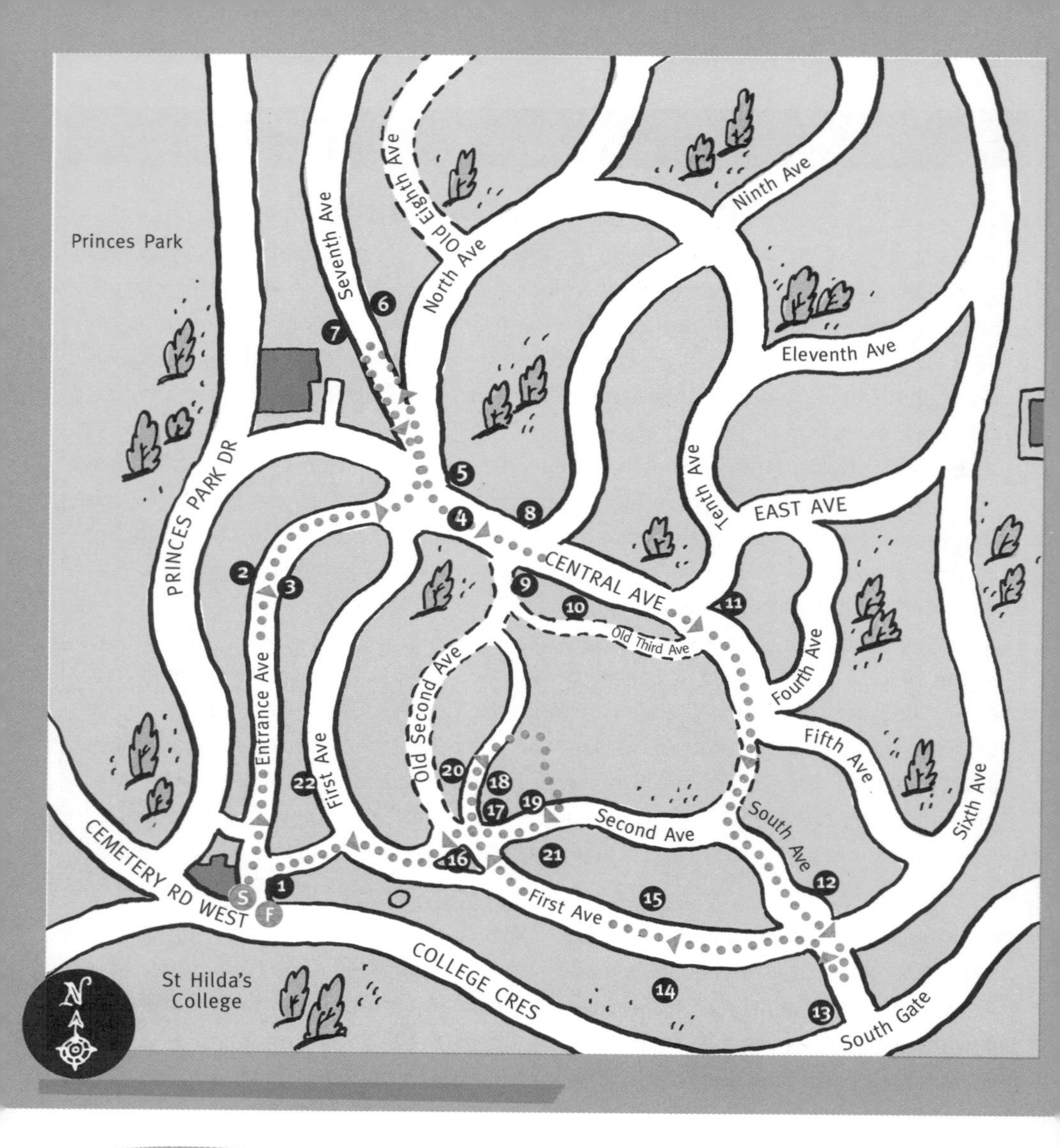

Walk key

1. Prime Minister's Memorial Garden | **2.** Graves of James Scullin and Arthur Calwell | **3.** Walter Lindrum grave | **4.** Mausoleum | **5.** Elvis Presley Memorial | **6.** Catholic Mortuary Chapel | **7.** Peter Lalor grave | **8.** Sir John O'Shanassy monument | **9.** Hungarian War Memorial | **10.** Robert Hoddle grave | **11.** Chinese ovens | **12.** Jewish Mortuary | **13.** Jewish Holocaust Memorial | **14.** Emily Mather grave | **15.** Marcus Clarke grave | **16.** Burke and Wills Monument | **17.** Sir Charles Hotham grave | **18.** Sir Redmond Barry grave | **19.** Price Family Monument | **20.** James Galloway grave | **21.** Frederick Baker grave | **22.** Samuel Thomas Gill grave

Walk No. 9

Melbourne General Cemetery

Monuments and memories

Start & Finish

Entrance in College Crescent – trams 1 or 15 along Swanston Street and get off at the corner of Elgin Street, or tram 19 along Royal Parade and get off at the corner of Gatehouse Street. In both cases there is a five-minute walk to the starting point.

Length/Time

2 km/1.5 hours

Melbourne General Cemetery is a historic and cultural treasure trove. It was established in 1850 and opened in 1853. Previously the city's cemetery had occupied the site where the Queen Victoria Market now stands. This 'tour' should be regarded as an introductory overview. There are hundreds of significant historic sites to be found, and those with a further interest can pick up a fairly detailed listing of the more famous sites from the administration office. Visit the National Trust in Tasma Terrace East Melbourne (9654 7111) for a copy of their excellent brochure, 'Tour of the Melbourne General Cemetery' (9654 4711); or contact Melbourne Cemetery Tours (9890 9288).

Start the walk at the main cemetery gate in College Crescent. On the left is the administration building designed in the Gothic idiom in 1934. The cemetery covers 43 hectares, and the whole area is classified by the National Trust. It represents an exceptional example of the Picturesque style in Victorian cemetery planning, a tradition that called for a flowing park-like design, with grand memorials that would evoke religious sentiment and moral renewal on behalf of the observer. But more than that, it serves as a sort of roll call of the citizens of Melbourne. Laid to rest are community leaders, law enforcers, union leaders, politicians, judges, artists, writers – the diverse range of people seminal to the development, growth and character of the city. There are also the infamous – scoundrels, criminals and miscreants of various types – who somehow managed to get a Christian burial. And there are the graves of ordinary people, where headstones tell stories of shocking levels of infant mortality, rampant disease, the growth of migrant communities, a diversity of religious belief, and a flurry of burial fashions over the decades.

Few burials are conducted here now, although there is a recently completed mausoleum and a few pre-booked sites elsewhere waiting to be filled. Parts of the cemetery are in a bad state of repair, and even some of the more significant historic graves have been neglected. For decades the cemetery was largely ignored by the general community; once most of the graves had been filled and occupiers had faded from immediate memory, many probably felt they had no need to visit a place that served only as a reminder of human mortality. Perhaps because it was so far from the view of public scrutiny, all sorts of unusual practices have been found to have flourished for many decades prior to 1980, including the overlaying of graves and the removal of bodies. The cemetery, since 1980, has been under the jurisdiction of the trustees of the Necropolis Cemetery in Springvale. In recent times significant attention has been paid to the conservation value of the site, and it remains to be seen if this growing interest will translate into some sort of major restoration project.

Eternal debate

Immediately to your right is the **Prime Ministers' Memorial Garden |1|**. Here lies Bob Menzies, Australia's longest serving prime minister. The garden also has a memorial to Harold Holt, who disappeared into the ocean at Portsea in 1967 while still prime minister. Prime Minister John Howard and Premier Jeff Kennett opened the memorial in 1996. At that time many were suggesting that, henceforth, all Australian prime ministers should be buried here, but retired Labor leaders disagreed, declaring a preference for Sydney as a final resting place, rather than a city known as the heartland of conservative politics.

Head north along Entrance Avenue. A little way up on the left are the graves of two Australian Labor leaders, **James Scullin**

(1876–1953) **and Arthur Calwell |2|** (1897–1973). Scullin was Australia's 13th prime minister, serving between 1929 and 1932, and headed the only government to be defeated in office after only one term. Calwell led the party from 1960 to 1967, part of a long period of Liberal rule, a time when Labor seemed in danger of becoming the party of perpetual opposition.

Opposite these graves is that of billiard champion **Walter Lindrum |3|** (1898–1960), one of the world's great players, if not the greatest. His tombstone is sculpted in the shape of a billiard table, complete with balls and cue.

Further along is the imposing bulk of the cemetery's newest addition, a **Mausoleum |4|.** These structures, catering for above-ground burials (this one is several storeys high, containing 1,416 crypt spaces) were illegal in the state until fairly recently when pressure from migrant groups who favour burial over cremation forced the government's hand. Just beyond this is an **Elvis Presley Memorial |5|,** which is regularly visited and tended by the King's many Melbourne fans.

Head along Seventh Avenue. Ahead is the **Catholic Mortuary Chapel |6|,** built in stages from 1870 to 1889. Further along on the left is the grave of one of the most significant figures in Australian history, **Peter Lalor |7|.** He led the Eureka uprising, the only armed insurrection on Australian soil, in 1854 (see Walk No. 14, Richmond).

Here, and further north, is the high point of the cemetery and the place to get an

Opening Times

Cemetery: Open every day. Office Tue 9am–11am and Thurs, Sat & Sun 9am–3.30pm (9546 9377).

Refreshments

Take your choice from the wide range of restaurants, cafes and bars in Lygon Street, about a 10-minute walk (See Walk No. 8, Carlton).

overview of the curving paths, 19th-century landscaping and the jagged horizon of tombstones, spires and monuments.

Multiculturalism here and ever after

Throughout the cemetery there are many areas dominated by Italian graves, bearing distinctive features such as black and grey granite, encased photographs of the deceased, and finely detailed marble or plaster statues of religious figures, particularly angels. In the 1960s, the cemetery authorities began selling off the border edges along the paths and roads, and these were snapped up by a community now firmly establishing itself in the wake of the massive post-Second World War immigration programs. In the face of general dereliction, the Italian graves tend to be remarkably well maintained.

Return to the Mausoleum, and cut along the side of the structure. There you will see the massive Celtic monument to Sir John **O'Shanassy |8|** (1818–83), thrice premier of Victoria. O'Shanassy was born Irish Catholic and at a time when those of that ilk were still suffering on society's outer edge, he made a point of advancing the interests of his church and community. His monument is one of the cemetery's most imposing.

Walk straight ahead along Central Avenue. On the corner, to the right, is the **Hungarian War Memorial |9|,** commemorating those who died in the fight to liberate Hungary between 1948 and 1956. Further along to the right is the grave of **Robert Hoddle |10|** (1794–1853), a master surveyor who laid out the central grid of Melbourne, beginning in 1837, just two years after European settlement. It is one of those ironic quirks of history that Hoddle Street, one of the most annoying roads in Melbourne from a driver's perspective, is named for this visionary town planner. And also on the right, a few metres along, is the grave of the first citizen buried in Melbourne General Cemetery. It belongs to John Burnett (1817–53), one of the first merchants to set up business in the new colony. At the intersection of paths you will see a distinctive Chinese-looking structure. This houses the **Chinese ovens |11|,** used for burning of offerings to the spirits to ensure the dead a safe journey. As mentioned elsewhere, the Chinese have been a presence in Melbourne from the earliest days of the colony, their numbers significantly increasing from the start of the gold rush. Have a look at the old Chinese graves nearby.

Continue towards the south fence line, following the loop in the road. On the right is a small path that lines up with a coffee-coloured ecclesiastical building – the **Jewish Mortuary |12|.** Continue on to this structure, built in 1854 and the oldest in the cemetery, and take time to have a look at the nearby Jewish War Memorial, which commemorates the victims of the two world wars. The path opens out onto First Avenue. Cross the road and walk down to the **Jewish Holocaust Memorial |13|,** a stark modern structure, constructed in the 1960s to honour the memory of those who perished. Now, retrace your steps to First Avenue and turn right.

The good, the bad and the questionable

A little way along on the left, fronting the avenue, is the grave of **Emily Mather |14|**. Mather was murdered by her husband in 1891, and her body was dismembered so that it would fit beneath the hearth. The community was outraged, particularly when it was discovered that the husband had previously disposed of his first wife, and their children, using a similar method. Emily's epitaph is one of the most evocative to be found:

To those hereafter who come reflecting
Upon the text of her soul ending
To warn her sex of their intending
For marrying in haste is defending
On such a fate, too late for amending.

Scan the area on the right for the grave of **Marcus Clarke |15|** (about halfway across the block). It can be identified by its intentionally broken column, meant to signify a life cut short. Marcus Clarke (1846–81) wrote one of the great novels in the Australian literary canon, *For the Term of His Natural Life*. He was also an exceptionally talented journalist who, according to his biographer, 'raised the quality of discursive writing in the colonial papers to a height which deserves to be called extraordinary'. He died at the age of 35, broke, despondent and angry at the Public Library for refusing to give him the position he cherished of chief librarian.

Continue on to the imposing stone bulk of the **Burke and Wills Monument |16|**, erected in 1873, a surprisingly modern looking structure given the usual excesses of the Victorians. It commemorates the ill-fated expedition by those most famous and tragic of Australian explorers, Robert Burke and William Wills. The pair set off in 1860 from nearby Royal Park with the aim of reaching the Gulf of Carpentaria. This they achieved, only to perish with most of the rest of their party on the return journey. The sole survivor of the expedition was John King, who is buried in the north-west section of the cemetery. That King was still around to tell the story was due solely to his willingness to heed the advice and accept the help of the Aboriginal people he encountered. Alfred Howitt, an explorer commissioned by Wills' father to find the expedition, eventually rescued King.

At the north-east corner of the monument is Second Avenue. Follow it a short way until you reach a large monument of reddish hued stone on the left. This is the grave of **Sir Charles Hotham |17|** (1806–55). Hotham was the first governor of the newly autonomous state of Victoria and is probably best known for his uncompromisingly harsh attitude to the gold miners of the 1850s, and his refusal to sympathise with their complaints about the licensing system (resulting, of course, in the Eureka Stockade). The soaring tower that marked the grave was removed recently because of fears it would topple over and do some serious damage. It is expected that a restoration will take place at some stage. Behind Hotham lies another founding father, Sir **Redmond Barry |18|** (1813–80). Barry was quite an amazing figure of the Melbourne scene. He founded the University of Melbourne and what is now the State Library of Victoria, and served for a time as chief justice. But he is probably best known as the judge who ordered the hanging of Ned Kelly who, at the sentencing, was reported to have prophesied the imminent death of Barry and, sure enough, several days later Barry passed over to the other side to join his nemesis. That Barry was not the perfect paradigm of the upright Victorian gentleman he might have appeared is proved by the fact that his mistress, and mother to his four children, is buried with him – although her name, Mrs Louisa Barrows, is not on the gravestone.

Just back and to the south of Barry's grave is the **Price Family Monument |19|.** Before coming to Victoria, the family's patriarch, John Price (1808–57), managed to secure for himself the reputation of being one of the most cruel commandants in the history of transportation, by virtue of his work at the penal colonies on Van Diemen's Land and Norfolk Island. He was the model for the brutal figure of Maurice Frere in *For the Term of His Natural Life*, and contemporary writer Robert Hughes described him as the 'last paroxysm of the system's cruelty'. He died as a result of injuries received when set upon by a gang

An historic gatehouse marks the entrance to Melbourne General Cemetery.

of convicts at Williamstown in 1857. His son, Colonel Tom Price (1842–1911), was an extraordinary administrator, and was responsible for a major reorganisation of the state's military services. However, like his father, it is for dark deeds that he is known. In the maritime strike of 1890 he called on his troops to fire on the striking labourers, earning himself a place on the blacklist of Australian union history.

About 30 metres north-west lies one of the great heroes of the union movement, **James Galloway |20|** (1828–60), a pioneer of the Eight-Hour Day in the 1850s. The monument of four columns topped by a platform bearing distinctive circular carvings is one of the more unusual of 19th-century landmarks, and one of the most intact thanks to recent major restoration work.

Opposite the Price monument, down a path flanked by graves bearing the names of Italia and Lo Ciuro, is the grave of **Frederick Baker |21|** (1850–88). This prominent singer and actor, who went by the stage name of Federici, died while performing in *Faust* at the Princess Theatre. His ghost, in full evening dress, has apparently watched many of the performances since then, and refused to be deterred even by the major renovations of the theatre in the 1980s.

Go back to Burke and Wills and head north along First Avenue. About 100 metres or so on the left you will find the grave of S.T. Gill. **Samuel Thomas Gill |22|** (1818–80) depicted the drama and colour of life on the goldfields, and remains today one of the most successful and sought after artists of that period. His life skills were not so developed. An habitual drunk, he was nearly always broke and utterly despondent. He died from a tumble down the stairs of the General Post Office. He was initially laid to rest in a pauper's grave, but was moved to this section of the cemetery in 1913.

Retrace your steps and turn right at the rose garden (where ashes are interred). Head down alongside the Prime Ministers' Memorial Garden, and you are back at the main entrance.

Walk key

1. Residence of Peter Jageur | **2.** Amess house | **3.** Naughton's Hotel | **4.** Residence of Sir Albert Coates | **5.** Munro Buildings | **6.** Site of former City Horse Market | **7.** Douglas Terrace | **8.** Northern Cattle Market wall | **9.** Mentone | **10.** Tasma | **11.** Old dairy | **12.** Parkville Post Office | **13.** Wardlow | **14.** Beaconsfield Terrace | **15.** College Church | **16.** Burke and Wills Memorial Cairn | **17.** Obelisk | **18.** African Rainforest | **19.** Tropical Rainforests of Asia | **20.** Butterfly House | **21.** Great Flight Aviary | **22.** Australian Bush Exhibit | **23.** African lions | **24.** Big cats | **25.** Australian fur seals | **26.** Lakeside Bistro by the Japanese Garden

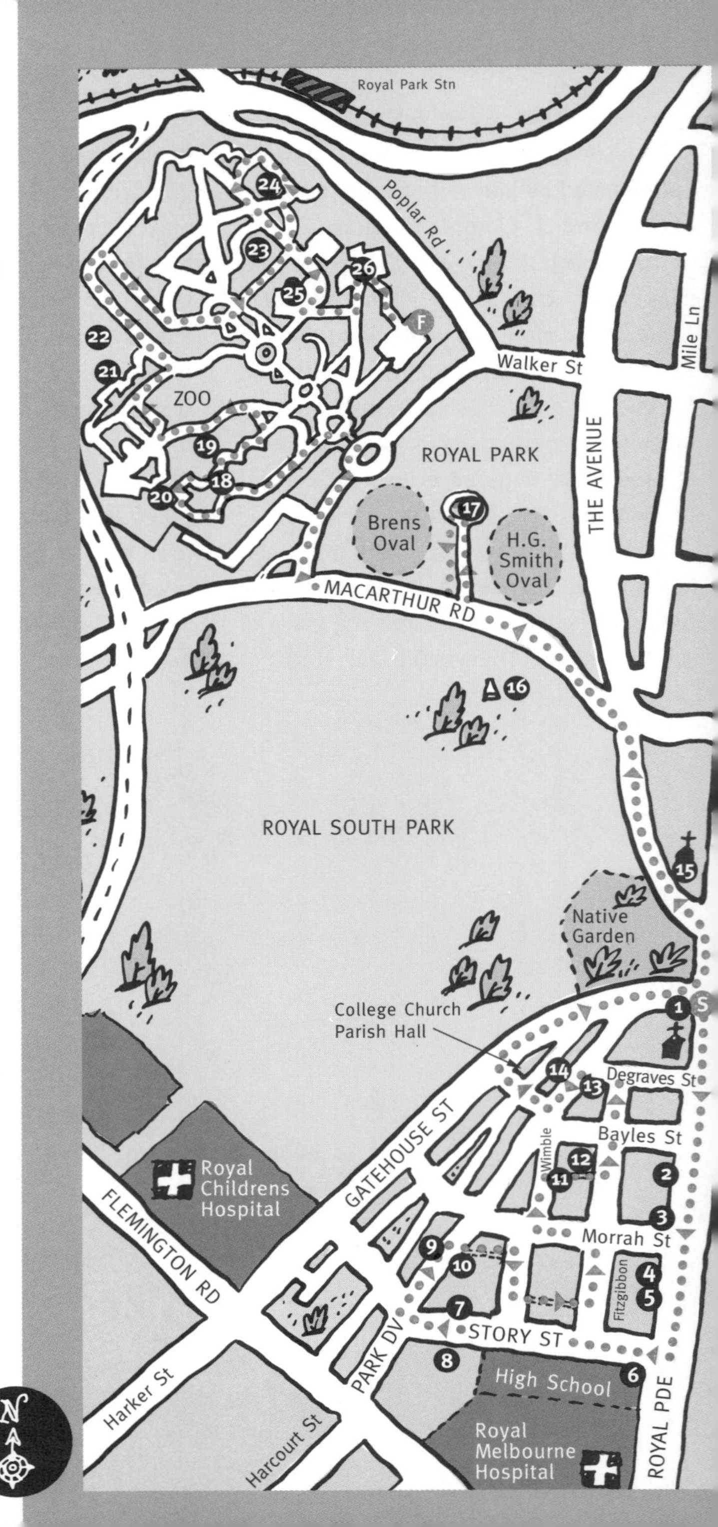

Walk No. 10

South Parkville & Melbourne Zoo

Studies of Victorian Australia and wildlife

Start

South corner of Gatehouse Street and Royal Parade, Parkville – tram 19 from Elizabeth Street in the city (takes about 15 minutes).

Finish

Melbourne Zoo, Royal Park – tram 55 and 56 or train from Royal Park Station to the city.

Length/Time

3.5 km
1.5 hours for South Parkville
2.5 hours for the Zoo.

South Parkville boasts some of Melbourne's most impressive Victorian streetscapes, many listed by the National Trust in 1972. A short walk away, across the grassy swathes of Royal Park, lies one of Melbourne's premier scientific institutions, and its most popular leisure destination – the Melbourne Zoo.

South Parkville was laid out in 1837, but the first residential sales of land did not take place until 1868, when the council realised it lacked the cash to develop the area as a major centre for business. After the gold rush period of subdivisions throughout the rest of inner Melbourne, the Melbourne City Council took great care to protect the integrity of its design for South Parkville. Allotments were jealously guarded (though not always successfully) against excessive subdivision and the Council even went so far as to dictate construction materials. Between the great depressions, and even as late as the 1960s, South Parkville, like all of Melbourne's inner-city suburbs, suffered economic and physical dilapidation. During this period many of the two-storey terraces had their verandahs covered up to maximise the room available for their use as boarding houses. While South Parkville still has student rental accommodation, it is now overwhelmingly the home of wealthy professionals and university and medical institutes and offices. With vigilance, South Parkville will likely remain a time capsule of a significant early period of Melbourne's history for many generations to come.

This tiny suburb is fortunate enough to have as its near neighbour a zoo that is ranked as one of the best in the world. The Royal Melbourne Zoological Gardens were founded in 1862. The first in Australia and only the third in the world, the Zoo was in part the product of the Victorian Acclimatisation Society (later the Zoological Society of Victoria), which insisted on importing exotic creatures to see how they would survive in the Antipodes. They also wanted to make what was still seen as an alien and dreary land more familiar and interesting to the early Europeans.

Covering 22 hectares (a map from the entrance gate is an essential navigation aid), the Melbourne Zoo is a consistent winner of tourism awards in the major attraction category. The Zoo has a mission to encourage conservation of the natural world and the world's remaining wilderness areas. It discharges this duty by caring for the needs of over 3,500 animals and thousands of plants, by providing exhibits with educational and amusement value, and by conducting joint research and breeding programs with national and international conservation organisations.

South Parkville

Start the walk at the south corner of Royal Parade and Gatehouse Street, Parkville South. Victorian Filigree, as a style, is largely defined by the use of cast-iron filigree 'screening' on the verandahs of buildings, which may be influenced by Classical, Mediaeval or Italianate themes. The widespread use of Victorian Filigree was mostly confined to Australia. Its deployment in South Parkville complements the other trademark characteristics of the period: two-storey verandahs, ornamental concrete mouldings and the use of thin classical columns. While architectural styles from later periods, including Art

Nouveau and Federation Queen Anne, are also represented in South Parkville, the feeling, particularly off Royal Parade, is overwhelmingly Victorian.

No. 127 Royal Parade was built in 1886 as the Residence of **Peter Jageur |1|**, a monument mason. His home stood in the middle of a large enclosure of stone works, now occupied by St Carthage's University Parish Church and the block of flats at No. 135, and it served as a landmark for north-bound travellers. The cast-iron filigree, along with most of the rest in South Parkville, was locally cast and chosen from standard iron-founders' catalogue designs. St Carthage's was built between 1934 and 1936 in the Inter-War Gothic style, perhaps with some mediaeval Scottish influence. Prior to Jageur's residence and business, the stretch of land from here to Morrah Street was owned by the Port Phillip Farmers Society. Here they conducted some of Melbourne's first agricultural exhibitions, forerunners to the Royal Melbourne Show.

Moving south to No. 73, note the ornate woodwork and angled gable of the classic Queen Anne style house Los Angeles, on the north corner of Royal Parade and Degraves Street; also the large mansion on the south corner of Bayles Street, which was built in 1886 and used for some years as a girls' grammar school.

No. 73 Royal Parade was erected in 1873 by **Samuel Amess |2|**, Lord Mayor of Melbourne from 1869–70 and one of the city's important early builders. Born in Scotland, Amess commenced his career in the colony

Opening Times

Zoo: Open every day of the year 9am–5pm, and in January and February Thur–Sun 9am–7pm when jazz bands play in the evenings until 9pm (9285 9333).

Refreshments

Naughton's Hotel is the only place in South Parkville that provides meals and beverages and is open seven days a week (9347 2283). At the **Zoo** there are numerous food and drink outlets, including a licensed bistro.

in 1853, after a brief sojourn at the goldfields. He built the Melbourne Post Office, Customs House, Kew Lunatic Asylum and the Ballarat Railway Station, among numerous other important works. The ornamentation of his house is decidedly restrained compared to that of its neighbour at No. 71 and the florid Grasmere at No. 75. The surreal motif of bearded heads running up the partition walls on either side of No. 71 and the overdone skyline are indicative of the lavish Boom period just before the 1890s depression, during which the house was built. Continue south to Morrah Street.

There are few signs of street life in Parkville other than that provided by the successive waves of youth attending the University of Melbourne. **Naughton's Hotel |3|**, on the corner of Morrah Street and Royal Parade, was established in 1873 and has been serving ale to those of drinking age since. It is one of Melbourne's best university hotels and provides a warm, friendly and often fun atmosphere, in keeping with its youthful clientele.

Just over Morrah Street, 33 Royal Parade was also built in 1873 and at one time was Mrs Grey's Cake Shop as well as a former **residence of Sir Albert Coates |4|**, when he was a student at the University of Melbourne in the 1920s. The original posted verandahs remain intact with the Corporation of the City of Melbourne symbol cast into the iron. Moving along, note Nos. 21 and 23, now annexes of the university, built in the Victorian Italianate style and once owned by **David Munro |5|**. Munro was the construction engineer whose firm worked on the second and extant Princes Bridge that links Swanston Street with St Kilda Road. Move to Story Street and turn right.

Story Street was formerly known as Market Street due to the early existence of markets in this area. The **City Horse Market |6|** was situated on the site of the current school oval from 1870 to 1917, and a general market was situated just beyond on the site of the current Royal Melbourne Hospital. The houses in Story Street date from 1880 to the 1920s and Nos. 28–38 provide a good example of Federation Filigree style terrace housing. Story Street blends the various architectural periods well, complemented by the inter-war structure of University High School. Moving towards Park Drive, note the ornate roofline of the Federation period Art Nouveau home at No. 54, before coming to **Douglas Terrace |7|** at Nos. 82–88. This terrace is one of only five named terraces in South Parkville and was built for Will McMurtie in 1882. Directly opposite is the old **Northern Cattle Market wall |8|** that was built in 1888. On the Story Street and Park Drive corner of the wall, do not miss the horse head figure, which was originally hung over the entrance to the market. Turn right, heading north along leafy Park Drive.

Park Drive was known as Park Street until 1965. It acquired its name at the time when Royal Park extended right up to the western edge of this expansive boulevard. A strapped council ensured further land was stripped off Royal Park and sold in 1875, much to the chagrin of landowners on the east side. Of the usurpers, the stately **Mentone |9|** at No. 81, on the western side of Park Drive, was built in 1885 and uses an elegant Georgian symmetry in the layout of its entrance and windows, behind the Filigree veil of a two-storey verandah.

Tasma |10|, across the road at No. 34, was built in 1887 by Robert Taylor and originally had an orchard next to it, now the site of a block of flats. Note the deeply recessed doorway and the freely perforated north wall. Head up the lane beside Tasma to Benjamin Street.

The wooden picket fence of the house on the south corner of the lane and Benjamin Street could be the original. The 14 houses in Benjamin Street – named after a former Lord Mayor of Melbourne, Mr Benjamin Benjamin – were built between 1881 and 1887. Before this, the land bounded by Benjamin, Story, Fitzgibbon and Morrah streets had been the Melbourne Pound for stray animals. Cross the street and go south to the lane closest to Story Street, next to 14 Benjamin Street, and moving east up the lane, note the round cut of bluestone at the intersection of the lanes. These were used to prevent houses being damaged by cartwheels. Note also the excellent rear view of some of the fine architectural features of the Federation terrace in Story Street, mentioned earlier, just before arriving at Fitzgibbon Street.

Fitzgibbon Street, like Benjamin Street, is entirely Victorian in date. The Boom period residence at No. 14 is the only Victorian two-storey house in South Parkville with double verandah posts. The frontages of South Parkville were supposed to be 25 feet wide, but on the east side of Fitzgibbon Street the two smallest houses in South Parkville, at Nos. 28 and 26, have frontages only 13 feet wide. Continue to Morrah Street and turn left towards Park Drive.

No. 44 Morrah Street was built in 1873, the design based on English and Tasmanian cottages of the period. Nos. 62 and 66, just past Wimble Street, were built in 1875, in a simple variation on the Victorian Regency style. Note the privy access lane between them that allowed the nightmen to empty the containers before you turn right at Park Drive.

Nos. 62–72 Park Drive were built between 1874 and 1876 by Farquahar Macdonald. The unadorned, recessed loggia verandahs owe something to Mediterranean arcade designs. The terraces across the road at Nos. 135–137 are three-storey abodes with basement levels, quite rare for Melbourne. The laundrette on the corner of Wimble Street was once the Post and Telegraph Office and later became a butcher's shop. Hook right into Wimble Street.

Wimble Street was named after F.T. Wimble, the first to manufacture printer's ink in Australia. Most of the other streets in South Parkville are named after bureaucrats and councillors, in keeping with the bureaucratic origins of this ordered suburb. York Place at 30–34 Wimble Street was constructed in 1884 by George Lockington, who built many houses in the area. The Federation period house at No.18 was once the main retail **dairy |11|** in Parkville when there were no fewer than four dairies in this tiny pocket of Melbourne. It is now a creche. Continue up the lane adjacent to No. 16, east towards Fitzgibbon Street.

At Fitzgibbon Street, turn left towards Degraves Street. The impressive No. 52 was among the first residential constructions in South Parkville and has some very interesting glasswork around its ornate door. The charming and elegant **Parkville Post Office |12|,** on the corner of Fitzgibbon and Bayles streets, was built in 1889 in the Victorian Gothic style. The lower level is leased out as a post office and the upper level is let as a private residence. Continue along Fitzgibbon Street, past the rather narrow Boom period cottages, turn left into Degraves Street and continue to Park Drive. From the corner of Fitzgibbon Street and Park Drive note the built-in upper-level verandah at No.20 Degraves Street, a reminder of the period when Parkville and the rest of inner-city Melbourne was down on its luck.

On the south corner of Degraves Street at 114 Park Drive is **Wardlow |13|,** built in 1888 by ironmonger John Boyes, whose family occupied these Italianate residential buildings for many years. To this day, the interiors are understood to have remained virtually unchanged. From this corner, cross Park Drive to see **Beaconsfield Terrace |14|** at Nos. 177–83, next door to the Federation Academic Classical twins at Nos. 185–87. Moving south towards Bayles Street, note

The Gothic styled Parkville Post Office sits well among the nearby rows of Victorian terraces.

the three variations of the Federation Queen Anne style houses culminating in Eire on the north corner of Park Drive and Bayles Street. Turn right down Bayles Street to Gatehouse Street, crossing the beginning of Levers Reserve. The lane heads south from here and turns into a serene patch of grass and eucalypts. Before turning right at Gatehouse Street towards the church hall, note the Egyptian heads on the window frame of the house on the south corner of Bayles and Gatehouse streets.

Cross over to Royal Park and follow Gatehouse Street towards Royal Parade. The College Church Parish Hall at 196 Gatehouse Street was built in 1888 for the Presbyterians as a temporary place of worship until College Church was completed. It was also

South Parkville High School for a number of years until the opening of University High School. The garden at the south-east corner of Royal Park is planted with Australian natives. It stands as the gateway to Royal Park's 202 hectares of parklands, sports ovals and sports facilities, including a golf course and the Zoo. Continue past the nature reserve to College Church, set back from the corner of Royal Parade and The Avenue. Note the Federation Arts and Craft style power substation along the way.

Built in 1897, **College Church |15|** was designed by R.A. Lawson and is understood to be unique in Australia for its crown tower, influenced by mediaeval Scottish design. It is also home to a late model Fincham organ dating from 1903, but unfortunately the church is not open to the public. The area behind the church in Royal Park was the spot from where horsedrawn cabs used to leave to ferry eager passengers to the Zoo. Cross The Avenue to Royal Park and follow the curve of the park along the road (which becomes Macarthur Road as you follow the bend) until you reach the **Burke and Wills Memorial Cairn |16|**.

Royal Park was approved as a Reserve in 1854 and, during the gold rush, was used as a rest-stop by the hordes battling their way to the northern goldfields. It served as home to the very early matches of the Carlton Football Club, and later as a pasture for the herds of cows serving Parkville's dairy businesses. Its main claim to fame so far, however, is in having played host to a pivo-tal piece of Australian history – as the starting place for the first European south–north crossing of the Australian continent, achieved by Burke and Wills.

The Burke and Wills Expedition left for the Gulf of Carpentaria from Royal Park in 1860. They assembled and were sent off with great fanfare from this area marked by the cairn. Facing north and attempting to visualise the north coast of Australia, somewhere in the distant horizon gives some inkling as to the scale of the adventure that these two men and their crew undertook.

With camels and saddles of provisions, Burke and Wills headed from here towards the Sarah Sands Hotel on the south edge of Brunswick, before turning west to Essendon and north again, thereon north to central Australlian deserts, death and the annals of modern Australian history.

The two-metre **obelisk |17|** across the road, just back from the north-west corner of Macarthur Road and The Avenue, has a curiously moving inscription. It commemorates a Lieutenant James G. Roberts, who was killed during the Boer War 'and used to play in this park as a boy'.

Continue along Macarthur Road to Elliott Avenue, and cross to the Melbourne Zoo.

Melbourne Zoo

Part of the beauty of Melbourne Zoo is that there are many different routes that can be taken by the visitor, according to an individual's interest. It is impossible to cover everything in a single visit, so that which follows should be taken as a recommendation rather than the definitive tour.

For the continued welfare of its animal and plant clientele, the Zoo has in recent years developed a 'bioclimatic' scheme of housing compatible species together. The mini-ecosystems that have been created demonstrate how important plant and animal life are to each other, encouraging visitors to appreciate the delicate, interlinked engine of life as it occurs and sustains itself in natural environments. Not to be missed is a visit to the **African Rainforest |18|.** Here mandrills and pygmy hippopotamuses may be seen as if cavorting in each other's company, while nearby is the display of treetop apes and monkeys. Among chimpanzees and orangutans, ebony leaf-monkeys and lion tamarins, the star attraction here is undoubtedly the enormously dignified western lowland gorilla. Melbourne's is the only gorilla group in the Australasian region and it has been incorporated by the Zoo into an international breeding program to help save the species from extinction. The Zoo made history in 1984 with the birth of Mzuri, the only surviving gorilla to be born with the help of artificial insemination.

A short walk from here takes you from the steamy depths of Africa to the **Tropical Rainforests of Asia |19|.** The main attraction here is the endangered Sumatran tiger which, paradoxically, will never be at home in captivity but may well survive in the long run because of it. Also of interest are the ferociously cute Asian small-clawed otters. The otters, particularly at feeding time, provide a jolly carnival of eating activity and associated play, which invariably leads to squeals of delight and intrigued laughter from the younger, less inhibited visitors.

Continuing the tropical theme, the **Butterfly House |20|** provides an exuberant yet delicate experience, and is modelled on a steamy section of Australia's northern tropical rainforests. For the survival of the exquisite and exotic inmates, such as the Ulysses butterfly, blue triangle or Australian birdwing, the temperature must not fall below 25 degrees Celsius. While this makes for a breathless and sweaty interlude, the delightful technicolour chaos of madly fluttering wings makes it well worth it. Do be careful to check your clothing and baggage on the way out – the odd camouflaged stowaway is not unknown!

Coasting from wing to wing, a visit to the **Great Flight Aviary |21|** is a real treat. As you walk through double protective doors into approximations of rainforest, scrubland and wetland habitats, you find yourself amid any number of stunning aviators. Female satin bowerbirds, cattle egrets, pied herons and black-winged stilts are among the feathered luminaries to be viewed from the carefully designed boardwalks. Here, as is the case throughout the Zoo, interpretive plaques are strategically located to enhance enjoyment of the animals; providing a little knowledge about origins, habits, and threats to existence among other things.

Further on is the **Australian Bush Exhibit |22|,** a new enclosure designed around the Zoo's ecosystem theme. It houses all the

Australian favourites, affording the delightful possibility of visitors mingling with many of the species. Soporific Victorian koalas, the majestic red kangaroo, blue-winged kingfishers, wombats, dingoes, emus and many more familiar and not-so-familiar faces can be seen. The exhibit is also home to a large collection of Australian plants, many of them endangered.

After detouring past the elegant giraffes and their savanna soulmates, the zebras, and after a possible peep at the nocturnal platypus display, you come to what are, for many, the number one attraction of the Zoo, the **African lions |23|**. As the 'kings and queens of the jungle' the lions have laid claim to probably the most impressive of the Zoo's single enclosures. Amid maximum-security high-wire fencing, stroll along the caged sky-walk for an aerial view of these formidable legends sunning themselves on rock-contoured lawns.

More **big cats |24|**, including cheetahs, Persian, black and snow leopards, pumas and jaguars, can be seen a little further on, next to the enclosures housing the astounding Syrian bears. For some frolicking good fun the **Australian fur seals |25|** are a must-see. At feeding time, public talks are given by the marine mammal-keepers on the habits and threats to the species. At this time the seals can be seen being individually fed from above the water, or you can go down to the viewing platforms below to see just how graceful these flippered galumphs can be. The new Asiatic elephant enclosure is, at the time of writing, yet to be completed.

By now, if you're a normal member of the human species, you're probably feeling somewhat overwhelmed by the experience and sheer variety of all the different creatures. You might, therefore, like to take in some refreshment at the **Lakeside Bistro by the Japanese Garden |26|**. Before sitting down to a meal or glass of wine, however, a brief saunter along the paths of the Japanese Garden will be rewarding. Designed by world renowned Japanese landscape architect, Shiro Nakane, the garden intends to capture a four-seasons' view and experience of nature in keeping with Japanese philosophy. A brief sit in the garden offers a moment of reflection and contemplation on one's encounters with all the creatures of nature's domain – before retirement to the culinary and beverage delights brought to you by homo sapiens.

Walk key

1. Ian Potter Museum of Art | **2.** Old Pathology Building | **3.** Architecture Building | **4.** Bank Facade | **5.** Raymond Priestley Building | **6.** Union Lawn | **7.** Wilson Hall | **8.** Old Quad | **9.** South Lawn | **10.** Baillieu Library | **11.** Old Arts Building | **12.** University House | **13.** Beaurepaire Centre | **14.** Grainger Museum | **15.** Conservatorium of Music | **16.** Trinity College | **17.** Ormond College | **18.** Newman College

Walk No. 11

University of Melbourne

Treasures and traditions of academia

Start & Finish

Ian Potter Museum of Art – trams 1 or 15 from Swanston Street or any other tram marked 'Melbourne University'; get off just before the corner of Elgin and Swanston streets.

Length/Time

2 km/1.5 hours

The University of Melbourne was established during a period of unparalleled public spending – the gold-rush years of the 1850s – and has steadily grown over 150 years to service some 30,000 users. This campus, which at 19 hectares is small relative to other Australian universities, offers a host of educational courses and cultural attractions and a range of buildings representing most of the major architectural styles from the last 150 years. Drawing together the diverse architecture and the many cultural and social strands of campus life is the internationally acclaimed landscape of winding paths, formal plantings, courtyards, expansive lawns and native groves.

The new and the old

The newest building on campus starts the walk. The **Ian Potter Museum of Art |1|** (100 metres north of the tram stop) moved into this building in 1998 from the Physics Annex next door. The building was designed by Nonda Katsalidis, an architect responsible for some of the more jaw-dropping structures of the 1990s around town, including the apartment building on the corner of Franklin and Queen streets in the city that is seemingly 'held-up' by the massive shapes of Classical figures. One remarkable element of the museum design is the spaciousness of the galleries, given what is essentially a tiny area of land. Another is the way it has incorporated the large Leckie Window, created by Napier Waller in 1935, which hangs suspended from the ceiling down the different levels of the gallery. Also incorporated into the design is the 1994 mural work on the facade of the building, named *Cultural Rubble* by artist Christine O'Loughlin. The building houses the bulk of the university's art collection, which is over 100 years old and covers 19th- and 20th-century Australia, international indigenous cultures and archaeological relics from Classical period. An institution of the Melbourne cafe scene, Brunetti, is located on the ground floor, where you can sit and read the graphics etched onto the street win-dows with quotes from famous artists, such as 'To paint is to love again'.

Head back towards the city along Swanston Street for about 30 metres and at Gate 3 take the walkway into the university. Along the course of this walk, look at the extraordinary campus landscaping. Expansion of the university was rapid, and by the 1940s many of the outdoor public meeting areas had either been lost forever to development, or were not particularly pleasant places to gather. The gardening budget tended to be spent on big showy displays of flowering plants, which were neither appropriate (given they flowered in the summer break) nor practical in a busy campus. All that changed in the early 1970s with the implementation of the Mortlock Plan, by Sydney architect Bryce Mortlock. This provided a series of outdoor spaces of varying size and atmosphere, conducive to large gatherings or private reflection, linked by curving paths and shaded by expansive European trees that alternate with Australian eucalypts.

On the right, about 50 metres in from Swanston Street, look out for the **Old Pathology Building |2|** (1884). Built in rough-cut freestone, it follows a mannered Romanesque style much used in university buildings of the period and a favourite style of prominent American architect, H.H. Richardson. A little further along, also to the right of the path, is the blond brick **Architecture Building |3|** (1963). It follows what is broadly called the Functionalist style, which dominated in the 1950s and 1960s, with post-modern features recently added to the skyline and exterior. The inside of this rather bland building is something of a surprise, with the classrooms and offices stacked up around a central atrium. The atrium space was originally constructed as an internal open-air court, but with the Melbourne climate it proved far too chilly to be useful. On the north side of the building is a small Japanese garden.

Just past Architecture, and facing the Union Lawn and open courtyard, is what is known as the **Bank Facade |4|**. The exterior of this building is the old facade of a Bank of New South Wales office from Collins Street, designed by Joseph Reed. It was given to the university in 1935 when the building was demolished. The facade provides a solid historical bookend to Union Lawn, which contains one of the univesity's many notable outdoor sculptures, *Sun Ribbon*, designed in the early 1980s by Inge King. On the west side of the lawn is Union House, where there are shops, cafes and various student facilities. The **Raymond Priestley Building |5|** (1969), on the south end of **Union Lawn |6|**, is another Functionalist structure. The generous bridging at ground level has made sure that this large building does not overwhelm surrounding buildings and open spaces. Travel underneath the building, and emerge at MacFarland Court. Directly ahead is **Wilson Hall |7|** (1957). This Modernist structure replaced a Gothic revival predecessor that was destroyed by fire in 1952. It is the university's major ceremonial venue with impressive murals and other decorative features set within a light-filled interior. It was the first example of large scale modern architecture on the campus.

Opening Times

Ian Potter Museum of Art: Tue–Wed 10am–5pm, Thurs 10am–9pm Fri–Sat 10am–5pm (9344 5148).
Baillieu Library: Mon–Thurs 8.30am–10pm, Fri 8.30am–6pm, Sat–Sun 11am–5pm. Semester breaks: Mon–Fri 9am–5pm (9344 5379).
Grainger Museum: Open Mon 10am–1pm, Tue 10am–4pm, Wed–Fri 10am–5pm (9344 5270).
College buildings: Trinity College and Chapel (347 1044), Ormond College (9344 1100), Newman College (9347 5577) are open by appointment, or with permission from reception desks. Grounds open at all times.
Underground carpark: Open at all times.

Refreshments

There is a cafe at the **Ian Potter Museum of Art** run by the Brunetti crowd from Lygon Street – the undisputed coffee making masters of Melbourne. **Union House** provides food and beverages during weekdays, but on the weekends these services can be rather thin. However, Lygon Street is nearby with its cafes and restaurants, and there are pubs opposite the university in Grattan Street and Royal Parade.

Historic centre

Just near the northern face of Wilson Hall is the entrance to the **Old Quad |8|**. Here you enter the 'heart of brightness' of the university, in that it was here that it all began. In 1854, shortly after Supreme Court Judge Sir Redmond Barry and others initiated the formation of the university, the foundation stone was laid here. The east and west wings to house the professors were completed by 1855 in Victorian Academic Gothic style with Tudor influences. The sense of tradition was intentional, with the layout and stylistic traits deliberately evocative of Oxford in England. The rest of the University of Melbourne emanates from this historic core. However, on weekends, you're as likely to trip over a bridal gown as an academic cape in these cloistered corridors, as the Old Quad seems to attract wedding parties and their photographers.

From the Old Quad a short stroll brings you to the expansive **South Lawn |9|**. Now here is a bit of the old grey matter at work. South Lawn sits above an underground carpark and trees grow down into hollow cocktail-glass columns, which provide both support and drainage. The lawn, pedestrian areas and watercourses were all designed in 1972 to provide a warm, human scale combined with a gentle sense of order conducive to easy reflection. In warmer months, it is a hugely popular area filled with students lounging about, book fairs, performances, political meetings and, of course, a location for intensive short courses in open-air romance.

Be careful to walk rather than cascade down the awkwardly proportioned steps leading from South Lawn to the **Baillieu Library |10|**. As you enjoy the scent of the natives, note the enormous *Mothering* bronze statue to the left of the foot of the steps. The Baillieu Library holds around a million books and is the university's central library. It was built with funds bequeathed by William L. Baillieu in 1959, supplemented by state and federal grants. While its architecture is a fairly mediocre rendition in the Modernist style, the Baillieu is a centre of Melbourne learning, providing a range of excellent though financially challenged services to academics, students and members of the broader community alike. The library holds a number of rare special collections, including the Morgan Collection of children's literature dating back to 1729, and the McArthur Collection with manuscripts from as early as the 15th century.

For a quick side trip, move south past the entrance of the Baillieu to the underground carpark. The two classical figures on either side of the entrance, nicknamed 'Soapy and Foamy', were carved in bluestone and came from an 1880 bank building in Little Collins Street. A look inside the carpark is worth it to see the supporting columns mentioned earlier, and to appreciate why this space is used by theatre practitioners for performances.

Retrace your steps past the Baillieu and head north to the **Old Arts Building |11|**, built in 1923 in a harmonious style to the Old Quad, with which it forms a second quadrangle. On most days, access may be gained from here to the Old Quad, and it is a pleasant little detour to saunter up and see how they connect.

Straight ahead is **University House |12|**, the staff club, and one of seven professorial residences until the early 1950s. Redmond Barry did much in his day to encourage an overlap between professions and culture and believed that the university needed to be a centre of socialisation as well as learning. The early residential use of campus buildings made this possible and University House stands as the last remnant of that tradition. The social club is closed off to the public and provides a convivial place for staff to relax. The posted verandah, once the exterior of one of Melbourne's earliest Collins Street pharmacies, was attached in the 1950s.

Still on Professors Walk, follow the faint whiff of chlorine until you reach the Functionalist style **Beaurepaire Centre |13|** around the corner. Built in 1956, it houses a 25-metre pool, sports activity rooms and a physical education research facility. It is part of the greater sporting complex of the university, which includes a cricket ground, running track, hockey field and gymnasium. Upstairs in the trophy hall there is a mural, *The Symmetry of Sport*, and some abstract mosaic work designed by Leonard French. The complex was made possible by the sponsorship of Melbourne businessman and Olympic swimmer, Frank Beaurepaire.

Head back along Professors Walk to the Babel Building and turn right. This will take you through the drafty narrow walkway under the Zoology building to the **Grainger Museum |14|**. The indomitable Percy Grainger was Australia's first internationally acclaimed modern composer, whose drive and imagination extended to, among other things, composition, scholarship, self-flagellation, and the erection of this functionalist museum. Housing a large collection of manuscripts, photographs and Grainger memorabilia, alongside collections detailing other Australian composers, the museum would not exist were it not for the persistence of Grainger and his artist wife, Ella Strom. Having bankrolled the museum for the university, and seen its design through to completion in 1938, Grainger returned 18 years later to discover that it had been used as a storeroom and had nearly been torn down. He and Ella persisted and set up the museum's main exhibits themselves, thus leaving the university an embarrassment of riches today.

Next to the Grainger Museum, just a bit to the south, is the **Conservatorium of Music |15|** and Melba Hall. These two buildings are the only Federation period structures on campus and both have been influenced by Art Nouveau. The Conservatorium was founded in 1894 and now forms part of the School of Music in the Faculty of Music, Visual and Performing Arts. This faculty now includes the Victorian College of the Arts as well as all of the university's artistic courses. Travel north from here along Royal Parade until you reach Trinity College Chapel and the college precinct.

University colleges

Trinity College Chapel was designed by North & Williams and built in 1915 in a blend of Federation Arts and Crafts and Gothic styles. A look inside is worth it for the wood carvings of possums and platypuses on the choir stalls and other decorative elements. The Anglican chapel is part of **Trinity College |16|**, the university's first residential quarters for students, established in 1872. The oldest part of the college, the Leeper Wing designed by Leonard Terry, is listed by the National Trust. The University of Melbourne has 13 colleges and residential halls, including Janet Clarke Hall, **Ormond College |17|**, Queens College and **Newman College |18|**, Despite their English ambience, the colleges have little in common with the older European prototypes. Melbourne's colleges were conceived as residential additions to the main university, while their European elders, such as Oxford and Cambridge, were Academic institutions in themselves. Most of the university colleges were exclusively male affairs until the early 1970s when the last enclaves of gynophobia were finally defeated. All the colleges are now 'co-ed'. Meander east through Trinity to the north end of University Cricket Ground.

From the 19th-century grandstand area you can see the rear of Ormond College, founded in 1881 by the Presbyterians and designed by Joseph Reed. A closer inspection of the building is worth it for architecture enthusiasts as Ormond is said to have one of the finest Gothic halls in the world (however, a look at the interiors is by appointment only). In the early 1990s this bastion of conservatism was rocked by a sexual harassment scandal that sparked enormous media interest. The college became the embarrassed subject of feature articles, public debates, a major television news documentary and at least two books; one, *The First Stone*, was written by author Helen Garner. From here follow the perimeter of the cricket ground, bearing south, and then go past the tennis courts into the grounds of Newman College.

Newman Chapel sits in sympathy with the magnificent Griffin-designed college building next door.

Of all the architecture of the university, Newman stands out in a class of its own.

The college was brought to the people of Melbourne in 1918 by the same team who designed Canberra – Walter Burley Griffin and Marion Mahoney Griffin. It is easy to see how the design would have been pilloried by the narrow and conservative establishment of the day. The genius of scale and proportion, the unique decorative elements, and the elevation of light, contrasted with battlement forms of rough-hewn stone, were radical departures from common architectural practice in Melbourne at the time. Though very beholden to the philosophy and pioneering work of American Frank Lloyd Wright, the Griffins were a style unto themselves and Newman is considered their finest completed and extant work in Australia.

The design of the chapel next door to the college, executed by the firm Connelly, Dale & Payne, picks up on many of the ideas utilised in the Griffin design. The structure was completed in 1942.

Walk to the corner of Elgin Street to get a tram, or to Lygon Street for a coffee at one of the many excellent cafes there.

Walk key

1. Upfield Railway Line | **2.** Jewell Railway Station | **3.** Duke of Edinburgh Hotel | **4.** Cumberland Arms | **5.** Town hall and library | **6.** Mechanics' Institute | **7.** Monument to 'free speech' campaign | **8.** Christ Church | **9.** St Ambrose Church | **10.** Methodist Church | **11.** Baptist Church | **12.** Mediterranean Wholesalers

Walk No. 12

Brunswick

Bricks, battlers and bluestone

Start

At the edge of Parkville, on the south-west corner of Park Street and Royal Parade/Sydney Road – tram 19 from Elizabeth Street in the city.

Finish

At the Mechanics' Institute, corner of Glenlyon and Brunswick roads – tram 19 back to the city or walk back to Jewell Station and catch a train.

Length/Time

3.5 km/2 hours

Brunswick was first surveyed in 1839, four years after the arrival and settlement of the city's founders, John Batman and John Fawkner. Situated 5 kilometres north of the City of Melbourne with an area of 1,101 hectares, it was subdivided into 20 large farming lots that backed onto the Moonee Ponds and Merri creeks, running east and west off Sydney Road.

After the gold discoveries north-west of Melbourne in 1851 and the re-routing of Sydney-bound traffic along Sydney Road, Brunswick enjoyed a retail and civic boom due to the increase in travellers. The development of brick-making and stone-cutting industries further consolidated local prosperity in the 1860s and 1870s. Rail and cable tram lines were laid and shortly after their electrification following the First World War, Brunswick became highly regarded as 'the town of the north'. Manufacturing industries emerged in the 1920s.

With the post-war migration schemes of the 1950s and 1960s, the cultural complexion of Brunswick changed markedly, occasioning yet another wave of growth and vitality. The majority of newcomers were Italians, followed by Greek and Turkish people, with Middle Eastern and African people more recent arrivals. Contemporary Brunswick has a distinctly Mediterranean feel, captured in the dizzying variety of shops on Sydney Road and the architectural casserole of its residential areas.

The digger's route

The boulevard of Park Street, as the southern boundary of Brunswick, exhibits architectural signs of the suburb's early wealth, when the area was a country retreat from the teeming industry of Melbourne. Many of the residences here were built in the Victorian Filigree, Italianate and Free Classical styles on reasonably large land allotments, but the wealthier residents moved away as the heavy brick-making and stone-cutting industries grew. After a prolonged post-war slump, these splendid houses are now once again considered prized real estate.

On the south-east and south-west corners of Sydney Road and Park Street are two reminders – Ye Olde Lodge (now apartments) and Princes Park Motor Inn – of the era when Sydney Road was the path to potential goldfield prosperity for many a traveller. At one time most of Sydney Road would have been a bustle of roving itinerants and traders tending to the traveller's every need. From the south-west corner looking north, notice the stately facade of the old Sarah Sands Hotel, now the Irish pub Bridie O'Reilly's. The Sarah Sands (1854) was for many years an icon that most people from other parts of Melbourne associated with the township of Brunswick.

West along Park Street, towards the beginning of the Upfield Walk and Bicycle Path, is the **Upfield Railway Line |1|**. Until as late as 1998 you could see the hand-operated railway gates across Park Street in action (the last of their kind in Melbourne), harking back to the first steam-powered locomotive that traversed these tracks in 1884. Today the screaming whistle is to be heard no more, but on a quiet day a traveller's thoughts can be interrupted by the most remarkable interjection – that of the roaring lions and hungry gibbons at Melbourne Zoo, just a kilometre away to the south (see Walk No. 10, South Parkville and Melbourne Zoo). Proceed on the east side of the railway line, along the bike path.

A different kind of transport

After nearly 50 years of settlement, Melbourne gained a railway system, which was first extended to Brunswick in 1884. The Upfield rail line is still fully operational 114 years after its creation, and was until recently held in high regard by rail heritage enthusiasts as an outstanding example of 19th-century rail infrastructure. Until 1998, much of the line's original detail remained in the form of railway buildings, signal boxes, hand- and wheel-operated gates, gatekeepers' cabins, original picket fences and remnants of early railway technology.

Near the Brunswick Road crossing, the gatekeeper's cabin on the north-east corner remains a memory of the hand-operated gates that were deployed throughout the Melbourne rail system. A system of bells used to rouse the gatekeepers away from their little fires and cups of hot chocolate to the task of locking off the pedestrian and vehicular access to the line until the train had cleared. The timber house on the north-west side of Brunswick Road was owned by the railways as a gatekeeper's residence and dates from 1884.

Just beyond the gates on Barkly Street is **Jewell Railway Station |2|**. A gem indeed, the east platform of Jewell is home to a Victorian Gothic style station house. While standing just to the left of the gabled entrance to the platform, you can look down the length of Wilson Street, stretching its way towards the west. The bottom of this street was the location of Brunswick's earliest brick- and pottery-making area, known then as Phillipstown.

The railway was not only important to commuters but was a great boon to the brick, stone and pottery-making industries in Brunswick. The brickworks relied heavily on the new system of transport, with sidings added to help those factories dotted from Phillipstown to Victoria Street. Continuing north along the bike path, the two-storey Union Street signal box is next. Built in 1889, it is the oldest operational

Opening Times

Churches: Open Sun and for services during the week.
Brunswick Town Hall: Mon–Fri 8.30am–5pm (9240 1111).
Brunswick Library: Mon–Thurs 11am–8pm, Fri 11am–5pm, Sat 10am–1pm, Sun 1pm–5pm (9240 2380).

Refreshments

Sydney Road provides a rich variety of tasty and inexpensive food – from Turkish to Japanese. There are a number of informal cafes along the stretch, but the best bet is the small espresso bar housed in the magnificent Mediterranean Wholesalers near the corner of Victoria Street (9380 4777).

signal box on Melbourne's metropolitan lines, continuing to operate a signalling system with levers. On the cleared land to the west of the signal box is the former site of the railway sidings that serviced Cornwell's pottery factory and Hoffman's brickworks. At its peak, Hoffman's produced 40 million bricks a year, making it the largest industry of its kind in the colonies.

A good drink and a yarn

Brunswick's hotels have seen much of its social history since the opening of the first establishment, the Retreat Inn, in 1842. From the 17th-century inn kitchen, to the 19th-century public house, and through to the 20th century's corner local, watering holes have always been important to Western societies, serving as sites for debate, refreshment and a good yarn.

Heading east along Union Street, towards Sydney Road, note the weatherboard cottage at the end of Little Gold Street. This was a typical abode for 19th-century workers. Next is the Paris Tavern. The hotel was built and named the Austin in 1866 and then renamed the Phoenix in 1871 due to its location on the Phoenix Estate of Michael Dawson. Over the years it has taken on many guises, and at one point it was thought to have a connection with Brunswick's most famous son, wartime Prime Minister John Curtin. While this is incorrect, Curtin had been a local in the area and had frequented the Union Hotel (400 metres west down Union Street), where he was caught, convicted and fined for drinking on a Sunday (before his ascension to Australia's highest office!). The left-wing association continued, with the Phoenix being bought by the Storeman and Packers' Union in 1972. The hotel was renamed as the R.J. Hawke, in honour of the then union leader and future prime minister, Bob Hawke. Another change of ownership brought another name, the Candy Tavern, with an interior refit in the unattractive 1980s fad decor. The Paris is currently trading as a local and is home to a Greek nightclub on the weekends.

Just across Sydney Road is the Brunswick Hotel. Built in 1852 in the Victorian Regency style, this pub was located to cash in on the gold-digger crowd and, interestingly, traded for a full two years before gaining its licence. It was rebuilt to its current configuration in 1907 and enjoyed huge trade from the booming population of workers in the local industries. Like many of Brunswick's hotels, life was good until just after the Second World War, when the closures of the brickyards saw a rapid decline in clientele. However, with the recent influx of young professionals to the area, there is the potential for a hotel revival. The successful Bridie O'Reilly's provides an example.

Travel north along Sydney Road and find the Retreat Hotel, next to the Mechanics' Institute and just north of the corner of Sydney and Glenlyon roads. It is the granddaddy of Brunswick's drinking establishments. Built in 1842 with a weighbridge to service the stone-cutting industry, the

Retreat was first a single-storey inn of the Victorian Regency style, built to its current two-storey form in 1892. Looking north from the town hall corner of Sydney Road, you can see the grand three-storey brick facade of the **Duke of Edinburgh Hotel |3|**. Built in 1868, the hotel was named after the Duke of Edinburgh, who passed it on his way to visit Pentridge Gaol. Its third licensee was Mrs Mary Wildman, whose son prompted a black-ban and picket of the hotel by unions in 1917. The Duke is now fully captive to the electronic gambling bug of the 1990s.

The Cumberland Arms |4| at Nos. 347–357 opened in 1857 and was the site of the first Brunswick Council meeting in the late 1850s as well as the first regular variety show in Brunswick commencing in 1860. It was rebuilt in 1882, having been home to travelling shows, boxing tents and circuses that entertained the public on open land behind the hotel.

Civil society and salutes to the Lord

The civic and religious centre of Brunswick remains, in form at least, where it began, clustered around the corner of Sydney and Glenlyon roads.

The town hall was erected in 1876. The original structure is now the busy community library. Later extensions were added in 1908 and 1926. The 1920s interiors of both the **town hall and library |5|** are well worth a look. Diagonally opposite is the **Mechanics' Institute |6|**, which started in 1868 with the objective of fostering greater learning and culture among Brunswick's adult population. Local bricks were used in its construction and the building now houses a range of community services. Outside the institute is a **monument to the 'free speech' campaign |7|** of the 1930s. The dove perched upon a covered cage commemorates a famous speech delivered by artist Noel Counihan from 'the cage' on the corner of Sydney Road and Phoenix Street.

Just off Sydney Road to the east, in Glenlyon Road, is the Anglican **Christ Church |8|**. The church is listed by the National Trust. It is a masterful and rare example of the Italian Villa Rustica style of church architecture in Victoria. Built over a period of 18 years from 1857, its patronage for many decades was predominantly working class.

There is another Italian connection at **St Ambrose Church |9|**, north of Glenlyon Road at 261 Sydney Road. This was Brunswick's first Roman Catholic Church and, despite the fact that most of the early patrons were of Irish descent, it gained its name from the patron saint of an early parishioner hailing from Milan, Italy. St Ambrose now has a strong following from Brunswick's Italian, Lebanese and Maltese communities.

The **Methodist Church |10|** at No. 354 (approximately 200 metres north of the Mechanics' Institute) was probably the first church in Sydney Road, opening as a small Wesleyan chapel as early as 1841. The church in its current Gothic, polychrome brick form was built in 1872 using local bricks. Its opening was packed to the rafters with 1,000 eager worshippers and

200 more outside. The Methodist Church is a fine example of early decorative brickwork. Loop back down to Glenlyon Road.

Industry and immigration

Head east along Glenlyon Road to Blair Street. Brunswick's very early wealthy residents tended to settle above Blythe Street on the hill or in Park Street next to the parklands and Parkville. With the growing population of workers and industry in the 1850s, the area gradually developed into an eclectic social mix of people whose economic position was broadly reflected in the land size and use of building materials for their homes: single-fronted timber for the poor, double-fronted two-storey mansions in bluestone or polychrome brick for the wealthy, and brick of varying dimensions for everyone else. The post-war migrations and growing population of the 1950s and 1960s led to the mass erection of flats and the 'Mediterraneanisation' of many a Victorian Filigree style home.

Less grand than its Victorian counterparts, the Brunswick Town Hall is nevertheless an imposing building.

Turn left and head north along Blair Street. This route through to Blythe Street provides a journey through the history of Brunswick domestic architecture. While no original rough-cut timber homes remain, mid-to-late Victorian weatherboards, built with the assistance of steam-powered sawmilling technology, are dotted along various locations en route. Late Victorian brick cottages peppered with 1960s Late 20th-Century Immigrant's Nostalgic style interlopers are to be found, as are Mediterranean–Victorian fusions. In the intersecting streets of Lydia and Laura, similar fusions and originals are to be found. Many of the more traditional dwellings are now the highly prized homes of young and moderately well-off professionals. Turn right down Evans Street and left at Ellingsworth Street.

Looking east from the south-east corner of Ellingsworth and Albert streets, you can see the grand, late Victorian, three-storey facade of the Brunswick Club Hotel (1888), a monument to the land boom of the period in which it was built. Cross Albert Street and walk up George Street to the right. This is a similar experience to Blair Street, yet with an even more alarming – or exciting, depending on your view – pastiche of styles, building materials and modifications. Cross Victoria Street and head right to Nash Street, which gives more of a true indication of the early architectural form of Brunswick's tiny streets. It is also interesting for the use of brick in late Victorian houses situated on tiny plots of land. This may be indicative of the fact that by the 1890s locally made Brunswick brick was a cheap alternative to weatherboard for many of the working poor.

Follow Nash Street and turn left into Blythe Street, where you can see something of the impressive contrast of lifestyles, means and tastes of last century in the generous allotments of land and some fine remaining examples of broad-berthed, two-fronted, or two-storey Victorian Filigree and Federation Queen Anne style homes. The best specimens lie between Cooraminta Street and Sydney Road. As you head west for Sydney Road, just as you pass the fire station do not miss the impressive, if odd, view, of the darkly Romanesque style apartments next to the **Baptist Church |11|** in Sydney Road.

A thoroughfare through time

Turn left from Blythe Street into Sydney Road and head back towards the town hall. Sydney Road was first called Pentridge Road, due to the excellent reserves of bluestone discovered to the north at Pentridge Village. This link continued with the establishment of Pentridge Gaol in 1850 and the use of convict labour to surface the road that, prior to this, was an unsealed bush track. Brunswick's early centre, with town hall, churches, hotels and banks, ran along Sydney Road between Albert Street and Glenlyon Road on the east side and between Phoenix Street and Glenlyon Road on the west. Sydney Road remains significant as a large, generally intact linear commercial area. Most of the shops of Victorian character have retained their facades and there is a degree of consistent architectural feeling provided by the uniform setback of the buildings. Unfortunately, early subdivision and planning showed little foresight, with the subsequent legacy of narrow and barely adequate thoroughfares. Yet this congested feeling contributes to Brunswick's charm.

Where Sydney Road once catered to the traveller, it is now home to the Australian type of socioeconomic potpourri of which so many in this country are proud. There are all sorts of goods for sale and items to peruse as you stroll along, and whether it's a Turkish restaurant, a new-age yuppie cafe, a Vietnamese bakery, or a Greek Bazaar, Sydney Road has got the lot. Don't miss **Mediterranean Wholesalers |12|** just near the corner of Victoria Street. Long the gastronomic lifeline of Brunswick's Italian community, in more recent years it has become a favoured shopping place fine pasta, related condiments and grains, coffee and delicious cakes and sweets.

Walk key

1. Mononia | **2.** Mon Sejour | **3.** 39–49 Brunswick Street | **4.** Cable-tram Engine House | **5.** Osborne House | **6.** Royal Terrace | **7.** Grantown House | **8.** Labour in Vain Hotel | **9.** Perseverance Hotel | **10.** Fitzroy Town Hall | **11.** The Black Cat | **12.** Binary Bar | **13.** Moran & Cato building | **14.** The Provincial Hotel | **15.** Mario's Cafe | **16.** Rhumberalla's

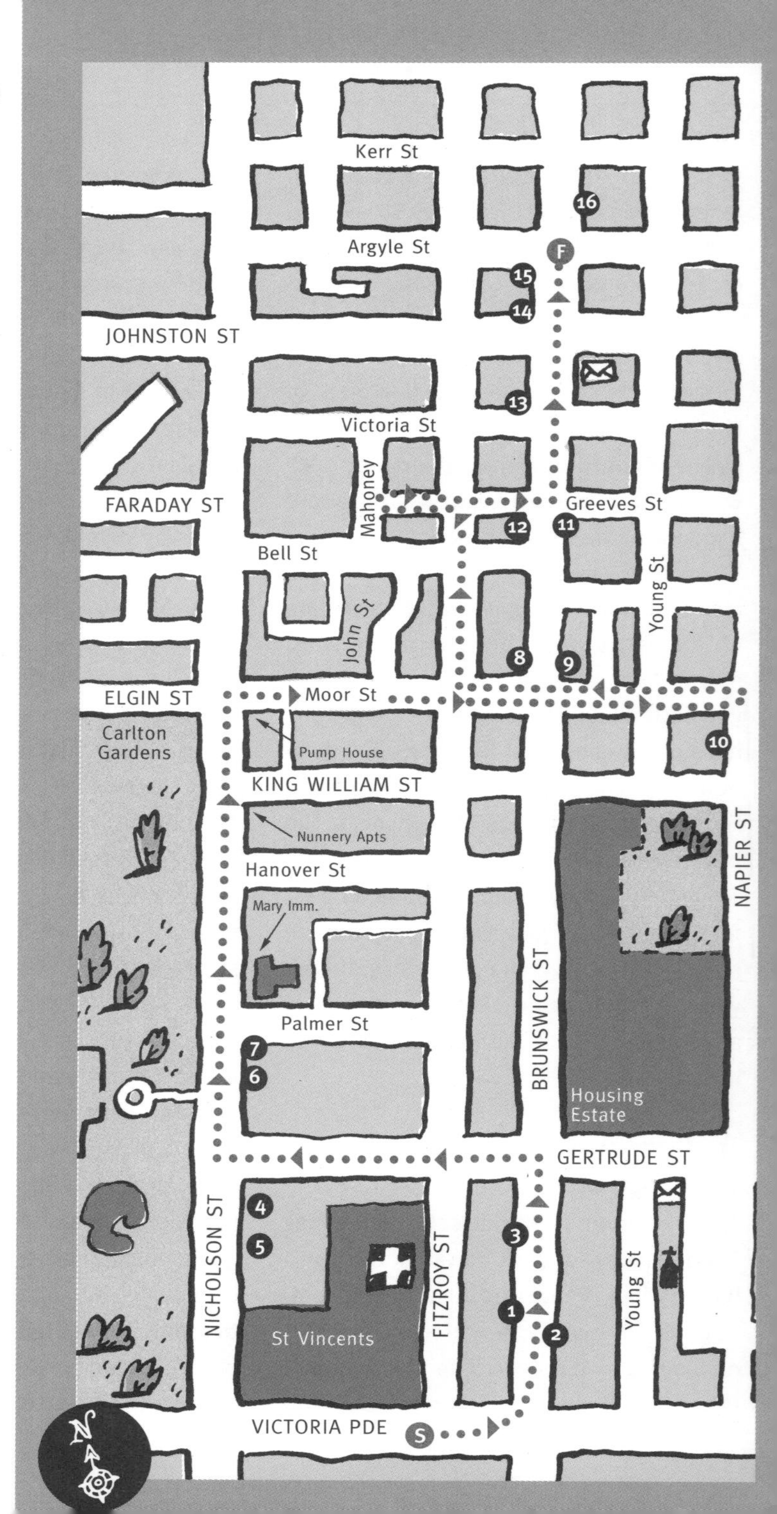

Walk No. 13

Fitzroy

From streets of mean to coffee beans

Start

Corner of Victoria Parade and Fitzroy Street – trams 10, 11, 12 or 42 from Collins Street in the city; or it is an easy walk.

Finish

Mario's Cafe, 303 Brunswick Street – any tram from the east side of Brunswick Street back to the city.

Length/Time

2 km/1.5 hours

Fitzroy is Melbourne's first, as well as its smallest, suburb. Its earliest homes were for the wealthy and were located on the rise to the north-east of the city. However, as the wealth accrued in the very south and east ends of the suburb, those who were less well off were also making the new quarter home. From the beginning, the wealthy and impoverished of Fitzroy lived shoulder to shoulder, co-mingling on the sidewalks of eventually densely packed and active streets.

By 1939, due to absurd subdivisions and the dividing and subletting of many a previously grand home, Fitzroy was not only the smallest suburb but also the most densely crowded municipality in Victoria. The smallness of the suburb made for a unique, community conscious atmosphere, which lasted until the depression of the 1930s when it was, in part, shattered by the mass evictions of the poor.

The well-to-do eventually departed Fitzroy, enticed away to quieter and more spacious locations. The suburb was left to the growing industries and their workers who, burdened by long hours and inadequate means of transport, needed to live close by. After the 1890s depression, the swelling numbers of poor and unemployed created slums and a very lively crime scene.

The focus of life and trade in the early years was within the boundaries of Nicholson, Gertrude, Smith and Johnston streets. The boom of the 1880s, when there were still many open spaces, attracted larger retailers and industries, displacing the smaller shopkeepers and craftsmen. In 1949 Fitzroy's major industries were clothing, footwear, and the manufacture of food and drink, but today the major activity is provision of hospitality services and culture.

The post Second World War waves of immigration gave Fitzroy a very multicultural feel from the 1950s on and nearly 50 per cent of the population by 1966 were new migrants. More recently, up-market professionals, students and artists have come to dominate the mix. Brunswick Street, in particular, is on the 'must-see' list for interstate and international visitors. Where street life may have been industrious or desperate over the years, it is now likely to have an air of carnival about it, especially during the time of the annual Fringe Festival Parade. While many of Fitzroy's older and more colourful characters have gone, the drive and invention of the new population ensures that the suburb's reputation will continue to 'punch above its weight'. We really can be grateful for the fact that Fitzroy is nothing if not unique.

Newtown architecture

Between 1850 and 1870 south-east Fitzroy was described as 'a comfortable walking suburb of fine villas and terraces'. At this time it was still called Newtown and, as home to Melbourne's elite, had become something of an architects' gallery. Some of Melbourne's earliest buildings remain in this pocket of Fitzroy. South-east Fitzroy contains the first parcels of land sold outside those of the city of Melbourne. After its salubrious beginning, the section of the once intensely fashionable Victoria Parade at the start of this walk and most of the rest of south Fitzroy was, by the early decades of the 20th century, the haunt of prostitutes, cocaine and liquor dealers as well as some of Melbourne's most violent criminals.

Fitzroy has a richly textured industrial and political history. As you commence walking you will see this represented in no small part by the building on the north-west corner of Brunswick Street and Victoria Parade, the former Belvidere Hotel. Between the 1850s and 1890s, Brunswick Street was a busy pedestrian and retail thoroughfare, with a concentration of industry and skilled workers. The Belvidere, later the Eastern Hill, was the establishment wherein the stonemasons held the first discussions, in 1856, that led to the winning of the Eight-hour Day. Turn into Brunswick Street.

A few metres along, there is a plaque commemorating the birthplace of Blessed Mary McKillop, just in front of the 19th-century mansion at No. 9. Next door, at No. 11, is a small museum celebrating the life of the woman set to become Australia's first saint. At No. 23 is **Mononia |1|**. This house was built in 1851 for John Mickle to the design of Charles Laing, and remains as a representative of the early days of colonial ale and frilly shirts. Mononia, now home to the religious order, the Sisters of Charity, is situated on a land allotment that, along with the other uneven allotments of the west side of this end of Brunswick Street, gives an indication of some of the earliest of Fitzroy's subdivisions before things got truly out of hand. By 1870, nearly one out of five houses in Fitzroy could be classified mansions, with six rooms or more. Yet, at the same time, the remaining houses and land blocks were generally smaller than those in the rest of Melbourne. **Mon Sejour |2|** at No.24 was built in the mid 1800s for a Melbourne businessman and next door is the Central

Opening Times

Central Hall: 9am–3pm weekdays (9417 3726).

Mary McKillop Pilgrimage Centre: Open Mon–Fri 9:30am–4:30pm; Sun 2pm–4:30pm (9419 9273)

Academy of Mary Immaculate and the Convent of Mercy: By appointment only (9419 3044 and 9417 2723 respectively).

Fitzroy Library: Open Tue, Wed, Fri 1pm–6pm, Thur 1pm–8pm; Sat 10am–1pm, Sun 2pm–5pm; closed Mon (9201 1540).

Refreshments

Brunswick Street, from King William Street to Alexandra Parade, offers a diverse range of meals and refreshments in establishments with the longest opening hours to be found in Melbourne. Recommended for a coffee or meal are **Mario's Cafe** (9417 3343), **Rhumberalla's** (9417 5652) and **The Provincial** (9417 2228).

Hall, built in 1902. Erected by the Catholic Church in response to the community needs of the Irish working class of Fitzroy, Central Hall is still owned by the church and is a venue for everything from karate classes to wedding receptions and ballroom dancing. It is worth taking a look inside for its colourful Edwardian interior.

Fitzroy is the birthplace of terrace housing in Melbourne, and of the buildings that remain intact, those at **39–49 Brunswick Street |3|** are the most distinctive. Still run down at the time of writing, this terrace designed by Charles Laing and built in 1856 was once absolutely prime real estate. Its two three-storey houses at either end are novel, and the one on the corner of Gertrude and Brunswick, newly renovated, had until recently been a surgery for more than 100 years.

Turn left into Gertrude Street and head towards Nicholson Street. But before doing so, it is hard not to notice the Housing Commission Estate occupying the north-east corner. This area was one of the worst slums in Melbourne's history, known as The Narrows, which once had the dishonour of being dubbed 'probably the most fetid spot in Australia'. This was at a time when the infant mortality rate for Fitzroy was higher than anywhere in Australia and when infestation and disease were also rife.

Due to the cramped conditions, street life was important in Fitzroy. For children, there was no other place to play, and a great deal of communication, swapping of stories and daily business occurred.

Detail of the old Cable-tram Engine House on Nicholson Street.

But for the establishment of the legendary Fitzroy Residents Association in 1969, Glass Terrace at 64–78 Gertrude Street, along with many other fine historic Fitzroy structures, would undoubtedly have been demolished. Glass Terrace is now the oldest surviving terrace in Victoria. The first two houses, attributed to architect J.E. Moore, were built in 1853 out of rough-axed bluestone. The rest were completed by 1858. The last house in Glass Terrace abuts Fitzroy Street. To the south, on the corner of Fitzroy Street and Victoria Parade, is the former site of the Cyclorama that showed the Battle of Waterloo as a popular attraction from 1889 until 1904.

Heading west along Gertrude Street, note the splendid dome of the Royal Exhibition Building dominating the skyline (see Walk No.8, Carlton). Gertrude Street at the turn of the century was still, despite this suburb's troubles of the time, a respectable shopping strip providing homemaker stores and a wide variety of skilled services.

On the south-east corner of Gertrude and Nicholson streets is the **Cable-tram Engine House |4|,** designed by Alexander Davidson in the same Victorian Free Classical style of the Exhibition Building. It was built for the Melbourne Tramway and Omnibus Company in 1886 in time for the Centennial Exhibition at the Exhibition Building. Cable-trams lasted in Fitzroy until just before the Second World War, when they were replaced with buses following the same routes. These were, in turn, replaced by trams in time for the 1956 Olympics.

Nicholson Street was named after William Nicholson, a former premier of Victoria, founder of the Bank of Victoria and the MP who introduced the bill for the Eight-Hour Day into the Victorian parliament. Just south along the street, at No. 40, is **Osborne House |5|**, one of the oldest surviving residences in Melbourne. The transformations that it has seen and endured over time mirror those of Fitzroy. Originally Osborne House was a ten-room, Victorian Regency style mansion built in 1850 for the McPherson family – a later descendant, John McPherson, was premier of Victoria from 1869–70. It then became an exclusive boarding house, and after the 1890s depression, a doss house. Just before the 1888 Centennial Exhibition the wings were added to the house, bringing the total number of rooms to 88. Go back to the intersection of Gertrude and Nicholson Streets. Cross over to the splendid Carlton Gardens.

From the Gardens, you are best able to gain a sense of the formal elegance and scale of **Royal Terrace |6|** at 50–58 Nicholson Street. Built in the Victorian Regency style in two stages between 1854 and 1856, the design of this stately row of bluestone terraces is attributed to John Gill. Cross Nicholson Street and note the palisade fences, which represent the first use of cast iron in Fitzroy. Each individual bar and its ornamental top was cast as one piece. The houses of Royal Terrace, after having served as boarding houses and low-cost rental homes for decades, are once more the homes of the very well-to-do. They have provided shelter for a great number of interesting characters. In 1858–59 artist Nicholas Chevalier lived here as did Melbourne society surgeon William Crook (1871–91), and Victorian Premier John O'Shanassy (1888–89). At one stage in the early 1900s, a detective David O'Donnel, who was known for thwarting the illegal gambling trade, was a resident. The night before he was to give evidence at a trial, a bomb was tossed through his window.

At 82 Nicholson Street (heading north) is **Grantown House |7|**. Often described as a wedding cake of a structure, it was built in the 1850s and initially designed by George Brown, with more extravagant extensions and ornamentation added over a 20-year period. The combination of a two-storey verandah and balcony with a three-storey residence is unusual.

At No.88 is the large bluestone Gothic Revival style Academy of Mary Immaculate and the Convent of Mercy, built from 1857 through to the 1890s. The fee-paying academy for girls was established by four women from Ireland's Sisters of Mercy. Next to the academy the sisters ran the maid-training House of Mercy for 'respectable young women out of situation' and a 'ragged school' for children forced onto the streets by poverty. The convent also absorbed the structures of Watson's and Wight's houses, designed by Newsom & Blackburn in 1850, which, along with Osborne House, are among the oldest houses in Melbourne.

The Nunnery, at 116–118 Nicholson Street, initially built for Melbourne physician Dr Thomas Hewlett, now provides backpacker accommodation. In 1944 it was purchased by the Daughters of Charity for the purpose of establishing St Vincent's Hall – a hostel for young working women. These nuns started working in Fitzroy in the 1930s, mingling with the locals in full 17th-century French peasant habits, replete with the winged headgear made famous on the Gidget TV series. (The closest you would come to that in modern Fitzroy would be a half-sober and scarcely reverent drag queen during the Brunswick Street Fringe Festival Parade!)

Heading further north, encounter the house at No. 122 on the corner of King William Street which, with its rather dour loggia verandahs, was erected in 1862 at the tail end of the gold-induced land boom. King William Street was named after William IV, who reigned from 1830 to 1837. On the north corner is the Pump House Hotel, a sedate drinking establishment with reasonably priced meals and excellent views of the Carlton Gardens. Continue to Moor Street, turn right, and then head east towards the town hall.

Pubs, gangs and the town hall

Moor Street is now part of a network of charming and elegant streets inhabited mainly by professionals and old bohemians who moved in when the properties could be bought quite cheaply in the early 1970s. However, just after the 1840s recession when the area was a shantytown of tents and other makeshift shelters, it was described as a place in which pigs 'would hardly condescend to wallow'.

Today the street offers a delightful cross-section of Fitzroy housing, with modest yet stately terraces through to tiny, elegant workers' cottages near Smith Street. The snaky contour of John Street, running left off Moor Street, is a reminder of earlier periods of haphazard subdivisions and slum-filled back streets. As early as 1856, the Melbourne City Council felt obliged to raze entire blocks of temporary housing to realign Fitzroy's streets.

The corner of Moor and Brunswick streets was an early location for the sly-grog trade. On the north-west corner is the recently reopened **Labour in Vain Hotel |8|** and on the north-east the **Perseverance Hotel |9|**. These hotels gained their names from two pubs in England that had, in the former's case, a billboard out front depicting someone vainly trying to scrub a black child white and, in the latter case, a billboard with white streaks beginning to appear on the same child. Today, Labour in Vain boasts a fine hand-carved, old-style bar and fittings, lovingly cluttered with collectors' items of 19th- and early 20th-century drinking, and drink advertising paraphernalia; and the Dutch-gabled Perseverance is a friendly and well-renovated local.

Just before reaching the town hall area, note Young Street, stretching off to the north, which used to run all the way south to Victoria Parade before the Commission flats replaced The Narrows. Young Street (as well as Fitzroy Street) was infamous for its violence from the 1870s. By the 1890s, this infamy had extended to all of Fitzroy and, by the turn of the century, it was seen as the receptacle of evil itself by many a respectable outsider. There were also reports of rival gangs of larrikins from Fitzroy and Collingwood – with names like the Checkers, the Woolpacks, the Little Campbells and the Fitzroy Roses – fighting weekly battles up and down Smith Street, particularly on a football day. During the First World War, Young Street, and other streets near Gertrude Street, were riddled with sly-grog shops and brothels, many doing a secondary trade in cocaine for returned soldiers and prostitutes.

In 1919 the gangs involved in these illicit dealings were led by 'Long Harry' Slater, and they fought with the Richmond gangs over territory and spoils. In what came to be known as the Fitzroy Vendetta, many of Fitzroy's brothels and sly-grog shops were systematically shot to pieces in night-time raids. Local myth suggests that famous local criminal Squizzy Taylor may have started the shooting because his girlfriend was beaten up in a Fitzroy grog shop. Fitzroy became emblematic for the problems associated with inner-city life; a case study for moral crusaders and welfare reformers alike.

Continue to **Fitzroy Town Hall |10|**. Work began on the building in 1873 amid a raging political controversy over its location, resulting in interminable delays. The *Fitzroy City Press* issued the sarcastic suggestion of mounting it on wheels, but the current site was eventually agreed upon. Built in the Victorian Academic Classical style, the Town Hall appears to the unwary modern pedestrian as a pompous, if awkward, interloper in the otherwise residential Napier Street. The small library (upstairs, off Napier Street) has a warm and resonant sense of Victorian grandeur.

After the depression of the 1890s a good deal of Fitzroy was purchased by absent landlords, who were primarily responsible for the suburb's physical degeneration for six decades thereafter. Even the politicians of the time were understood to have participated, with the legendary King O'Malley apparently owning bug-infested rental property in the area. Poor, rent-paying people in the era didn't have many options for alternative housing. The speculative interest of outsiders meant that when the times got very hard, 'no longer could rents be held over by appeals to a sense of neighbourliness, or evictions staved off through the pressure of local opinion'. Even the council failed to bear many representatives from Fitzroy at the time. Retrace your steps to Brunswick Street, turn right and head north to Greeves Street.

La Boheme

By the late 1980s, Brunswick Street had become the artistic and 'alternative culture' centre of Melbourne. After the Second World War many European immigrants moved into the area, sometimes combining earnings to purchase properties. This started the renovations that eventually pulled Fitzroy out of its decades of neglect. Even so, Brunswick Street remained virtually devoid of street life from the 1950s until 1982, when two cafes – Bakers Cafe and **The Black Cat |11|** – were opened. The latter, on the south-east corner of Greeves Street, was established by European cabaret artist Henry Maas. It is this cafe, in particular, that is credited with starting a veritable onslaught of young bohemian interest, caught awkwardly in the last days of hippie culture, with no real place to go. Brunswick Street now has some of the best pubs, cafes, restaurants and boutiques in Australia. Cross Brunswick Street and travel west along Greeves to Mahoney Street.

Greeves Street was named after Augustus Frederick Adolphus Greeves (1805–74), a surgeon, journalist, publican and mayor of Melbourne. The section west of Brunswick Street is the first streetscape to have been listed by the National Trust. It was designed by Alfred Kursteiner, built in 1870–71, and comprises 30 single, and four two-storey houses at the Fitzroy Street intersection, as well as two more at the Mahoney Street intersection. Mahoney Street was named after Fitzroy mayor, Daniel Mahoney, who built the Greeves Street housing complex. Return to Brunswick Street and detour right towards the Binary Bar.

Binary Bar |12|, at 243 Brunswick Street, opened early in 1997 and was the first fully licensed Internet bar in Australia. Providing free Internet access to customers, a game of pool, or a go on a near-ancient Space Invaders machine, Binary heralds a new wave of eccentric and trend-setting establishments in Fitzroy.

At 265 Brunswick Street (heading north again), see the former home of the supermarket-grocery-milk bar run by the Pizziola family until the mid-1990s (now a trendy shoe shop). The Pizziolas used to sell the best Mediterranean produce and theirs, at four decades, was the oldest surviving small business of its kind in Brunswick Street until ill health and age forced their retirement. Like so many new Australian and other cosmopolitan businesses of character, the Pizziolas' was one that played a pivotal role in refurbishing people's interests in the inner-city suburbs of Melbourne.

Continuing north, note the impressive Mannerist bulk of the old **Moran & Cato building |13|**, on the north-west corner of Victoria Street. F.J. Cato, one of the partners of the cash and carry retail grocery syndicate, was a devout Methodist and local philanthropist, and the firm was an important and fair employer in the suburb. Moran & Cato had eight suburban branches by 1884, and 30 by 1890. When it moved into importing and manufacturing the headquarters were here in Brunswick Street, but the onset of the 1890s depression prompted a shift to Haw-thorn. Cato had built the empire into 170 branches employing over 1,000 people by the time of his death in 1935.

The Provincial Hotel |14| on the north-west corner of Johnston Street was, until late into the 1980s, known as a retreat for bike gangs and certain colourful figures of Melbourne's underworld. Taken over and transformed by Max Fink and partners in 1992, it is now a chic yet relaxed complex comprising two restaurants, a cafe and bar.

Mario's Cafe |15| at 303 Brunswick Street has, since 1986, been serving some of Melbourne's best coffee. It has also become synonymous with cafe cool, the meeting place of artists, famous and obscure. (Don't worry if the waiters give you a bit of a hard time; it's all part of the act.)

Further north along Brunswick Street is a wealth of legendary bars and fine restaurants. These include the bar that couldn't find a name – Bar Open – at No.317; the dimly lit and sophisticated Gypsy Bar at No.334; the open-plan and colourful **Rhumberalla's |16|** at No.342; cool heaven in summer, Charmaine's ice-cream parlour at No.370; local mecca for alternative music right next door, the Punter's Club Hotel; the Veggie Bar on the north-east corner of Rose Street, if you enjoy a good vegetarian meal; and Bakers Cafe at No.384; to name a few.

Together with excellent bookstores, restaurants, alternative clothing stores and street buskers, Brunswick Street provides a sophisticated and highly cultured experience to the visitor. If you wish to return to the city, catch the number 10 tram.

Walk key

1. Richmond Bridge | **2.** Bryant & May | **3.** Dimmeys Store | **4.** Christine Abrahams Gallery | **5.** St Stephens Anglican Church | **6.** St Ignatius Church | **7.** Peter Lalor | **8.** The Vaucluse | **9.** Orwell Cottage | **10.** Former home of murderer Martha Needle | **11.** Australia Hotel | **12.** Richmond Town Hall

Walk No. 14

Richmond

From riches to rags and priceless institutions

Start

Richmond Bridge, southern boundary of Richmond – train to South Yarra from Flinders Street Station, the trip takes about 6 minutes; Frankston, Pakenham, Cranbourne and Sandringham lines go to South Yarra; Get out at South Yarra, exit station to Toorak Road, walk east to Chapel Street and turn left. Richmond Bridge is about 300 metres to the north. Alternatively, catch a tram 8 from Swanston Street. It takes about 30 minutes to get to the corner of Toorak Road and Chapel Street.

Finish

Richmond Town Hall – trams 75 or 48 back to the city. Board on the south side of Bridge Road for trams running west.

Length/Time

2.4 km/1.5 hours

Richmond was laid out in the 1830s by surveyor Robert Hoddle and created as a borough in 1855 along with Prahran and Collingwood, before being declared a city in 1882. Prior to this, the land was home to the Yarra Yarra and the Jaga Jaga indigenous communities.

Richmond was named after the salubrious parkland suburb by the Thames in London, and in its early years was a fashionable place to live, with sprawling properties fronting the Yarra River. As with many areas in Melbourne, the population of the suburb grew rapidly after the gold discoveries of 1851. Where a clutch of hilltop estates with clear air and fine views predominated in the early 1850s, the Richmond river flats became home to a shantytown of itinerants who had either failed at the goldfields or who were on their way to try their luck.

From the earliest days, Richmond had a diverse ethnic complexion. Although predominantly from the British Isles, immigrants also came from the Mediterranean and China, particularly during the gold rush and, in the 20th century, after the Second World War. When Australia abolished its White Australia Policy in the late 1960s a new wave of Asian immigration began, particularly from Vietnam. This has led to the wonderful colour and vibrancy of Victoria Street, full of Vietnamese businesses and inexpensive restaurants.

Richmond has also been home to some of Australia's defining political characters, such as financier and gambler John Wren (said to be the model for Frank Hardy's novel *Power Without Glory*), and some of the country's most famous criminals (among them Ronald Ryan, the last man to be hanged in Victoria; and Squizzy Taylor, considered by some as a Robin Hood and by others as a murderous gangster).

For years seen as unfashionable due to its heavy industry, Richmond is now once again prized, particularly for its streets containing heritage housing, such as the tiny workers' cottages, once threadbare homes in an age of slums. In more recent years, cleaner business and industrial acti-vity and a vigorous retail sector have given the suburb a new lease of life.

Tough as nails

Richmond Bridge |1| was opened in 1924 by the Earl of Stradbroke. Before this, goods and people alike had to use Brander's Ferry to access Prahran and beyond. From the west side of Richmond Bridge, looking north towards the spire of St Ignatius Church on top of Docker's Hill, it is evident that this part of Richmond is still a place of industry. It evokes historical Richmond, one of Australia's defining industrial suburbs with a long history of hard blue collar work, political and union activity. By 1914 south Richmond was a densely crowded slum, home to very hard-working families. Most of the early industrial businesses such as abattoirs, tanneries and wool-washing took place here by the river.

Just north of the bridge, on the west side you can see the site of the old Richmond power station, designed by architect and engineer Charles D'Ebro in 1891 and now listed on the Victorian Trust Register as an important example of a 19th-century coal-fired power station. The engine, boiler houses and original offices remain intact. Head along Church Street.

On the corner of Balmain and Church streets is one of Richmond's defining industrial icons, the former home of match-manufacturer **Bryant & May |2|**. Now occupied by a variety of businesses, access to the interiors is off limits to the public, but take a stroll into the complex to see the clock tower, chimney stack and courtyard areas that preserve the character of a bygone industrial era. The lavish use of brick and the pleasing proportions have a sense of humanity, which was reported to be a quality of the employer in those early years. Bryant & May staff had access to tennis courts, bowling greens and a host of other sporting and social activities. One sporting activity included a women's football team, which played a social game against the seconds of the professional league. An early photograph of the team demonstrates something of the character of the suburb. Strong arms are folded in grim determination – these women were not about to be messed with.

Before moving further north to Swan Street note the tiny workers' cottages in Willis Street, just opposite Bryant & May. The dimensions of these homes provide an indication of the unscrupulous land subdivisions that took place throughout the latter half of last century – 'barely enough room to swing a cat without concern for its head' as one commentator put it. Further north, past Adolph Street, note the East Richmond Station from the railway bridge as a good example of 19th-century Victorian railway architecture. Also from the bridge, looking west, is another Richmond icon, the Dimmeys Clock Tower. At Swan Street turn left towards **Dimmeys Store |3|**.

Swan Street, named after the black swans that used to inhabit the Yarra at Richmond Bridge, is one of three retail strips in the modern-day suburb. Dimmeys, at No. 140, has been its pride and joy. Built in the Federation Free Classical style with an extraordinary landmark tower, Dimmeys has long been synonymous with the bargain-filled great Australian general store and continues the tradition with everything

Opening Times

Dimmeys: Mon–Tue 9am–5.30pm, Fri 9am–9pm, Sat 9am–5pm, Sun 10am–5pm (9427 0442).
St Stephens and St Ignatius: Open every day, approx. 8am–6pm, but sometimes later (9429 3574 and 9428 1212 respectively).
Richmond Town Hall: Mon–Fri 8.30am–5pm (9205 5555).
Christine Abrahams Gallery: Tue–Fri 10.30am–5pm, Sat 11am–5pm (9428 6099).

Refreshments

There are numerous pubs and cafes along the way. While there are several cafes in Swan Street, Bridge Road offers a far greater variety, and is a surer bet on a Sunday. The **Richmond Hill Cafe and Larder**, 42 Bridge Road (9421 2808) comes highly recommended. By far the best Vietnamese eating strip in Melbourne is in Victoria Street. Get there by walking north down Church Street for about 15 minutes from Bridge Road, or catch trams 78 or 79 along Church Street (run every 30 minutes). Head west along Victoria Street for the restaurants. Recommended is **Thy Thy** at 142 Victoria Street (9428 5914), one of the more established eateries.

from a cheap shovel to a five-dollar haircut. The remnants of the old mechanical money dispatch system can still be seen hanging from the ceiling throughout the store.

Rifles and residences

From Dimmeys, head west down Swan Street and turn right into Stanley Street. The journey from here through to Bridge Road reveals a cross-section of well preserved historic architecture, centred on and around Docker's Hill. In 1853 the Reverend Joseph Docker engaged in a deliberate land subdivision strategy to enable land ownership by an economically diverse population. By 1855, the large estates occupying Docker's Hill were surrounded and penetrated by smaller cottages. Cobblers, painters and doctors lived here, and John Monash, who was to become Australia's leading wartime general in the First World War, grew up on land obtained from Docker's division, at 34 Clifton Street, two streets east of Stanley Street.

As you move towards Gipps Street, soak up the ambience of wood, iron, posted verandahs and small cottages. There is an interesting double-fronted Art Deco style home at No. 32, and note the 'butterfly house' at No. 60. Most of the really narrow allotments fall on the west side, and the east side shows Immigrant Nostalgic influences in the ad hoc renovations and additions to exterior forms. When you reach Gipps Street you will see the hulk of the Melbourne Cricket Ground brooding against the backdrop of the city.

Turn right into Gipps Street. At No. 27 is the **Christine Abrahams Gallery |4|**, which has been displaying contemporary Australian art since 1981. Parts of the interior of the new Bauhaus style building straddle the former sites of one of Richmond's earliest power substations and a dress-manufacturing factory. Go next to the south-east corner of Gipps and Docker streets.

As a result of the Crimean War, concern for matters military abroad had impressed itself upon the imagination of the local residents, spawning the Richmond Rifle Corps. The old drill hall at 37 Docker Street was the Victorian Carpenter Gothic style home to the Corps. The crack squad of riflemen was to defend the fledgling colony against the Russian invasion. This was no doubt a sensible precaution, considering the envy Richmond must have attracted by spawning a brand new, outstanding code of football! (The first recorded game of Australian Rules was played in Yarra Park, home of the subsequent Richmond Football Club, in 1858.) It is unclear whether the members of the Rifle Corps were related to the Richmond Volunteer Rifles. Photographs of the RVR show a uniformed and sombre cadre of bearded men with tall furry hats, assembled to fight the rebels at Eureka Stockade.

Howlands, on the north-east corner of Gipps and Docker streets, was built for the founder of the Alexander chain of stores in 1889. This Classical Revival style building has a stylistic soulmate at 29 Gipps Street, which was initially a fancy warehouse, later converted to residences. The use of Classical Revival in these and other buildings dotted around the area provides a welcome contrast to the widespread use of Victorian Filigree, an interesting example of which can be seen in the two-storey terrace at 39 Docker Street, on the corner of Gipps.

Move north along Docker Street towards Richmond Terrace and the summit of Docker's Hill. A look west down Richmond Terrace provides an engaging view of the city. Enter the churches area from Richmond Terrace via the entrance to **St Stephens Anglican Church |5|**. From here move east until you reach Church Street, then track around the front of St Ignatius to reach The Vaucluse. Reverend Docker offered the Anglicans this prime piece of land for St Stephens Church in 1849. The church opened in 1851 (giving Church Street its name) but was not completed until 1876, due to a shortage of labour resulting from the rush to the goldfields. Where St Stephens had been the hilltop bastion of the local gentry, **St Ignatius Church |6|**, in all its Gothic Revival glory, was home to the Irish-Australian working class. The first stone of St Ignatius was laid in 1867 and the spire, the second tallest in Melbourne, was not completed until 1928. The proliferation of churches continued along Church Street with Central and Uniting churches to be found further north down the hill. Before walking back along the north side of St Ignatius Church to The Vaucluse, a detour down to 293 Church Street, the former home of Peter Lalor, may be of interest.

Peter Lalor |7| led the miners at the Eureka Stockade, and built this mansion house when he became a politician. While his heroism is the stuff of Australian legend, his personal misfortunes remain obscure. It is hard to imagine a more tragic destiny than the one that befell this Australian icon. In this very house his wife died of a mysterious ailment, his daughter committed suicide by throwing herself off the balcony, and his son, who was a doctor and had his surgery downstairs, hanged himself. Lalor died of unexplained causes on the site in 1889.

Go back up to the north side of St Ignatius and move west down **The Vaucluse |8|**. Since its creation in the early 1860s, The Vaucluse has been an exclusive retreat, home to politicians, merchants, newspaper editors and professors. The mansions on the north side have since been demolished to make way for the expansions of the Convent of the Faithful Companions of Jesus, who established themselves in the area in 1882. Brinsley Place at Nos. 12–14 was built in 1878 and conforms to the glorious Filigree style, the identifying feature of which is ornate iron lace. No.10 is apparently a variation upon the Old Colonial Georgian theme. The Vaucluse becomes Rowena Parade; head down to Lennox Street and turn right towards Bridge Road.

Lennox Street has a number of fine terraces from the 19th century as well as turn-of-the-century dwellings, with modern apartment buildings crowding in upon the formerly elegant streetscape. For popular

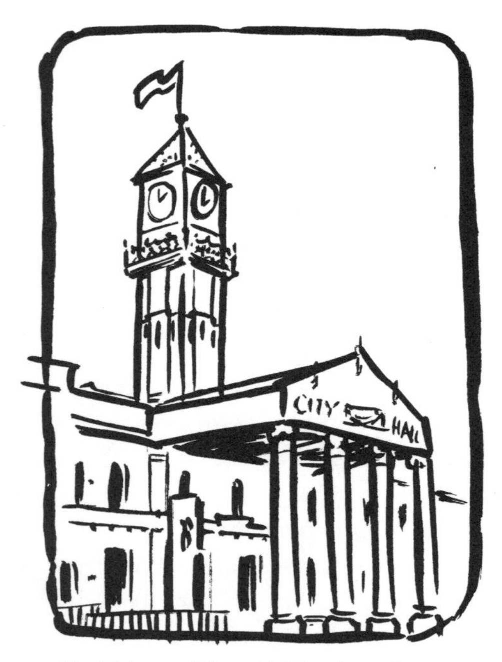

The Richmond Town Hall has been home to some furious political stouches over the years.

culture fans, the two-storey building on the south-east corner of Lennox Street and Rowena Parade was the birthplace of the Johnny Young Talent School. At 221 Lennox Street is **Orwell Cottage |9|**. If, as is thought to be the case, it was built in 1848, Orwell Cottage is the oldest standing building in Richmond. Head north to Bridge Road and cross Goodwood Street.

Arsenic and old con men

Bridge Road was constructed by convict labour housed in a stockade near Hawthorn Bridge. The first cable car in Victoria ran down this thoroughfare in 1885. Bridge Road can claim several other firsts, such as the production of eucalyptus oil by chemist Joseph Bosisto, and the first piano made of Australian wood by W.R. Blazey. Throughout its history, this road has been a vibrant site of commercial activity and has been traversed by Australian legends such as famous singer and local girl Dame Nellie Melba, who made her debut as an eight-year-old at a popular concert on the site of what was later to be the Richmond Town Hall. Plaques on the shops between Punt Road and Church Street provide details of the original businesses of Bridge Road.

Just to the west of Lennox Street, at 137 Bridge Road, is the **former home of murderer Martha Needle |10|**. Needle married in Adelaide, had three children and moved to Melbourne. Between 1885 and 1891 her husband and three children died one after another of mysterious causes. It was only when she remarried, to the saddler Otto Juncken whose business was here at No. 137 (and who became prone to subsequent and violent bouts of mysterious vomiting), that a doctor discovered Needle had been giving Juncken cups of tea containing enough arsenic to kill several men. Martha Needle was hanged in 1894.

Further east along Bridge Road, on the corner of Waltham Street, is the former **Australia Hotel |11|**. This was previously known as the Star and Garter and was the venue for the first Richmond Council meeting in 1856. Further down towards the town hall, note the two-storey timber house at the end of Eucalyptus Street as an interesting example of timber-clad (weatherboard) housing, made possible by the advent of the steam-powered sawmill. Across the road, at No. 267, is a commemorative plaque with a photograph of Bridge Road in 1872. Continue east down the hill to the town hall.

The **Richmond Town Hall |12|** was built in the late 1800s, then remodelled to its current Inter-War Free Classical style in 1934. James Scullin delivered his policy speech here before being elected prime minister in 1929. Richmond has virtually always been a very safe Labor seat and has seen much internal party warfare over the years. As the centre of civic politics the town hall harboured much of the political behaviour that has been part and parcel of politics in the suburb. Stories of procurement of prostitutes for mayoral balls, loaded revolvers drawn at council meetings, dead men voting, insurance scams, and many an encounter or chase down a local back lane contribute to the sometimes unsavoury but always colourful past of local government and life generally, in this lively suburb. The walk ends here. Take a tram along Bridge Street back to the city, or head north up Church Street for a cheap Vietnamese lunch on Victoria Street – Little Saigon as it is known.

Walk key

1. St John's Southgate | **2.** Southgate Plaza | **3.** Southbank promenade | **4.** Sheraton Towers | **5.** Esso House | **6.** Sandridge Railway Bridge | **7.** Queens Bridge | **8.** Crown Entertainment Complex | **9.** King Street Bridge | **10.** Spencer Street Bridge | **11.** Melbourne Exhibition Centre | **12.** Melbourne Maritime Museum | **13.** Charles Grimes Bridge | **14.** Melbourne Convention Centre | **15.** World Trade Centre | **16.** Victoria Police Museum | **17.** Batman Park | **18.** *Vault* | **19.** Proposed aquarium site | **20.** Old Customs House | **21.** Banana Alley | **22.** Flinders Walk |

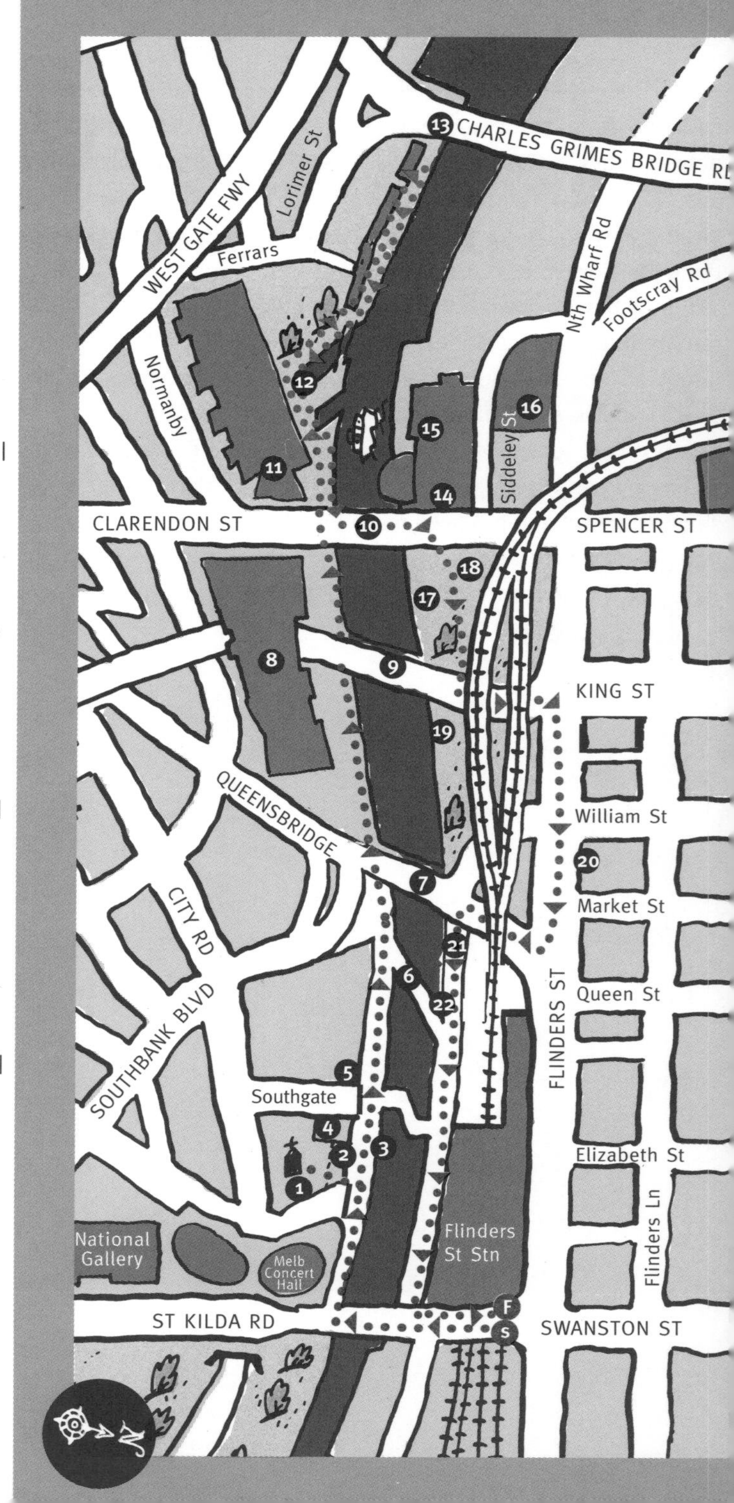

Walk No. 15

Yarra River West

From mercantile wharf to pleasure precinct

Start & Finish

Flinders Street Station – trams 3, 5, 6, 8, 16, 42, 48, 64, 67, 72, 75, City Circle tram; buses 216, 219, 220.

Length/Time

4.5 km/2.5 hours

The walk explores the banks of the Yarra River between Princes Bridge and Charles Grimes Bridge. The once thriving port that developed below the falls, congested with tall ships and lined with warehouses, became something of an industrial waste-land after 1930, with the relocation of the major port facilities further downstream. Only in the last two decades of the 20th century has the focus of Melbourne again turned to the river, revegetating its bushlands and developing new park-lands, and creating cultural and leisure precincts that have transformed the city's traditionally conservative image.

The lower reaches of the Yarra River, west of Princes Bridge, incorporate the oldest area of European settlement in Melbourne. Charles Grimes, the first white man to sail up the river in 1803, was unimpressed by its winding snag-ridden character, dismissing it as an unsuitable place for settlement. More than 20 years later, arch-rivals John Batman and John Pascoe Fawkner settled on the slopes above today's Queens Bridge.

In June 1835 Batman stumbled upon the Yarra while he and his party were returning to their ship after exploring Merri Creek. It was in this vicinity that he made a treaty with local Aboriginal people, later claiming to have purchased some 240,000 hectares of land in exchange for a collection of cheap trinkets. Batman came upon the Yarra at a place where a rocky reef created a large pool of fresh water, which cascaded down to meet the tidal saltwater below. He was reputedly so impressed with this spot that he wrote in his diary his oft-quoted words: 'This will be the place for a village'.

A party of men, under Fawkner's instructions but not accompanied by him, reached the falls area in August 1835. They were captivated by the site and several weeks later built a small wooden dwelling for Fawkner on the nearby hillside. Imagine Batman's reaction when he returned to settle on the land he claimed to have bought, only to find Fawkner's humble abode already there. In April 1836 Batman settled his wife and family on Batman's Hill but he became ill some years later, a result of exposure during a night ride, alcohol and suspected nasal syphilis. He died in 1839. Fawkner became one of the settlement's most prominent citizens, playing a significant role in its early development.

Southgate precinct

Cross Princes Bridge from Flinders Street Station. Ahead of you is the large circular edifice of the Melbourne Concert Hall. At the end of the bridge, turn right to the south-west bank and walk down the steps to the upper level concourse. If you walk over to the riverside parapet you can look back and get a good view of Princes Bridge, the oldest remaining bridge in the city.

The first bridge over the river, an inadequate wooden structure, was erected in 1845. In 1850 Lieutenant-Governor La Trobe opened the first Princes Bridge, which comprised a bluestone and granite single arch with a 150-foot span (almost 46 met-res), designed by David Lennox. The pre-sent bridge dates from 1886 and was designed by Jenkins, D'Ebro & Grainger (the last was the father of pianist and composer Percy Grainger). Opened in 1888, the name honoured the then Prince of Wales, later Edward VII. Its three equal spans are supported by solid bluestone piers. Inset into the lamp standards are the coats of arms of municipal councils that contributed to the cost of construction. Decorative cast-iron lacework is a feature of the spandrels, which bear additional crests.

If it is Sunday you can visit the weekly art and craft market, held underneath the bridge supports. On other days walk west, past Aromas cafe and towards the dark grey stone edifice of the three-tiered Southgate Plaza. To the left are the high-rise towers of the Herald Sun and IBM buildings.

It is worth making a short detour along the path that runs off to the left. It opens onto a courtyard; turn left and in front of you is the small **St John's Southgate |1|**, a Lutheran church dwarfed by the surrounding office towers. The original St John's was built in 1928 on the south side of the present church, at 50 City Road, but was demolished to make way for the Southgate development in the early 1990s. The new church, designed by David Cole of Buchan, Laird & Bawden, was opened in March 1992. The interesting octagonal design features small stained-glass windows around the building depicting 10 different Christian symbols, including the fish, the hand and the dove. The church steeple and bell line up with the Arts Centre spire. Most of the furnishings in the chapel are from the old church. The organ, made of Tasmanian oak, was designed and built in Australia by Knud Smenge. Dominating the wall behind the altar is the cross, made of river red gum. As well as a place of worship, St John's is a venue for music, drama and dance. Visitors are welcome and might hear the organist playing.

Retrace your steps back to the upper-level riverside promenade and enter **Southgate Plaza |2|**, opened in 1992. This shopping, eating and leisure precinct linking the St Kilda Road arts complex with the

Opening Times

St John's Southgate: events program information (9682 4995).
River cruises: Southgate–Williamstown Ferry runs daily llam, 1pm, 3pm & 5pm (9506 4144); Southgate River Cruises: (9682 5711 after 10am); *Spirit of Melbourne* riverboat restaurant departs daily (bookings essential, (9696 0311).
Bay Ferry to Williamstown: (9506 4144) departs landing stage, Exhibition Centre.
Old Customs House: Open daily 10am–5pm (9927 2700)
Victoria Police Museum: Mon–Fri 10am–4pm (9247 5215).
Melbourne Maritime Museum & *Polly Woodside*: Open daily 10am–4pm (9699 9760).

Refreshments

Southgate restaurants: Blakes, Ground Level, lunch and dinner daily (9699 4100); **Simply French**, lunch and dinner daily 10am–late (9699 9804); **Walter's Wine Bar**, Level 3, snacks, lunch and dinner Sun–Thurs from 11am, lunch Fri–Sat (9690 9211).
Crown Casino restaurants: Cecconi's (9292 6887), **The Duck** (9696 5432), **Silks** (9292 6888).

river is a Melbourne success story. People congregate here day and night to meet friends, to shop, or simply to enjoy the street entertainment and river activities. It has become a favoured venue for New Years Eve celebrations and the focal point for many cultural festivals and events.

On the upper level are the fashionable cafes of Walter's Wine Bar and Simply French. Walter's is Southgate's most awarded restaurant, with excellent food, an extensive wine list and great views. Opposite is the Ken Duncan Gallery, where you can browse or buy one of the renowned photographer's stunning Australian landscapes. Descend the stairs to **Southbank Promenade |3|**. At the quayside is an information kiosk and below is the Southgate landing, where a number of cruise boats are moored. There are tours up and down river, across to Williamstown and out to Hobsons Bay. Enquire at the information booth or at one of the ticket offices on the promenade. Continue past the multitude of restaurants and cafes that front the river. At the end of the plaza, at ground level, is Blakes, famous for its innovative modern Australian cuisine. Behind Blakes rises the luxury hotel **Sheraton Towers |4|**. On the right, the Yarra Footbridge, erected in 1989, leads across to Flinders Street Station.

Past the Sheraton is **Esso House |5|**, constructed as the headquarters of the petroleum company in 1993 to a design by Pedder Thorpe. The garden 'conservatory' at the front of the building is planted with species indigenous to the banks of the Yarra. The stone-bedded waterways wind among grasses and shrubs outside the building, against the backdrop of the larger plants growing in the semi-circular 'glass-house'. This is not a building that invites public viewing, but you can obtain a good look at the garden from the perimeter.

Walk on past three low-level, glass-fronted office blocks. At the end of this section is the old **Sandridge Railway Bridge |6|**, which once carried trains between Flinders Street and Hobsons Bay. In use until 1986, this is now a bridge that leads nowhere, a solid mass of iron lying forlornly across the water, its tracks bearing nothing but weeds. There has been talk of converting it to a footbridge, but at present it remains something of an anachronism. (Premier Kennett raised the issue of the bridge's future in January 1999, declaring to the residents of Melbourne that they must 'use it or lose it'. For several days the media was swamped with suggestions – ranging from the sublime to the ridiculous.)

The wide pavement leads to the traffic lights where you cross Queensbridge Street. Just before the lights is a rather incongruous piece of sculpture, formed from about 20 toilet bowls placed one on top of the other – perhaps the artist's statement about the Casino across the road!

Entertainment precinct

If you cross to the protective wall that fronts the river, you can view **Queens Bridge |7|**, dating from 1889. The first river crossing on this site was a timber footbridge, Falls Bridge, erected in 1860 over the rocky reef. Large ships could not go beyond this point and were forced to turn around in what was referred to as the 'turning basin'. Government and private wharves stetched from this point downstream beyond Spencer Street. The rocks forming the falls were blasted away in 1888 to allow boats access to the rapidly developing industrial suburbs such as Richmond, upstream. The following year the new bridge, designed by a Mr Rampant, honoured Queen Victoria. The drawings were completed by Carlo Catani, chief engineer of the Public Works Department.

The first building in the massive Crown Entertainment Complex (opened in 1997) is Crown Towers, a luxury hotel. It is worth stepping inside to have a look at the foyer, with its black Italian marble atrium and intriguing light and water displays. Once outside again, follow the Yarra Promenade along the river. At ground level, fronting the river, the **Crown Entertainment Complex |8|** comprises a number of shops selling imported designer labels and a multitude of restaurants and cafes. Two of the most notable eateries are Cecconi's near Crown Towers and The Duck, about halfway along the complex. Outside The Duck is an aquatic display where streams of water gush out at intermittent intervals from holes in the pavement. Children, delighting in trying to dodge the water spouts, find the area irresistible. At this point you pass underneath **King Street Bridge |9|**. Built to connect busy King Street in the central business district with South Melbourne, it first opened in 1961, but 15 months later a crack appeared in one of the steel girders. Forced to close for repairs, the bridge did not reopen until 1965.

Across the river there is a helicopter pad, and to the right the towering glass form of Rialto Towers (see Walk No.1, Historic Collins Street). At the end of the block cross Clarendon Street.

Old wharf precinct

Walk across to the timber boardwalk and look back to view **Spencer Street Bridge |10|**, first called Batman Bridge when it opened in 1930. Construction was carried out by the Board of Land and Works under the authority of an Act of Parliament, which was passed on 28 September 1927. At the south-west end of the bridge is the **Melbourne Exhibition Centre |11|**, opened in February 1996 by Victorian premier, Jeff Kennett. Commonly known as 'Jeff's Shed', this 30,000 square metre space hosts major trade exhibitions – it is reputedly large enough and the roof strong enough to support a jumbo jet. Designed by Denton Corker Marshall, it makes the most of its river frontage and has a number of significant architectural features. Apart from the spectacular welcoming gesture of its entrance, a concourse runs the entire length of the 450 metre long building, enclosed by a sloping glass curtain wall 8 metres high – the longest and largest glass wall in Australia. The signage on the building, conceived by Emery Vincent, one of Australia's top design firms, is considered an exceptional melding of architecture and graphics.

Between the Exhibition Centre and the river is a pleasant landscaped area of lawn and trees. A small landing is a departure point for one of the tour boats to Williamstown (tickets can be purchased on board). The parklands also encompass the **Melbourne Maritime Museum |12|** and its well-known exhibit, the *Polly Woodside.* The museum depicts the history of the port of Melbourne in displays, old photographs and film footage, and its 1875 timber-framed dry dock is the only one of its kind remaining in the world.

The *Polly Woodside* was built in Belfast in 1885 and was used to transport coal between Europe and South America. The small barque traded in New Zealand waters between 1904 and 1924 and then, unceremoniously demasted and derigged, was used as a coal hulk in the port of Melbourne. She was acquired by the National Trust in 1968, restored to her former tallship glory and opened to the public.

Walk along the boardwalk, past Lime Wharf and over a retractable footbridge set on pontoons. The museum entrance is about halfway along a series of historic cargo sheds. These sheds date from around 1888 and were built for the Melbourne Harbour Trust, which was founded in 1876 to dredge the silt from the lower reaches of the river. Under a grand plan devised by English engineer Sir John Coode, the river was straightened, deepened and widened by the construction of a 2,000-foot canal in 1887, and by the mid-1890s the first docks were operating. The mud collected was deposited as landfill on the marshy swamps adjacent to the banks. The South Wharf sheds, really one continuous building, are the oldest remnants of the city waterfront. The roof has a raised skylight along the entire length to allow light into the interior.

The Polly Woodside *is the star attraction of the Melbourne Maritime Museum.*

At the end of South Wharf is a series of landings where cruise boats are moored. These are mainly hired for functions. In front of you, and marking the turning point of this walk, is the **Charles Grimes Bridge |13|**. Opened in 1966 as the Johnson Street Bridge, it was renamed after the surveyor Charles Grimes (1772–1858), who was sent from Sydney to explore Port Phillip at the beginning of 1803. He discovered the Yarra River on 2 February but reported unfavourably on its suitability for settlement. He and his party were the first known Europeans to sail up the river, going about 32 kilometres before their passage was halted by rapids, later called Dights Falls.

Across the river is a line of dilapidated cargo sheds. This area is targeted for restoration. Retrace your steps along the river back to the Spencer Street Bridge. Cross the river. At the end of the bridge the Centra Hotel is on your left. Next to it is the **Melbourne Convention Centre |14|** and behind that the **World Trade Centre |15|**. The latter housed Crown Casino for a number of years while the gambling house awaited the construction of its opulent home at Southbank. The World Trade Centre is worth a detour to visit the **Victoria Police Museum |16|**, a small museum showcasing the history of policing in the state.

Opposite the Centra Hotel is the entrance to **Batman Park |17|**, established in 1982. Part of the redevelopment of the Yarra River that was prompted by an *Age* newspaper campaign in the late 1970s, the park is named after co-founder of the city, John Batman. Close to the Spencer Street perimeter is Ron Robertson-Swan's 1979 controversial painted steel sculpture, ***Vault* |18|**, dubbed the 'Yellow Peril'. Commissioned by the city council to adorn the 'new' city square in 1980, it was subjected to fierce public criticism and vandalism and was eventually removed to this less prominent part of Melbourne (a case of out of sight, out of mind). Walk through the park to its junction with King Street. Turn left, walk under the three railway viaducts and cross to the front of the Waterside Hotel. A favoured haunt of waterside workers, the pub's traditional opening hours were from 6am to 6pm. This lower end of King Street, rather down-at-heel, is characterised by its old brick and bluestone warehouses and butter factories, many of them converted into night-clubs and discos.

Cross King Street and walk along Flinders Street, rather insalubrious at this particular section. Cross Highlander Mews (if you glance down here you will see a number of particularly old warehouses) and walk to William Street. Construction work at the time of writing mars the riverscape between here and King Street – this is the site of the **proposed aquarium |19|**.

Across Flinders Street on the river bank is a small plantation of eucalypts encircling a rusting anchor embedded in the earth – one of a number of increasing memorials to the old wharf precinct (the area is undergoing rapid development). Queens Wharf was built just downstream from the shelf of rock that formed the falls. The rapids prevented navigation of the upper reaches of the river by all but the smallest of craft. Officially opened in 1842, the wharf comprised landing berths stretching from Queen Street to Spencer Street. Two companies had established earlier wharves at the Spencer Street end, the first being Cole's in late 1841, but by 1868 these had been incorporated in Queens Wharf. After the execution of

Coode's plans in 1888 to deepen the river, the wharf became a colourful and busy maritime precinct. It declined after 1930, when Spencer Street Bridge made the river unnavigable by large vessels.

Fronting the former Queens Wharf, on the corner of Flinders and William streets, is the **Old Customs House |20|**. A sandstone building was erected between 1838 and 1841 under the direction of Robert Russell to a design by the colonial architect's office in Sydney. Another building was constructed in 1855–58 in front of the first, following a design by Knight, Kemp & Kerr. The earlier Customs House was then demolished. In 1871–76 a third building, incorporating the 1850s structure, was completed to a design by John James Clark. Built of brick, the stucco facade is Regency inspired in its style. A fine bluestone fence with a cast-iron railing runs along the front and sides. Elegant lamps with cast-iron standards top the fence supports.

A highlight of the Customs House interior is the magnificent Long Room on the first floor. It was here that customs officers inspected incoming goods unloaded from the nearby Queens Wharf. The Long Room is all that remains of the unfinished 1858 Customs House. It was incorporated into the 1876 building that stands today. Architect Paul Kerr modelled the Ionic columns and door architraves on details of the Erechtheion temple in Athens, which had been built in about 400BC.

Some restoration of the interior of the Customs House was done in 1969 before it was taken over for the use of visiting parliamentarians, but the most extensive restoration work was carried out in 1998. Now part of the Museum of Victoria, it houses two separate entities: an Immigration Museum, showcasing the immigration experience and celebrating the state's cultural diversity and resulting Australian identity; and the Hellenic Archaeological Museum, featuring some of the finest antiquities ever to travel outside Greece.

On the William–Flinders Street corner an inscribed stone in the pavement commemorates the 'landing' of John Batman 'near this spot June 1835' and gives his words 'This will be the place for a village'. Batman's rival, John Pascoe Fawkner, owned the first Melbourne dwelling on this site – a small wooden cottage constructed by Fawkner's landing party in about September 1835 – before building his hotel and store the same year further up the hill.

Opposite the Customs House, on the other corner of Market Street, is the rather neglected Holyman House, a three-storey bluestone warehouse. It was designed in 1858 by John Gill for wool producer and trader Richard Goldsbrough, who used it as his headquarters until 1864. His business was the precursor of the international woolbroking firm Goldsbrough Mort & Co., established in 1888, about two years after Goldsbrough's death. The building was used as a warehouse until 1936, when it was bought by W. Holyman & Sons Pty Ltd, shipowners and agents, as the booking office for their White Star Line.

Railway precinct

Walk a little further along Flinders Street and cross to the single-storey red-brick building under the railway line. This is **Banana Alley |21|** and contains the Banana Alley Vaults. The railway viaduct, designed by William Henry Greene, chief engineer of the Victorian Railways, was built in 1891–92 to link the stations of Flinders Street and Spencer Street. The vaults were incorporated within the viaduct, and many were used by fruiterers to dry bananas. Fishmongers also used them as a place in which to open oysters. There are 18 vaults, each 5 metres wide with arched barrel ceilings. During the 1960s the alley was the location of the Pieteria, one of the city's first 24-hour cafes. The Victorian Wine Centre was based here for a time in the late 1980s, when an attempt was made to turn the vaults into a tourist precinct. Sadly, the project was a failure, largely because of the success of Southgate on the opposite side of the river. Its location, wedged in between major roads, is also not particularly pedestrian-friendly. The area has fallen into disuse, apart from several vaults at the far end occupied by a gymnasium trading under the name of Underworld Health and Fitness.

Go back to the Queens Bridge end of Banana Alley and walk along the river side of the vaults. The trail becomes **Flinders Walk |22|**, leading you underneath the Sandridge Railway Bridge and up to the Yarra Footbridge, opposite Southgate Plaza. At this point you can turn left and follow the underground tunnel to the station or through to Flinders Street. Alternatively you can cross the bridge to Southgate, or continue straight ahead to the steps that lead up beside Princes Bridge to Swanston Street.

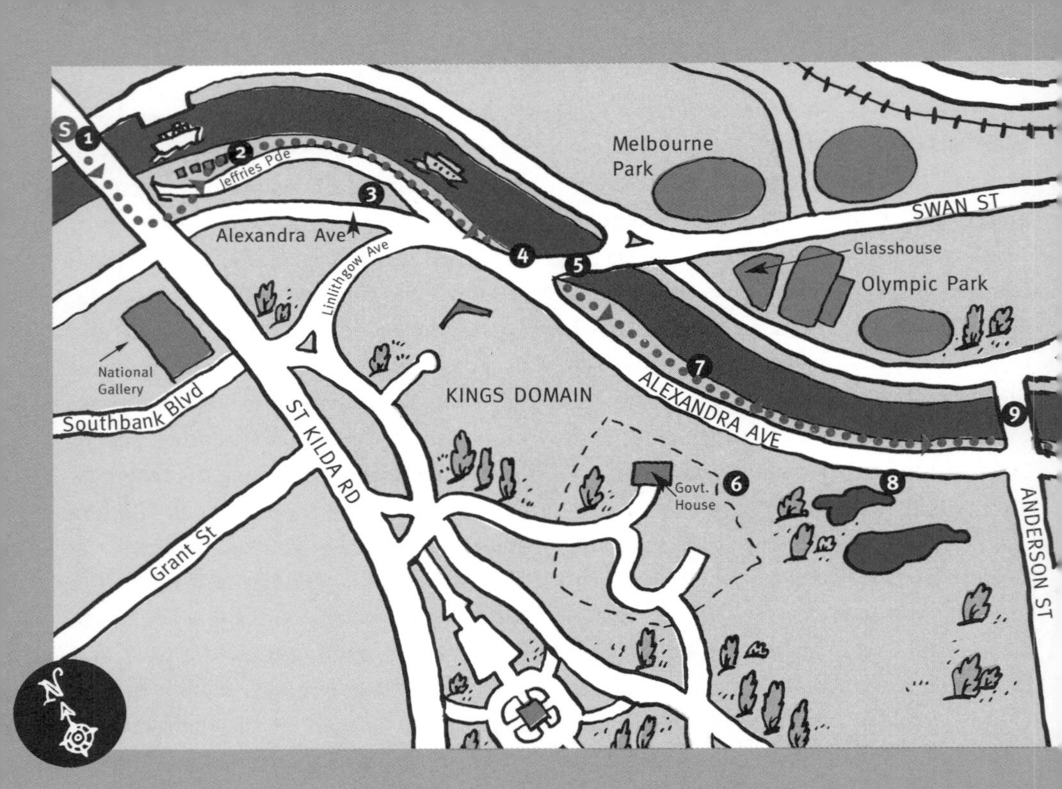

Walk key

1. Princes Bridge | **2.** Boatsheds | **3.** Alexandra Gardens | **4.** Henley Landing | **5.** Swan Street Bridge | **6.** Royal Botanic Gardens | **7.** Domain Tunnel site | **8.** Tan Track | **9.** Morell Bridge | **10.** Melbourne Girls Grammar School | **11.** Hoddle Bridge | **12.** Melbourne High School | **13.** Church Street Bridge | **14.** Herring Island Park | **15.** Como Park | **16.** Royal South Yarra Lawn Tennis Club | **17.** Como House

Start

Flinders Street Station – trams 3, 5, 6, 8, 16, 42, 48, 64, 67, 72, 75, City Circle tram; buses 216, 219, 220.

Finish

Corner Williams and Toorak roads – tram 8.

Length/Time

4.5 km/2 hours

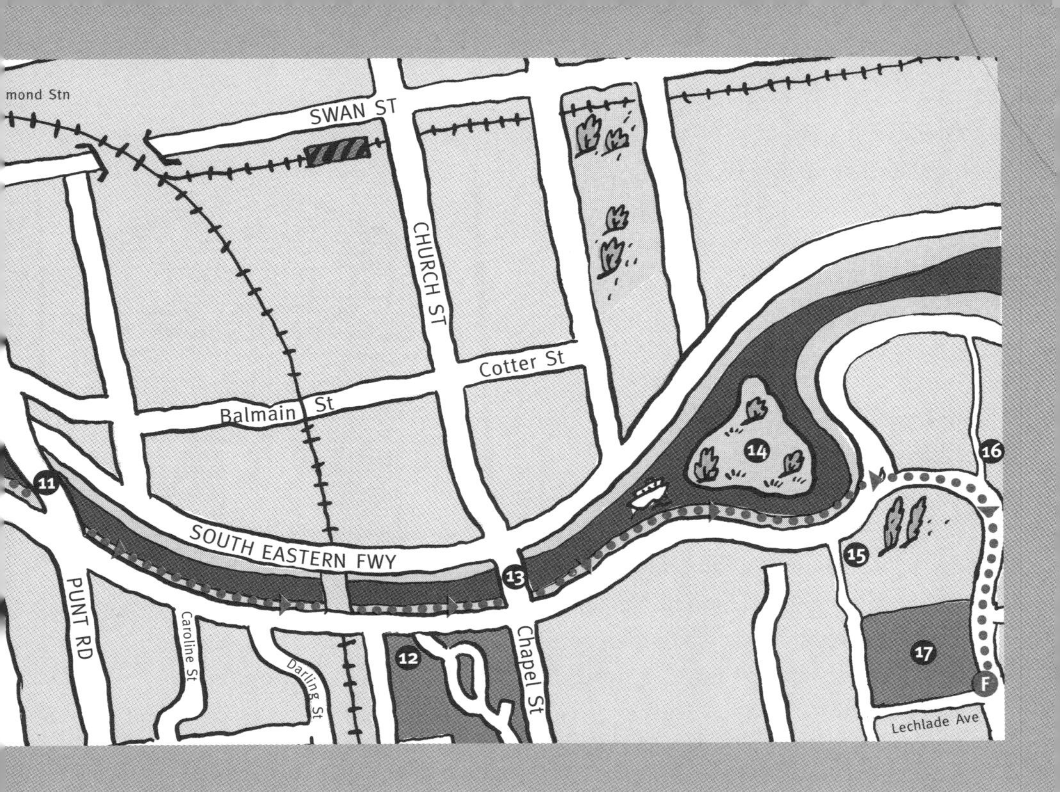

Walk No. 16

Yarra River East

Picturesque parklands beside the lazy river

This walk by the Yarra River follows part of the Capital City Trail, a 29-kilometre walking and cycling track that winds around the perimeter of Greater Melbourne, allowing you to explore its parklands, leafy boulevards and natural waterways. It also follows Alexandra Avenue, arguably the city's most beautiful roadway. The thoroughfare is at its most spectacular in spring, when the elm and plane trees display the vibrant apple-green foliage that is such a recognisable feature of the season of renewal in European climes.

The leaves in summer form a natural arch across Alexandra Avenue, and in autumn they turn the avenue into a kaleidoscope of reds, yellows and browns. We recommend you do this walk on a sunny day when the river looks its best; in wet weather you will find there is little shelter.

Princes Bridge to Morell Bridge

Cross to the east side of Swanston Street and turn right. Cross **Princes Bridge |1|**. At the end of the bridge, a path winds down through a stand of tall Canary Island palms to the Alexandra Gardens. The area was a swamp for most of the 19th century before reclamation work was carried out in 1904. The path ends on the river bank below Princes Bridge. (The art and craft market operates on Sundays under the bridge.) The riverside walking and cycling track is called the Capital City Trail. Turn right, away from Princes Bridge, and pass a series of **boatsheds |2|**, in which rowing clubs store their racing shells.

Rowing has long been a popular pastime and sport on this section of the Yarra. The first eight-oared race between New South Wales and Victoria was fought out here in 1873. Schools practise along this stretch of water for the annual Head of the River, although the race itself is held on the Barwon River in Geelong. The Moomba festival in early March sees the river bank a frenzy of activity, with side-shows, water pageants, international dragon boat races and waterskiing championships.

Nineteenth-century boatsheds add picturesque charm to the city aspect of the Yarra River.

The first boatshed is Richmond Rowing Club, established in 1863. Next is Melbourne Rowing Club, established in 1862. This boatshed is used by a number of girls' schools, including Lauriston and Melbourne Girls Grammar. The last boatshed belongs to the University of Melbourne. Although some remodelling has been carried out to the side of this building, the old weatherboard facade, painted white and blue, is original.

The trail continues, rimmed by the river on one side and the **Alexandra Gardens |3|** on the other. The trees along here are mostly elms, with a few large plane trees and some stands of Canary Island palms. Across the river you can see the roof of Melbourne Park. A little further and you can see the Swan Street Bridge. A small Classical stone structure at the water's edge is the Oarsmen's Memorial Judges Box

1914–18, erected by the Victorian Rowing Association in 1930 and designed by F.S. Nason. You are now approaching the end of the Alexandra Gardens.

As you come to the Swan Street Bridge you draw level with the white steel structure of Melbourne Park, otherwise known as the National Tennis Centre. The impressive stadium has a retractable roof, allowing play during the Australian Open (January) to continue whatever the weather. This is also a venue for live music concerts, international entertainers and even opera. Beyond are the light towers of the Melbourne Cricket Ground (MCG). The Melbourne Cricket Club (MCC) was founded in 1838, received land from the Crown in 1853 and the MCG was established on this site. Regarded as one of the great sporting stadiums in the world, the ground has a seating capacity of around 90,000. This was the main stadium for the 1956 Olympic Games, and it is the venue for Test Cricket and AFL football matches (including the AFL Grand Final on the last Saturday in September). Within the complex is the MCC Museum and Library and the excellent Australian Gallery of Sport and Olympic Museum. A covered walkway links the MCG with Melbourne Park.

The riverside path widens at **Henley Landing |4|**, the focal point of the water activities during the Moomba festival every March. You can see to the right the sloping lawns and large trees of Kings Domain, and through the trees the sail-like roof of the Sidney Myer Music Bowl. Outdoor concerts

Opening Times

Royal Botanic Gardens: Open daily dawn–dusk; free guided walks (9252 2300); or self-guided audio tours (contact the Gardens Shop 9252 2341).
Herring Island: Access by punt or row boat (131963). Southgate Boat Hire, Lower Promenade, Southgate (9741 9715).
Como House: Open daily 10am–5pm. House only open to guided tours, generally every hour (9827 2500).

Refreshments

Lakeside Tea Rooms, Royal Botanic Gardens. **Cafe Como** at Como House for light lunches and Devonshire teas. There are drinking fountains along the river bank, one located on the city side of the Morell Bridge.

were held in the Royal Botanic Gardens in the 1930s and Sidney Myer was a strong advocate for the construction of an outdoor venue in the vicinity. The Second World War intervened but in the 1950s the council commissioned Yunken, Freeman, Griffiths & Simpson to design a shell-shaped music venue similar to one in California. Funded by the Sidney Myer Trust, the bowl was named after the great benefactor and opened in 1959. It has been an immense success with Melburnians, hosting Carols by Candlelight every Christmas Eve. The bowl and surrounding lawns can hold around 15,000 people. For part of the year, between April and October, it is transformed into an ice-skating rink.

Just past the Henley Landing the path leads under the **Swan Street Bridge |5|**, opened in August 1952. Just past the bridge you have a clear view of the northern section of the Domain, and the tower barely visible, topped with a flag, is Government House. If you look across the river at this point you get a view of the MCG light towers and the back of the Great Southern Stand. On the opposite bank is the glass-windowed facade of the Melbourne Sports and Entertainment Centre (the Glasshouse), built as the major aquatic centre for the 1956 Olympic Games. The pools have long since gone and the place is used for concerts and basketball matches.

This section of the river bank is lined with bluestone gas barbecues, and is very popular with picnickers. At road level the trail now passes the **Royal Botanic Gardens |6|**. The magnificence and world acclaim of these gardens, spreading over 35 hectares, is due to the genius and vision of German botanist Ferdinand von Mueller and horticulturist and landscape designer William Guilfoyle. It was Lieutenant-Governor Charles La Trobe who chose the site in 1845. Mueller was director from 1857 to 1873 and was responsible for planting a wide range of Australian species. His layout, following the form of a scientific herbary, was somewhat rigid in style. It was Guilfoyle, director from 1873 to 1909, who really gave form to the spectacular landscaping you see today. He rearranged Mueller's plantings, creating great expanses of sloping lawns, winding paths and spectacular ornamental lakes.

On the other side of the river, past the Glasshouse, are the remains of the old Olympic Park. This section of the walk is where massive works were undertaken during 1997–99 to construct the **Domain Tunnel |7|** under the river, Botanic Gardens and the Domain. About 17 of the huge elms were temporarily relocated during construction, each set above ground complete with its own sprinkler system for a period of about two years.

You are now at road level and the Botanic Gardens rise quite steeply from the **Tan Track |8|**, which encircles the gardens. On the slope is a small classical ornamental structure, the Temple of the Winds. It was designed by Guilfoyle in 1902 to commemorate the founder of the gardens, Charles La Trobe. Moulded staghorn ferns decorate the top of the 10 columns. The gardens

Royal Botanic Gardens

In addition to the superb landscaping, historic architecture and ornate statuary, the Royal Botanic Gardens has an extraordinary range of 'theme' gardens, which provide fascinating insight into the natural and social history of botanic pursuits both here and abroad. The Rose Garden, established in 1978, charts the evolution of that most famous flower with its impressive collection of old species roses, as well as examples of roses produced by the process of hybridization. The Herb Garden, radiating out from an old sundial in a traditional design, has seven sections containing an enormous collection of medicinal and culinary species. The Australian Rainforest Walk winds past an impressive collection of plants representing some of the most ancient species on earth, while the Australian Lawn provides a native haven for eucalypts and bush birds. The Water Conservation Garden demonstrates how to create a stunning garden using resource-friendly plants and the Grey Garden is a revelation on how to plant using colour as the main theme. Other gardens and plantings include the Arid Garden with species drawn from the great deserts of the world; the Tennyson Lawn, housing the first trees, English elms, to be planted in the gardens; and the Oak Lawn, looking like a grand English country parkland, and planted with species originating from all parts of the Northern Hemisphere.

To get the best out of these magnificent gardens take a guided tour, leaving at 11am and 2pm from the Herbarium Building (Gate F) on Birdwood Avenue, every day except Saturday.

descend to road level beyond here and you can see very little without venturing inside.

The barbecue facilities continue along this stretch of river bank between the Swan Street Bridge and the **Morell Bridge |9|** completed in 1899. Commonly known as the Anderson Street Bridge, the latter is particularly interesting because it was built on dry land and the river was diverted under it. It was designed and built by Sydney firm Carter, Gummon & Co. and was one of the first reinforced concrete structures in Victoria. The cast-iron balustrade is an elegant feature and the spandrels boast some decorative mouldings, featuring winged serpents. The engineer for the bridge was John Monash, later to become the distinguished general of the First World War (he rose to become Commander of the Australian Army in France in 1918). The bridge leads to Anderson Street, the east boundary of the Royal Botanic Gardens and the location of **Melbourne Girls Grammar |10|**. The school dates from 1893 when it was started by two Englishwomen in a house in nearby

Domain Road. Called Merton Hall – a name that persists to this day – it was sold in 1898 to W.E. Morris, and Mary and Edith Morris became its principals. In 1900 Mr Morris bought the Anderson Street land on which the school now stands.

The river bank is quite steep here and there is no view of the road. Continue under the Morell Bridge.

Morell Bridge to Church Street Bridge

You can now see on your left the end of the South Eastern Freeway, which rises over the north end of the **Hoddle Bridge |11|**, named after Melbourne's first surveyor-general, Robert Hoddle. It was he who mapped out the city of Melbourne in a grid pattern in 1837. The bridge is rather utilitarian in appearance, lacking the elegance of other bridges such as the Morell, but it is one of the busiest river crossings in Melbourne. Five spans rest on pier supports and the light standards display Art Deco features. From the mid-1850s passengers and drays were ferried across the river here by punt, the origin of the Punt Road name. In about 1866 a footbridge was built in the vicinity and this survived, with some remodelling in 1899, until the erection of the Hoddle Bridge in 1938. The punt ceased operation when the Morell Bridge was opened downstream at the turn of the century.

The huge billboard rising above the north-east end of the Hoddle Bridge has been a landmark for decades; a clock at the top displays the time one minute and the temperature the next. The trail rises close to the road as you approach the bridge and you get a glimpse of the Punt Road hill.

On the south-west corner of Alexandra Avenue and Punt Road is a magnificent golden elm. It is worth ascending to road level to take a look. While the height and enormous spread of this beautiful tree have justified its listing by the National Trust, its exact age remains unknown. Walk under the Hoddle Bridge. The other side of the river is quite built up with factories and warehouses. A little timber jetty juts into the river just past the bridge, one of many such structures. If you are lucky you might see one of the city's water birds drying its wings in the sun while perched on one of the timber pylons. Here, too, is a line of peppercorn trees. Pass about five of these and you will see a large rock set in the ground above you at road level. Just past the rock there is a spot where you can actually clamber up the bank. A bronze plaque in the stone commemorates the site of the first crown land sale in Prahran on 10 June 1840. (A Mr R.H. Browne bought Lot 1, which had a frontage of 650 feet to Gardiners Creek Road – now Toorak Road – and was bounded by Punt Road and the Yarra, with an area of 28 acres at £24 per acre.)

Take a look at the large apartment buildings that predominate along this section between Punt Road and Darling Street, many built in the 1920s and 1930s in Art Deco style. Descend back to the river. The peppercorn trees continue along the bank. The path rises up to the road level opposite the end of Caroline Street. Here are some particularly impressive Art Deco buildings. On the west corner of Caroline Street, with Tuscan coloured rendering and window boxes on the upper level, is Durham Hall (No. 119); on the other corner is the four-storey Dorrington House, with decorative embossing on the facade between the bay windows. Coloured pink, the central section, incorporating the stairwell, is open, with an arcaded balcony at the third-floor level. Next is the somewhat smaller York House, cream with bay windows on the second level, and topped with turreted roofs lined with timber shingles. Next is Kildare, painted dark green. Then Riverview at No. 79, then No. 81 on the corner of Darling Street. More blocks line Darling Street as it rises to a sweeping bend. On the bend Nos. 61–63 are two large Art Deco blocks, part of the same complex, called Beverley Hills. From this point the Darling Street residences degenerate into rather ugly brick boxes – flats that probably date from the 1960s.

You are still at road level. At the edge of the road there are some beautiful eucalypts with smooth trunks. Pass the end of the Darling Gardens (on the other side of Alexandra Avenue) and you continue under a massive wrought-iron rail bridge, which carries the main line to the south-eastern suburbs. On the right, running the length of this stretch of the Yarra, is **Melbourne High School |12|**, grandly sited on Forrest Hill, overlooking a large playing field on its west side. It is an imposing red brick building. The school was originally part of the Model School, a coeducational establishment founded in 1854 in Spring Street. In the late 1920s the boys were moved to this South Yarra site, and the girls were relocated to MacRobertson Girls High in Albert Park.

You are now approaching the Church Street Bridge, which links the south-bound Chapel Street with north-bound Church Street. Diagonally opposite, on the south-east corner of Chapel Street, is a block of apartments, part of the Como Project, a grand 1980s scheme that originally envisaged creating a Little Venice on this side of the Yarra, with a system of interconnecting canals. The project floundered when the costs blew out, coinciding with a recession.

Church Street Bridge to Williams Road

Take the path under the **Church Street Bridge |13|**, dating from 1923, and one of the more attractive of the Yarra River bridges. It comprises three spans, two over the river and one over the South Eastern Freeway. The large lamp standards are tapered at the top and have decorative wreaths on the sides; four lamps adorn each standard. Crests decorate the bridge supports and the spandrels are arcaded. Half-circle Classical columns adorn the lamp standards on two sides.

The other side of the river is quite industrial, although apartments are going up in places. There are small stands of eucalypts and wattle along this section, the latter a blaze of yellow in August. A couple of old flowering gums are laden with cream flowers in early spring. Ahead the river divides, making its way either side of a small island. The land, once the site of an old basalt quarry, was isolated in 1929 when the Board of Works constructed a canal to eliminate a bend in the river. This is **Herring Island Park |14|**, accessible only by boat. In the late 1940s the Australian Scouts Association negotiated to lease the island for use as a training centre. It was formally handed over to the Chief Scout, Sir Edmund Herring, in 1851 and became known as Herring Island. The scouts used the island throughout the 1950s and 1960s. From 1970 to 1994 it was administered by a committee of local council and government representatives. Now a sanctuary managed by Parks Victoria, the island has undergone an extensive native revegetation program and features an environmental sculpture park. Created from natural materials such as stone, earth and wood, the sculptures are site-specific. The triangular stone work that is visible at the west end of the island is Steerage, by Jill Peck. The prow of the sculpture, emulating the bow of a boat, points downstream – a metaphor for water, journeys and knowledge.

The track ascends to road level once more. The buildings here are a mix of private homes and small apartment blocks, displaying a variety of 20th-century styles. The streetscape changes as rocky cliffs rise above the road. Massive luxury homes dot the ridge top and a large residence of contemporary design is built into the cliff. These places face the river, with large windows to allow great city views. The trail winds around a bend in the river and on the right can be seen a green expanse of parkland, **Como Park |15|** and playing fields. An Aboriginal camp was once located on part of this site. At the west end of the park is a rock embedded in the ground, with a bronze plaque commemorating the work of Sidney Myer. His generous donations to Prahran City Council and community during the depression years of 1930 and 1931 facilitated the regrading of Como Park and the river bank, providing much needed local employment.

Cross Alexandra Avenue (it turns left here) and the clubhouse of the **Royal South Yarra Lawn Tennis Club |16|** is slightly to the left. The club was founded in 1884 and had courts in Portland Place, South Yarra, before moving to its present site in the early 1920s. It is one of Melbourne's most prestigious clubs.

You are now in Williams Road, which marks the boundary between the suburbs of South Yarra and Toorak. Make your way to the set of traffic lights and cross over to Como Park. Walk up Williams Road hill. Past the end of Washington Street you come to the entrance of **Como House |17|**, one of the most historically significant homes in Australia. The house is Regency in style, with Italianate features, and has an air of restrained elegance. It is the oldest surviving residence in Melbourne. Only 2.1 hectares remain of the original 21.9-hectare property, which once stretched between Toorak Road and the Yarra. Before the arrival of Europeans the land was occupied by the Woiworung people.

Construction of the magnificent residence commenced in 1847 with the erection of a villa for solicitor Edward Eyre Williams (later Sir Edward Eyre Williams). This is the ground level central section of the house that still remains. Williams owned the Como estate from 1846 to 1852 and possibly named it after Lake Como where he is reputed to have proposed to his wife, Jessie.

After a brief ownership by property investor Frederick Dalgety, the house was purchased by wine merchant and land speculator John Brown. He and his wife had eight children and the modest residence was far too small for them. Brown, a master builder by trade, embarked on an extensive building program in 1855, adding the main features of the house that stands today, including the second storey, the verandah and various outbuildings. The cast iron for the verandahs was imported from Edinburgh. Brown employed landscape gardener William Sangster to design the grounds. Little remains of Sangster's original plantings, but the fountain terrace, croquet lawn and some old bunya pines date from this time. Modifications have been made by subsequent landscape designers: in the 1970s Ellis Stones designed the small rock garden and pool in the north-west section of the property. Beyond the house gardens, picturesque orchards once stretched down to the river. Sadly, John Brown's fortunes declined and at the end of 1864 the house was auctioned.

Charles Armytage, the new owner, was an early member of a well-known pastoral dynasty. He added a two-storey wing designed by Arthur E. Johnson, comprising a billiard room and ballroom downstairs and addtional bedrooms upstairs. The ballroom features a magnificent chandelier, and exquisite curtain pelmets decorated in gold and hung with gold silk, brought from England in 1853, a decade before Charles purchased the property. The house contains an extensive collection of original furnishings. There are beautiful marble objets d'art from Italy, gilt-framed mirrors from Paris and finely crafted dining room furniture made in Melbourne from local timbers. The Armytage family lived at Como House for 95 years, until its acquisition by the National Trust in 1959.

Walk key

1. Queen Victoria monument | **2.** Lady Clarke Rotunda | **3.** King Edward VII | **4.** Floral Clock | **5.** *The Pathfinder* | **6.** Walker Fountain | **7.** King George V monument | **8.** Pioneer Women's Garden | **9.** Sir Thomas Albert Blamey | **10.** Sir Edward 'Weary' Dunlop | **11.** Boer War Monument | **12.** Earl of Hopetoun | **13.** Sir John Monash | **14.** Edith Cavell | **15.** Malta George Cross Memorial Arch | **16.** Edward George Honey | **17.** Simpson and his donkey | **18.** Shrine of Remembrance | **19.** Old Melbourne Observatory | **20.** National Herbarium | **21.** La Trobe's Cottage | **22.** Macpherson Robertson Fountain

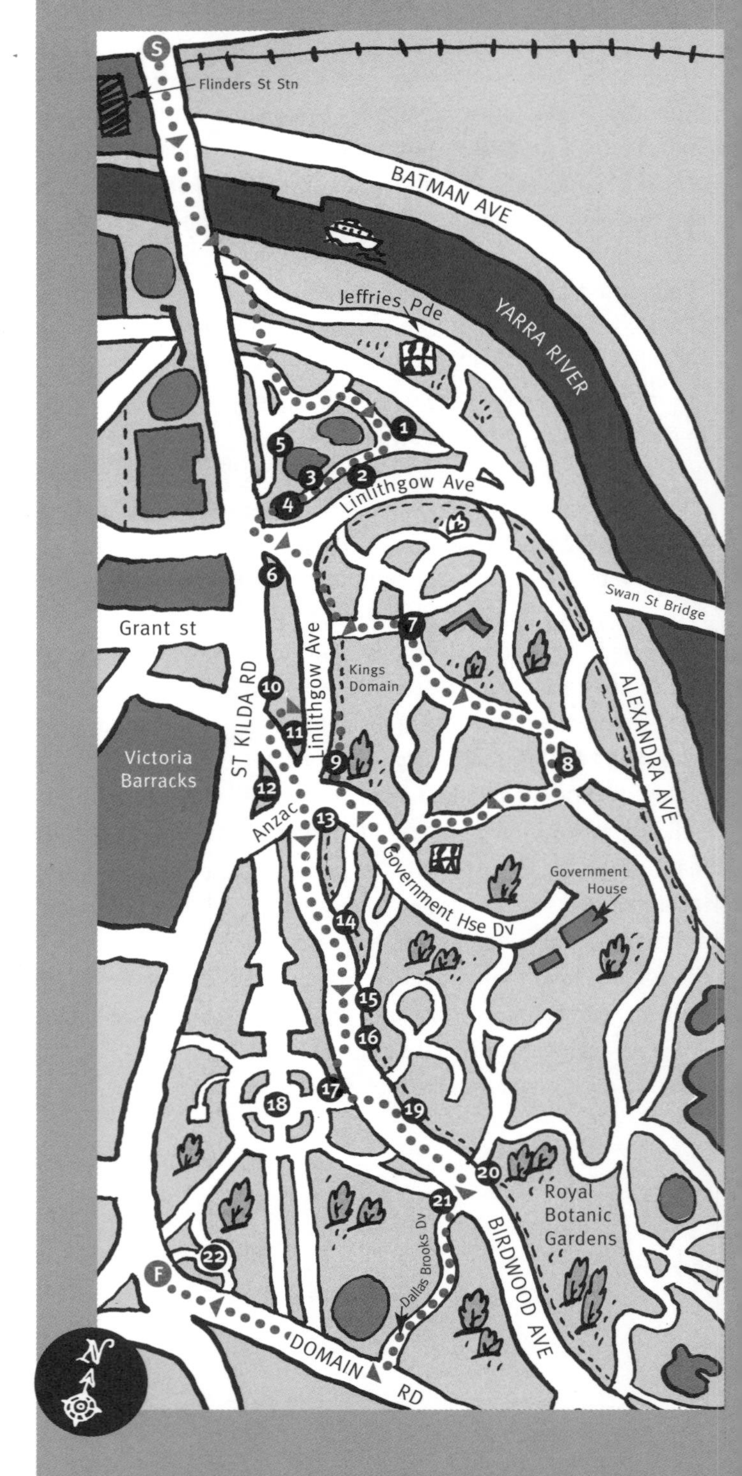

Walk No. 17

Kings Domain

Historic monuments in a parkland setting

Start

Flinders Street Station – trams 1, 3, 5, 6, 8, 11, 12, 16, 22, 42, 64, 67, 72, 109; buses 216, 219, 220.

Finish

Corner of St Kilda and Domain roads – trams 3, 5, 6, 8, 16, 64, 67, 72; buses 216, 219, 220.

Length/Time

3.5 km/2.5 hours

For many years Victorian vehicles carried the sobriquet 'The Garden State' on their number plates, a testament to the extraordinary wealth of parklands, particularly in the capital. The expansive 31-hectare Kings Domain, lining the city end of St Kilda Road and enfolding the western sections of the Royal Botanic Gardens, is dominated at its southern end by the Shrine of Remembrance. Among its rolling lawns, beneath the shade of its large variety of mature trees, and alongside its extensive shrubs, perennial borders and colourful annuals, the walker finds a vast collection of statuary, monuments, memorial shrines and commemorative plaques. They tell a little of the history of Melbourne, its British traditions and, in particular, the part played by its citizens in times of war.

Proclaimed in 1854, only 20 years after the foundation of the city, and envisaged by Ferdinand von Mueller as a massive pine plantation, the Domain's final landscaping was the work of William Guilfoyle, the man who contributed so greatly to the design of the adjoining Royal Botanic Gardens. The walk starts at the edge of the central business district and extends into the Queen Victoria Gardens, but generally follows the western section of the Tan Track, which encircles Kings Domain and the Royal Botanic Gardens.

Queen Victoria Gardens

Start the walk on the south-east corner of the Flinders–Swanston Street intersection. The intricate metal tower across the river to the right is the Victorian Arts Centre spire. As you cross Batman Avenue, the flags and umbrellas of the fashionable Southgate cafe precinct are visible on the right (see Walk No. 15, Yarra River West). Continue on, past the steps leading down to the Alexandra Gardens (see Walk No. 16, Yarra River East), and across busy Alexandra Avenue.

Directly opposite the Arts Centre spire turn left and descend the steps into Queen Victoria Gardens. Among the most picturesque in Melbourne, these gardens date from 1905 and were established to complement the imposing monument to Queen Victoria that stands on a high rise at the eastern perimeter. It was thought that Melbourne should have a fitting memorial to the long-reigning monarch (1837–1901) after whom the state was named. The gardens feature sunken ornamental lakes, floral parterres, mature elm, plane and Moreton Bay Fig trees, and small ferny retreats.

Walk past two small busts, one of Hercules, denoting 'strength and service', and the other of the sun god Apollo, representing 'beauty and light'. Keeping both busts on your right, continue along the path and turn right at the end. On the riverside of the gardens the path leads to the **Queen Victoria monument |1|**, surrounded by Canary Island palms and rising above beautifully landscaped gardens, including two small lakes fringed with pampas grass and beds of roses. The statue, carved from Italian Carrara marble and portraying the Queen in ceremonial robes, holding sceptre and orb, was unveiled on Empire Day, 24 May 1907. Four figures, supported by Swedish granite columns, represent qualities much prized in the 19th century – Progress, History, Wisdom and Justice. The personal life of this English monarch, queen of the British Empire and self-proclaimed Empress of India, was the subject of an award-winning film, *Her Majesty, Mrs Brown*, which deals with the controversial relationship between the queen and her Scottish manservant, John Brown. In the smaller of the lakes are two appealing statues, *The Water Nymph* sculpted by Paul Montford in 1925, and *The Phoenix* by Baroness Yrse von Leistner in 1973.

Continue round to the right to the **Lady Clarke Rotunda |2|**, erected in 1913 to

Equestrian statue of Edward VII, a reminder of Melbourne's strong links with the British Empire.

commemorate the philanthropic work of Sir William Clarke's second wife, Janet. Their home Cliveden in East Melbourne stood on the site now occupied by Melbourne's Hilton Hotel, and from there Lady Clarke administered food and clothing to the poor and destitute during the depression of the 1890s. The shady rotunda, resembling a Greek temple, is a favourite photographic haunt for newlyweds.

Continue along the path, past a small avenue of plane trees on the right, to the statue of Queen Victoria's son, **King Edward VII |3|** (1901–10), sitting majestically on horseback in the uniform of a field marshal. He was the eldest son of Victoria and Albert, and assumed the throne relatively

Opening Times

Government House: Guided tours of Government House and La Trobe Cottage start from La Trobe's Cottage, Mon, Wed, Sat & Sun. It is essential to ring first (9654 5528) as Government House may be closed for an official function. Cottage open Sat–Thur 11am–4.30pm (9654 8488).
Australian Centre for Contemporary Art: Tue–Fri 11am–5pm, Sat–Sun 2pm–5pm, closed Mon (9654 6422).

Refreshments

There are drinking fountains throughout Kings Domain. Near the end of the walk you can turn off to the **Domain Bakery and Cafe** (part of the Botanical Hotel complex) or a range of takeaway food outlets, near the corner of Domain Road and Park Street. For a luxury lunch indulge yourself at **Lynch's**, 133 Domain Road.

late in life (he was 59) due to his mother's long reign. The reconciliation between Britain and France, achieved after years of war, earned him the name of 'Peacemaker'.

The bronze figure of Edward VII faces St Kilda Road, and forms an impressive backdrop to the **Floral Clock |4|**. A commemorative plaque notes the presentation of this timepiece to the city by the watchmakers of Switzerland in 1966. Cleverly arranged plantings of 7,000 annuals – changed twice yearly – form the markings of the clock.

On the city side of the clock, through the trees, you can catch a glimpse of a little recorded statue of an athlete – ***The Pathfinder*** **|5|** – a hammer thrower, skilfully sculpted in bronze by John Robinson in 1974. It is well worth the short detour for a closer look at this impressive figure. It stands in a particularly picturesque corner of the gardens.

Kings Domain

Walk away from the city, cross Linlithgow Avenue and approach the **Walker Fountain |6|**, presented by Barbara and Ron Walker when he was Lord Mayor of Melbourne (1974–76). Pass the fountain, cross Linlithgow Avenue again and turn right onto the Tan Track. You are now in the parkland of Kings Domain. A short distance along the track a path to the right leads to the **King George V monument |7|**, a rather ugly structure of granite and sandstone, against which the proportionally small figure of the king is somewhat eclipsed. He stands in the robes of the Order of the Garter, surveying the broad path down to St Kilda Road. On the reverse of the column is a bronze depiction of Britannica, with two small children resting beneath each outstretched arm – representing the dominions and the colonies. On the northern aspect a small heraldic lion is counterbalanced by a seated horse on the south side. Facing the front of the statue, take the path that leads off to the right.

When the path divides, veer to the left, continue on and when it forks again (there is a signpost), take the left track once more. Straight ahead is a small hedge surrounding the **Pioneer Women's Garden |8|**. This sunken jewel was constructed in 1934 as a tribute to the pioneer women of Victoria and also commemorated the state's centenary. The small garden is finely conceived, the main feature a pool in the shape of a cross bordered by stone paving. Waterlilies bloom in the arms of the cross and weeping elms stand on either side. The entrance to the garden is on the lower slope on the river side, but there is an enchanting view from the stone balustrade that borders the higher elevation. When you enter you look directly at an unusual feature at the end of the pond – not visible from the balustrade above. A semicircular grotto, lined with blue tiles, shelters a small statue of a woman set among fernery. One out-stretched arm reaches up to touch water falling from the top of the half cupola. Other statuary includes a clover-shaped water receptacle on one side of the small lawn and a sundial on the other.

A plaque explains that within the base of the sundial lies 'a casket containing the sheets of remembrance to the pioneer women of Victoria, 1834–1934'. The sheets list the names of hundreds of female pioneers – inscribed by all those Melburnians who in 1934 paid a shilling for the privilege of having their ancestors named. An atmosphere of seclusion and serenity pervades the space, heightened by the shadows cast by two sentinel cypress trees at the edge of the entrance steps.

Go back to the path on the higher level of the garden and continue on (away from St Kilda Road). Take the first path right, which leads around the outskirts of the grounds of Government House. Completed in 1876, this impressive building rendered in ivory-coloured stucco is barely visible from the road. Continue on the path until you reach Government House Drive. Turn right and walk down towards the Tan Track.

Set back a little from the track stands an imposing statue of **Sir Thomas Albert Blamey |9|** (1884–1951), in a military vehicle. He served during the First World War at Gallipoli and in France, reaching the rank of brigadier-general. In the Second World War he was commander-in-chief of Australian military forces. (His military credentials are listed on a plaque.)

Turn right along the Tan Track. A very short distance along, on the lawn between Linlithgow Avenue and St Kilda Road, is a rather modest statue (in comparison to its neighbours), facing the tree-lined esplanade. This is **Sir Edward 'Weary' Dunlop |10|** (1907–93). Dressed in a suit, which caused some comment by those who would have preferred him in army uniform, he wears a red peace poppy in his lapel. During the Second World War he served in the Middle East, Greece and Egypt, but is most remembered for his actions as a medical officer while prisoner of war in the camps along the Burma–Thailand railway. Among the survivors of this indescribable horror, Weary was revered as a 'saint' who kept them alive despite the unbelievable brutality, deprivation, sickness and disease. Twenty-two sleepers leading to the statue symbolise the 22,000 Australian POWs captured by the Japanese, and the eight steps above commemorate the 8,000 POWs who died.

Facing St Kilda Road, turn left and walk across the lawns to a memorial shrine on the corner of Government House Drive. This is the **Boer War Monument |11|**, erected by the 5th Victorian contingent in memory of their fallen comrades in South Africa during the Boer War, 1901–02. Plaques on all four sides of the sandstone list the war dead. Australia sent 16,000 men to support Britain's war effort, almost 3,500 of them from Victoria.

Continue on, across Government House Drive, to the equestrian statue of the **Earl of Hopetoun |12|**. Lord Hopetoun, Marquis of Linlithgow, was the first governor-general of Australia (1901–02), and governor of Victoria (1889–95).

Directly opposite, on the other side of Birdwood Avenue, also on horseback and in full uniform, is the statue of **Sir John Monash |13|** (1865–1931), Commander of the Australian Corps in France, 1918.

Continue along the Tan Track as it follows Birdwood Avenue. The track here is lined with large poplars, most picturesque in autumn. The Shrine of Remembrance is visible in the distance through the trees on the right. A little way along on the left, shaded by the canopy of an old elm, is a small bust of **Edith Cavell |14|**, an English nurse shot by the Germans during the First World War for allegedly helping 'persons to escape'. Small bronze panels show her arrest and execution by firing squad on 12 October 1915. She is particularly remembered for her heroic and selfless statement before death, ending with the words: 'I realize that patriotism is not enough. I must have no hatred or bitterness to anyone'.

A little further along, the **Malta George Cross Memorial Arch |15|** leads off the Tan Track, a tribute to the island of Malta which withstood incessant bombing in the Second World War. Four plaques proclaim Faith, Hope, Peace and Charity. There are quotes by Franklin D. Roosevelt, and King George VI, who awarded the George Cross to the tiny island fortress.

Next to the track is a large stone set in the ground. This commemorates Melbourne journalist **Edward George Honey |16|** (1885–1922) who, while living in London, first suggested the solemn ceremony of silence now observed on special days in former British colonies in remembrance of those who died in war.

Shrine gardens

Cross the road and walk towards the Shrine of Remembrance. You come first to a miniature statue simply inscribed 'The Man with the Donkey'. After the landing at Gallipoli, Private John Simpson Kirkpatrick, with his donkey Murphy, worked day and night taking water to the front line and carrying the wounded back to the ambulance station. **Simpson and his donkey |17|** were killed by a shrapnel shell on 19 May 1915. The nearby pine tree was grown from a pine cone brought home by one of the survivors of the Gallipoli campaign. This legendary story of a wartime 'Good Samaritan' is a favourite with all Australian schoolchildren.

The **Shrine of Remembrance |18|**, built of granite, freestone and marble as a memorial to those who died in the First World War, is situated on a hill at the southern end of Kings Domain, positioned to dominate the horizon to the south from Swanston Street and to the north from the St Kilda end of St Kilda Road. The stepped pyramid roof is supported by broad bases, typical of the Classical Temple style. One remarkable feature is the Eye of Light in the top of the pyramid, which sends filtered light into the inner shrine. The imposing monumental exterior serves as a protective shell for the darkened, solitary spaces within. In the forecourt, added as a memorial to the fallen of the Second World War, the Eternal Flame burns continuously. On the west side, the Remembrance Garden honours servicemen and women of the more recent conflicts in Korea, Malaya,

Borneo and Vietnam. A dawn service is held every year on Anzac Day (25 April). Space does not permit a detailed description of the Shrine's many other features, but it is worth spending some time here, whether to reflect on the tragedy of those who died – Australia lost 60,000 men in the First World War, 19,000 from Victoria – or simply to marvel at the interior and exterior design.

Across the road from the Shrine is the **Old Melbourne Observatory |19|**, at the time of writing undergoing impressive renovation and redevelopment. Further along is the **National Herbarium |20|**, where you turn right into Dallas Brooks Drive. On the corner is **La Trobe's Cottage |21|**, Melbourne's first government house and the home of Lieutenant-Governor La Trobe. Charles La Trobe was never provided with a government residence, and the cottage was shipped from England in 1839. It has been in various locations before the move in 1998 to its current position.

Halfway down Dallas Brooks Drive is the Australian Centre for Contemporary Art, a small public gallery focusing on recent developments in Australian and international contemporary art. At Domain Road turn right, unless you wish to make a detour for refreshments. On the opposite side of the road is an impressive assortment of bluestone buildings. This is Melbourne Grammar, one of the city's major private schools, founded in 1856. As you approach St Kilda Road the magnificent **Macpherson Robertson Fountain |22|** is visible on your left. Donated by a famous Melbourne confectioner, it features bronze frogs, seahorses and ducks, and the crowning statuary is a boy holding a dolphin.

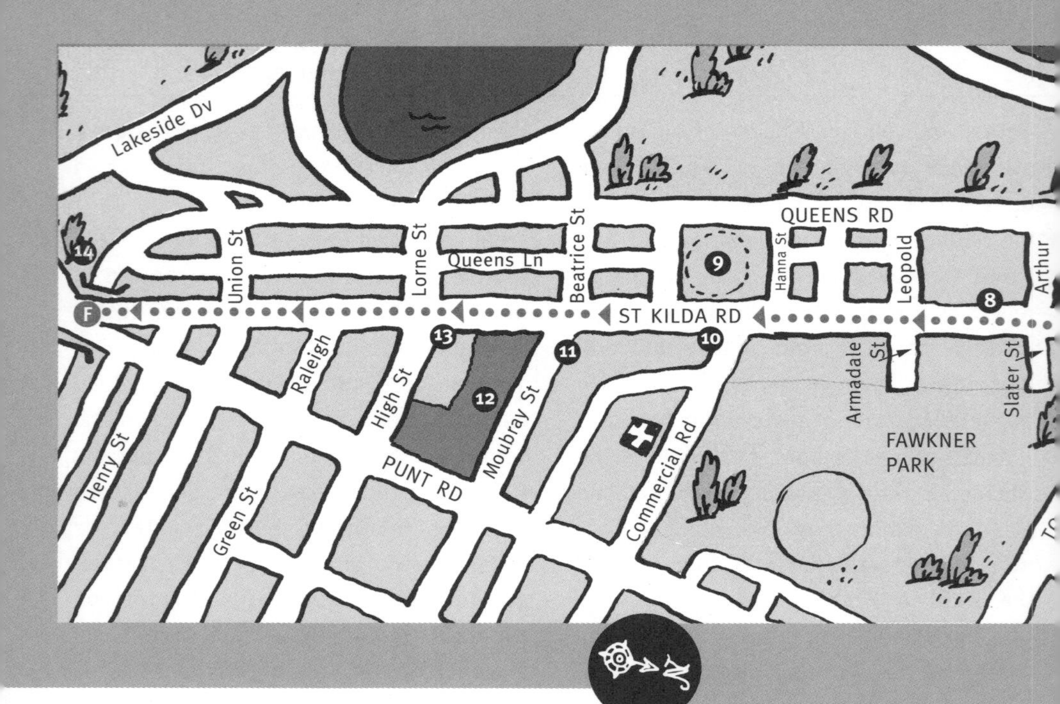

Walk key

1. Government House | **2.** Victoria Barracks | **3.** First Church of Christ, Scientist | **4.** Shrine of Remembrance | **5.** Melbourne Grammar School | **6.** Boer War monument | **7.** Synagogue of the Melbourne Hebrew Congregation | **8.** The Willows | **9.** Albert Cricket Ground | **10.** Chevron Hotel | **11.** Royal Victorian Institute for the Blind | **12.** Wesley College | **13.** Victorian College for the Deaf | **14.** Albert Park Native Forest Restoration Reserve

Start

Flinders Street Station – trams 3, 5, 6, 8, 16, 42, 48, 64, 67, 72, 75, City Circle tram; buses 216, 219, 220.

Walk Finish

St Kilda Junction – trams 3, 5, 64, 67; bus 246.

Length/Time

5 km/2 hours

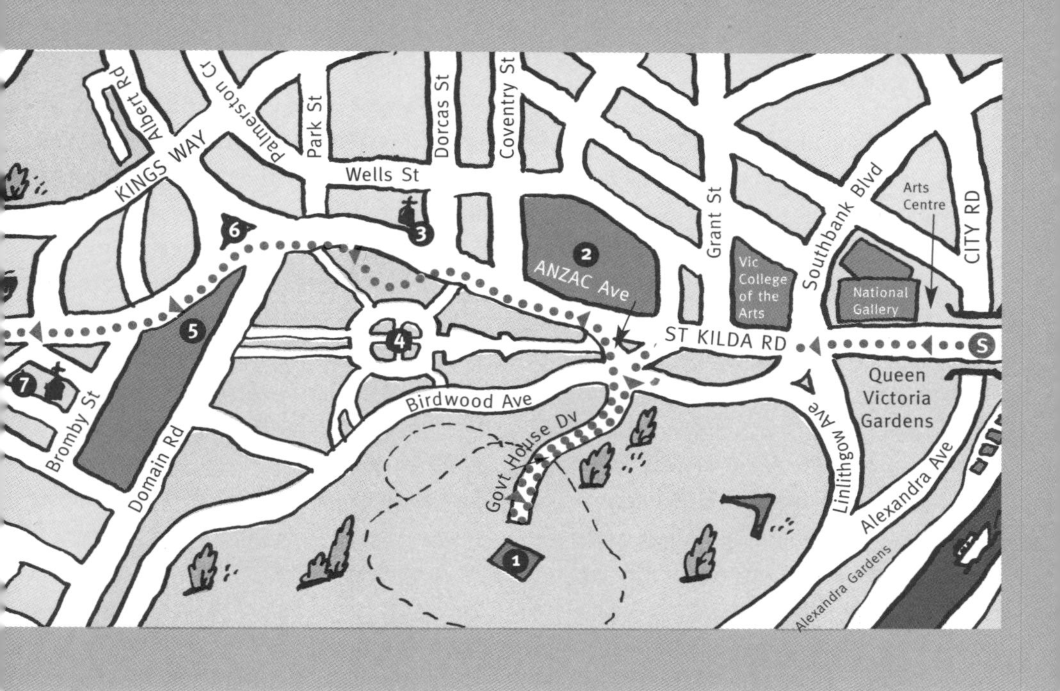

Walk No. 18

St Kilda Road

In search of the past

Melbourne's grand boulevard stretches from Princes Bridge, the southern gateway to the city, to St Kilda on the shore of Port Phillip Bay. Most of the gracious stately homes that once lined this thoroughfare have long since gone, replaced by office towers and luxury apartments. In the 1840s the road was no more than a rough track to St Kilda, used by pleasure seekers going to the bayside suburb for picnics. In the 1850s the north-west section of the track overlooked a huge canvas town, which sprawled out over present-day South Melbourne and was inhabited by those not able to afford even modest dwellings. The road could be dangerous, as shown in a famous painting of the time by William Strutt, which depicts a group of travellers bailed up by bushrangers in 1852.

In 1861 Ferdinand von Mueller directed the planting of blue gums along St Kilda Road, but these had been removed by the late 1880s. Some 400 trees were planted in 1883 (presumably many of these were poplars because in 1963 about 365 poplars were replaced with English plane trees). In 1886 cable trams were introduced and traffic increased, but it was the proposed royal visit in 1901 – the Duke of York had been invited to open the first parliament – that prompted the landscaping which gave form to the boulevard as we know it today. In the 20th century the road witnessed many momentous occasions: servicemen taking part in Anzac Day parades, runners in the 1956 Olympic marathon and anti-war protesters in the Vietnam moratorium marches of the 1970s. In the 1990s the north end has become a cultural precinct, presided over by the National Gallery and the Melbourne Arts Centre.

Palatial grandeur and memorial shrine

Walk across Princes Bridge, which separates Swanston Street from St Kilda Road. You pass the Alexandra Gardens on your left and the Queen Victoria Gardens, opposite the National Gallery of Victoria. Cross Linlithgow Avenue (from here Kings Domain stretches as far as Domain Road, see Walk No. 17, Kings Domain). On the right side of St Kilda Road, past the gallery, is the Victorian College of the Arts, a secondary and tertiary institution devoted to training future performing artists.

At Government House Drive on the left you can make a short detour to the gates of **Government House |1|**, although you will not see much of the building unless you take a tour. Designed by William Wardell in 1871 in Classical Renaissance style and built between 1871 and 1875, this is hailed as the grandest residence in the country. Set on a hill overlooking 11 hectares of garden, the ivory-painted stuccoed brick facade is dominated by a tall parapeted tower – less of a landmark than it used to be because of the surrounding trees. There are 200 rooms, including a ballroom and state and private sections. The huge ballroom comprises the whole south wing and is lit by three massive crystal chandeliers.

Back in St Kilda Road the large bluestone complex on the west side is **Victoria Barracks |2|**, which extends to the corner of Coventry Street. The building was prompted by the state's participation in the Crimean War in 1854 and dates from 1860. British regiments were billeted here until their withdrawal in 1870, leaving the barracks deserted. In the following years the buildings were used for a multiplicity of purposes, including a refuge for neglected children; a home for the sick and aged; a barracks where mounted police were trained and quartered; and the defence headquarters of Australia in 1901. There are several fine bluestone buildings in Classical and Georgian styles. The building dominating the St Kilda Road streetscape is 'A' Block, its three-storey section dating from 1860 and its matching five-storey

The Shrine of Remembrance dominates the north and south aspects of St Kilda Road.

extension built between 1914 and 1920. It housed the conference room used by the War Cabinet during the Second World War. The original section was designed in the Victorian Classical style by Public Works Department architect Gustav Joachimi, who also designed 'J' Block, a fine two-storey barracks hospital to which timber and iron verandahs were added later.

At Anzac Avenue you can get a great view looking straight up to the Shrine of Remembrance. Between Coventry and Dorcas streets are some of the glass office blocks that now characterise much of this once gracious Victorian thoroughfare.

On the south corner of Dorcas Street is the **First Church of Christ, Scientist |3|**. A stuccoed building, it is a copy of a domed temple with large Ionic columns to the

Opening Times

Government House: Guided tours commence at La Trobe's Cottage, Mon, Wed, Sat & Sun, subject to availability and bookings are essential (9654 5528). **Shrine of Remembrance:** Open daily 10am–5pm.

Refreshments

A number of office blocks and hotels have cafes at street level: **Romanis Cafe** is at No. 437; **Java Palms Brasserie** on the corner of Hanna Street; and **Pristkars** in the Parkroyal hotel.

portico. Designed by Harold Dumsday for Bates, Peebles & Smart, it was built in 1922 and features some Art Deco detailing.

Walk up the grassy slope to look at the **Shrine of Remembrance |4|**. Designed by Hudson & Wardrop and completed in 1932, the Doric columns replicate the Parthenon and other features are after the Mausoleum at Halicarnassos, considered to be one of the seven wonders of the ancient world. (For a more detailed discussion of the Shrine, see Walk No. 17, Kings Domain.)

Halls of learning

Beyond the end of Park Street, the road curves to the left. On the south corner of Domain Road is **Melbourne Grammar School |5|**. This part is the Middle School, Wadhurst. The older section is better observed from Domain Road. The school grounds extend for several blocks, down to Bromby Street. Construction of the original bluestone buildings, designed by Charles Webb and Thomas Taylor, began in 1856, and the school opened in 1858 with 24 boarders and 53 day boys. The Gothic Revival style followed the architecture of English colleges, and the bluestone is lightened by sandstone detailing and white painted timber window surrounds. The impressive tower and cloisters were part of the original design but were not added until 1876 due to lack of funds. This is the oldest denominational school in Victoria to operate continuously on its original site.

On the right, situated in a triangular reserve at Albert Road, is one of the several Melbourne monuments to the **Boer War |6|**. Designed by Irwin & Stephenson and unveiled in 1924, the rather austere obelisk is decorated with a simple cross.

On the left at the corner of Toorak Road is the **Synagogue of the Melbourne Hebrew Congregation |7|**, designed by Nahum Barnet in 1929. Palladian in design it features a Corinthian portico and a copper-clad dome. The spacious interior can accommodate 1,300 people.

Cross Toorak Road and continue past the office blocks and apartments that line the west side of the street. On the north corner of Arthur Street (Slater Street runs off to the left), at No. 452 is an old residence, Airlea. This is the childhood home of Stanley Bruce, later Lord Bruce, who attended the nearby Melbourne Grammar School and was prime minister of Australia from 1923 to 1929. The large white residence has recessed arcaded verandahs on the upper level (those on the left side have been glassed in) and a balustrade along the top and bottom of the upper floor. The verandahs located on the ground floor echo the style of those of the second storey, and a large bay window faces St Kilda Road. The residence became a guesthouse in the 1930s, offering accommodation to visiting businessmen from country and interstate.

On the left at No. 437, at the southern junction of Slater Street, is Romanis Cafe, a possible refreshment stop for a coffee or snack. The Romanis, a 19th-century Prahran family, were early members of the local branch of the Mechanics' Institute.

A few doors down from Arthur Street on the right is Scalaci at **The Willows |8|**. The existing structure is all that remains of a larger 16-room single-storey villa called Estella, built for bookmaker Leon Cohen in about 1890. At some point, the two beautiful weeping willows were planted in the front, and the house became known as The Willows. It is a rather unusual remnant of a bygone era, with elaborate porches rising above double bay windows that frame the centrally located entrance. The square towers surmounting the porches feature moulded Roman ornamentation and urns mounted at the four corners. In the middle, above the entrance, a statue of a woman has lost its head. Restaurateur Tansy Good has taken over the beautifully situated restaurant and the food and ambience have won great critical acclaim.

On the left, at Nos. 449–453, is Kia-Ora Flats, originally built for the Dixon family of Kia-Ora foods fame. This wonderful piece of Art Deco architecture was built in 1936 to a design by Gawler & Drummond and was leased to long-term tenants. Considered extremely fashionable in its day, it comprises two moderately large brick buildings, each containing 30 apartments.

Over Armadale Street, on the right side at No. 478, is Charsfield. This lovely old residence was converted to a boarding house between the wars when it became the Nangania Guest House in 1931. Designed by Charles Webb and dating from 1889, the two-storey building features a colonnaded verandah and pillared portico with attractive ornamentation on the pediment. Leadlight windows incorporating a design in plain glass are at each end of the ground-floor terrace, which retains its original tiled floor. The facade is divided by a two-storey tower with Italianate windows on the upper level. The perimeter cast-iron fence with cast-iron pillars is a rare piece of original Victoriana.

On the left is the crescent-shaped Sheraton Close at Nos. 485–489, built in the 1950s. At No. 490 on the right side of the road is Landene, dating from 1897. This was the home of Mr and Mrs McHenry England. Born in the United Kingdom in 1847, he became a tea merchant, chartering ships and making many trips between China and Australia. He was a keen sportsman and a director of the Shamrock Brewery, which was later to become part of Carlton & United Breweries.

On the right, at the corner of Hanna Street, is the **Albert Cricket Ground |9|**. This is the site of the old Warehousemen's Ground where, in 1908, more than 7,000 spectators packed the pavilion and temporary stands to watch Norman Brookes and Anthony Wilding play America in the Davis Cup. The Cup was inaugurated in 1900 and Australia first took part in 1905. This 1908 match was the first time Australia hosted the event. The Davis Cup was held at the St Kilda courts again in 1912.

On the south-east corner of Commercial Road is the **Chevron Hotel |10|**, built in 1934 to a design by Leslie Perrott. Once a residential hotel for the wealthy, the 1950s saw

St Kilda: the suburb at road's end

St Kilda, the suburb that marks the end of this walk and gives its name to the spacious esplanade, was given its appellation in 1841 by then Superintendent of the Port Phillip District, Charles La Trobe. Picnicking by the sea he remarked on the picturesque sight of the small boat *Lady of St Kilda* in the bay, declaring that the delightful seaside retreat should be named after the vessel. The history of the boat's namesake, Lady Grange, was far more gruesome. She had been exiled in 1734 to the small remote island of St Kilda in the Outer Hebrides, off northern Scotland, for harbour-ing Jacobite secrets, and imprisoned there until her death 17 years later.

During the gold decade of the 1850s, wealthy Melburnians built mansions on the hillsides overlooking Port Phillip Bay and the cool sea breezes attracted crowds in the summer months (the railway linked the suburb with the city as early as 1857 and cable trams rattled along St Kilda Road from 1886). The picturesque area became a little like the English seaside town of Brighton, with pleasure palaces, amusement parks and sea baths along the foreshore.

The suburb was hit by the depression of the 1890s and lost its air of respectability as the wealthy turned to the more fashionable residential areas, such as Hawthorn and Toorak. Between the World Wars St Kilda developed a rather seedy reputation – a place of prostitution, strip shows and drug addiction – a mantle it wore well into the 1970s. However, concurrently with this fall from grace, the area became the refuge for a large number of Jewish immigrants, fleeing from the pre-war Nazi regime of 1930s Germany. They brought a vibrancy and cosmopolitan 'feel' to the area, establishing cafes and shops along Acland Street that were reminiscent of those of Vienna. The 1990s has seen a transformation of St Kilda to a stylish cafe precinct.

its transformation into a popular night spot. Today, after a long lull, the night club is popular again with a whole new generation of hip-hoppers. Further along on the other side of the road is a hotel of more recent times, the Parkroyal, on the corner of Roy Street. Its restaurant at street level, Pristkars, is a good place for a coffee fix.

As you approach Moubray Street you pass the **Royal Victorian Institute for the Blind |11|**, established in 1886. The solid bluestone building is unusual in its use of sand-coloured brickwork with some red brick decoration. Across the road, on the corner of Beatrice Street, is Warwillah, a Federation style red brick apartment block with Tudor features including timber decoration on the gables and corner turrets.

Over Moubray Street you come to the grounds of **Wesley College |12|**, built around 1865 with extensions dating from 1872. In 1942–44 the school was taken over by the US army and the pupils attended Scotch College in Hawthorn. Prime ministers Sir Robert Menzies and his successor Harold Holt were students here. In 1978 the school became co-educational and the last boarders left in 1980.

On the north-east corner of High Street is the **Victorian College for the Deaf |13|**, another impressive bluestone structure. The three-storey facade is more ornate than the Blind Institute, and features towers, spires and turrets. It makes use of polychrome brickwork, particularly in the window surrounds. Ferdinand von Mueller donated some plants for the garden.

Glass towers and an old tree

Past High Street, St Kilda Road generally reverts to office blocks. However, there is one small structure of interest in front of No. 615, the Tattersalls building. Adjacent to the pavement is a finely detailed brick and stucco one-storey building. This is the former Gas Valve House, built for the Metropolitan Gas Company some time between 1876 and 1881 to service one or both of the gas-holders at this outstation. Note the company's insignia on the northern and southern pediments. Historically the structure is important as one of the last pieces of evidence of the gas industry of the 1870s in Melbourne. The building houses the Tattersalls Heritage Collection, a small museum of Tattersalls memorabilia, not open to the public.

Cross to the west side of St Kilda Road. On the south-west corner of Union Street at No. 628 is a turn-of-the-century three-storey apartment block, displaying Tudor features similar to those seen earlier in the walk.

At No. 630 is a two-storey Victorian residence now owned by the Australian and New Zealand College of Anaesthetists. Called Ulimaroa, a Maori word for Australia, this Italianate mansion, built in 1890, was first occupied by John Traill, whose family lived here until 1946. The front entrance portico is incorporated in a three-storey tower, off which leads a verandah with a beautiful cast-iron balustrade. It is said to have fine stained-glass windows, but these are not visible from the street.

You are now approaching St Kilda Junction. In the parkland ahead on the right, the **Albert Park Native Forest Restoration Reserve |14|**, is an old 40-metre-high river red gum dubbed the Corroboree Tree. Claimed to be more than 300 years old it was said to mark the location where Aboriginal people held ceremonies and perhaps camped at the time of European settlement, hunting on the nearby wetlands for freshwater delicacies such as tortoise and eel. It is particularly fitting that there is a natural memorial to remind passers-by of the Aboriginal people who lived here for more than 40,000 years.

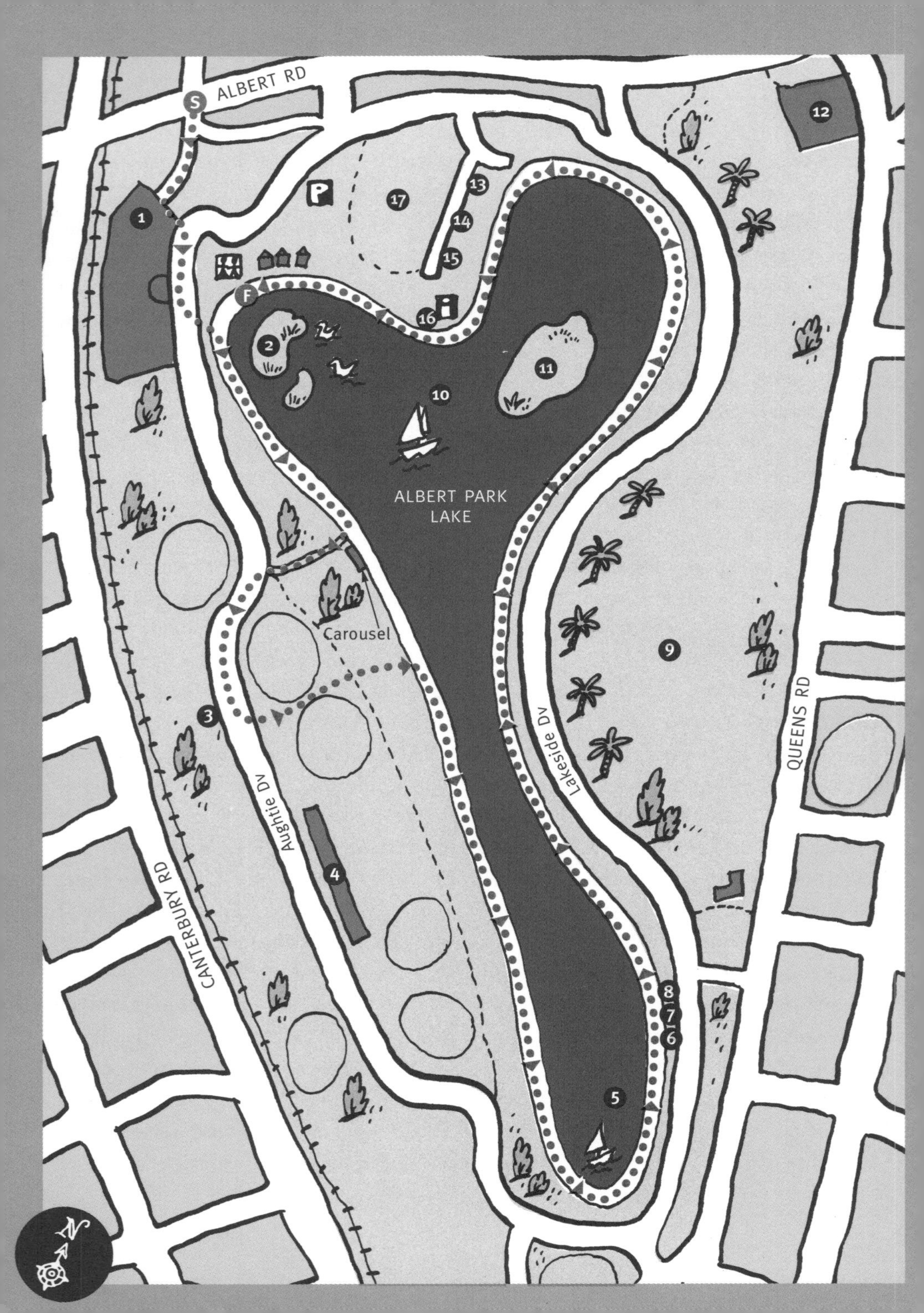

ALBERT RD
S
F
P
1
2
3
4
5
6
7
8
9
10
11
12
13
14
15
16
17
ALBERT PARK
LAKE
Carousel
Aughtie Dv
Lakeside Dv
CANTERBURY RD
QUEENS RD
N

Walk No. 19

Albert Park Lake

Palm-fringed oasis between the city and the bay

Start & Finish

Corner of Albert Road and Cecil Street – tram 12; light rail 96.

Length/Time

5 km/1.5–2 hours

Walk key

1. Melbourne Sports & Aquatic Centre | **2.** Wetlands | **3.** Children's Adventure Playground | **4.** Albert Park Indoor Sports Hall | **5.** Model yacht racecourse | **6.** Power House | **7.** Brighton Grammar Boat Shed | **8.** YWCA Rowing Club | **9.** Albert Park Public Golf Course | **10.** Fountain | **11.** Gunn Island | **12.** MacRobertson Girls High School | **13.** Albert Sailing Club | **14.** Boat-hire facilities and kiosk | **15.** Albert Park Yacht Club | **16.** Parks Victoria Information Centre | **17.** Bob Jane Stadium

Albert Park was once part of a swamp that stretched from the south bank of the Yarra to the bay. When the first Europeans settled in Melbourne after 1836 the lake, or lagoon as it was then called, was about the same shape as it is today. The lake and its surrounds were declared a park in 1864, and it was named after the Queen's consort, Prince Albert, who had recently died. Although its size has been whittled down over the last 100 years, its 225 hectares include a large number of ovals and ever-improving facilities. At different times of the year you will see men, women and children playing cricket, tennis, bowls, golf, soccer and hockey, while on the lake people enjoy yachting, rowing, boating and canoeing. In addition to this, walkers, joggers and cyclists beat well-worn tracks along the lakeside paths.

A park for all ages

If arriving by tram at the corner of Albert Road and Cecil Street, the **Melbourne Sports & Aquatic Centre |1|** is immediately in front of you when you get off the tram. Opened in 1993 this huge sports facility is the largest of its kind in the Southern Hemisphere. Its aquatic features include a depth-adjustable multipurpose pool, a water slide, a wave pool and a pool for toddlers. It provides facilities for martial arts, basketball, squash, table tennis and volleyball. The state-of-the-art gymnasium has a creche and cafe. When you reach the end of the complex cross Aughtie Drive and walk to the edge of the lake.

The closest section of water is designated the **Wetlands |2|**. Planted with a variety of aquatic plants the area is a habitat for a number of birds, including ducks and swans. Living in the water are turtles and a profusion of silver and golden perch. The wetlands play a vital role in controlling sediment in the lake. Walk along the lakeside track and take in the pleasant view across the water. On the right of the park are sweeping lawns, dotted with large poplars and the occasional eucalypt.

When you reach Lakeside Kiosk (adjacent to the Carousel restaurant) there is a track leading back to Aughtie Drive. If you take this detour you will come to the **Children's Adventure Playground |3|**, located on the western side of the road. This facility was constructed in May 1993 by local residents to a design incorporating the ideas of American Robert Leather.

Within the park boundaries there are 25 playing fields and ovals (including Bob Jane Stadium and Junction Oval). The sports grounds are named after prominent individuals who have had an association with Albert Park, such as cricketing legends Bill Woodfull and Lindsay Hassett. Parks Victoria has installed informative signs that give details about the various personalities.

Grand Prix racing

Back on the lakeside path the stretch of water narrows. Several tracks verge off to the right, passing some of the playing fields and leading to the **Albert Park Indoor Sports Hall |4|**, a complex of low buildings that caters for junior and senior netball and soccer players. In the first week of March it undergoes a transformation when it becomes the pit area for the four-day Formula One Grand Prix, which arrived in Melbourne in 1996 and is held around the lake on the first weekend in March. The first Australian Grand Prix was held here in 1953.

Continue on to the lake's southernmost point, where the track veers left round the St Kilda end of the lake before turning to follow the opposite shore to that you have just traversed.

Palms and city views

A short distance along, just south of the Power House building, is an area of water that is used as a **model yacht racecourse |5|**. The lake is a mecca for model boat enthusiasts, and the members of the Albert Park Model Yacht Club enjoy the thrills of big yacht racing without getting wet. Races are held at this spot on Sunday afternoons.

Power House |6| has its origins in the activities of the Victorian Sea Scout Troop, which was formed in May 1912. The organisation broadened its base in the 1920s and became associated with the Lord Somers Camps, which aimed at bringing together boys from all walks of life. Girls were included in the 1990s.

During the Second World War, Power House became a meeting place for servicemen and Saturday night dances here became a feature of Melbourne life. It ran into trouble with the Health Department, concerned that this unprepossessing boatshed was hosting dances for more than 1,000 people without conforming to health regulations. Attempts to close the venue to this Saturday night activity succeeded in 1945. Clandestine dancing still continued under the guise of club activities and the ban was lifted in 1949. By the 1960s this building had become the home of the Power House Football Club and now offers rooms for social functions.

At the south end of the Power House complex is the Wesley College Boatshed. On the north side is **Brighton Grammar Boat Shed |7|** and next to that the YWCA Rowing Club. In the mid-1960s Albert Park's committee of management insisted that improvements be made to these southern shore structures, namely the addition of brick veneer facades. The YWCA offers rowing tuition on Sunday mornings (9529 8596). The **YWCA Rowing Club |8|** was

Opening Times

Albert Park: Open to vehicles, pedestrians and cyclists 24 hours a day.

Parks Victoria Information Centre: Aquatic Drive. Open daily 9am–5pm. (131963)

Albert Park Indoor Sports Hall: (9696 6900).

Albert Park Model Yacht Club: (9557 1353).

Albert Park Public Golf Course: Open daily dawn–dusk (9510 5588).

Albert Park Yacht Club: (9690 5418).

Albert Sailing Club: (9571 5047).

Jolly Roger School of Sailing: (9690 5862).

Melbourne Sports and Aquatic Centre: (9926 1555).

Power House: (9510 3644).

Refreshments

The Keg and Swan restaurant & bar: open daily (9510 8416). **The Point:** casual cafe and fine dining, open daily for breakfast, lunch & dinner (9682 5566). **Jolly Roger Kiosk:** open Mon–Fri 9am–dusk (closed Mon in winter), Sat–Sun 9am–5.30pm (9690 5862). **Lakeside Kiosk:** open weekends and public holidays 10am–4pm. **Cafe Aqua:** Melbourne Sports and Aquatic Centre, open daily for breakfast, lunch and dinner (9926 1555).

founded in 1910 to provide the opportunity for girls and women to enjoy the sport of rowing in a safe and friendly atmosphere.

A short distance past Power House you will see the edge of the **Albert Park Public Golf Course |9|** on the other side of Lakeside Drive. The golf course office is located here, along with The Keg and Swan restaurant. A golf club has been in the vicinity since 1902 and the Albert Park Golf Club was founded in 1914 as a nine-hole course. In the early 1930s the course was extended to 18 holes and a new clubhouse in Queens Road was officially opened in 1936. Incredibly, the park committee still sanctioned the grazing of horses in the park and as golf enthusiasts grew in number, so did the complaints about the damage done to the golf course by wandering animals. Golfers also had to contend with the ruts and holes left by mushroomers, particularly during difficult economic times such as the war years. The golf club struggled for the right to impose restrictions on outsiders, but finally lost the battle in 1947 when it became a public course.

You now have a lengthy walk along the track that is bordered by the lake on one side, and Lakeside Drive, rimmed by Canary Island Palms, on the other. In the middle of the lake you will notice a large water spout or **fountain |10|** and a little further along you draw level with **Gunn Island |11|**. A proposal some years ago to develop the island and link it to the shore by a bridge was thwarted by boat owners, concerned about the effect on established boating courses. In 1992, when the lake was emptied and dredged, the subsequent development of wetland areas included Gunn Island, which became a habitat for a variety of flora and fauna.

The wetlands of Albert Park Lake provide an ideal habitat for a range of waterbirds.

The north edge of the lake is not far from **MacRobertson Girls High School |12|**, near Kings Way. This highly regarded government school started in 1905 as a co-educational establishment in Spring Street in the city. In 1912 it was renamed Melbourne High School but in 1928 the boys were moved to South Yarra. Saddled with a dilapidated building the renamed Melbourne Girls High School looked around for a new home. In 1930 it took up temporary residence at Government House. In 1933 noted philanthropist and chocolate-maker Sir Macpherson Robertson came to the rescue and donated £40,000 for a new school, which was built here in 1934.

A sporting legacy

At the north edge of the lake, Lakeside Drive veers off to the right. Keep to the lakeside track. To the left are a group of buildings bordering the shore. The first is **Albert Sailing Club |13|**, the vision of Bill Hooper, who grew up by the lake. After his return from the war he wanted his daughter, Sue, to learn to sail. When he discovered that there was no sailing club on the lake catering for female members, he helped to establish the club. The clubhouse on Aquatic Drive was constructed in the 1950s and conducts races on the lake on Saturdays.

The next building is occupied by the Jolly Roger School of Sailing. Bill Hooper's father had owned Hooper's Boathouse at the north-east end of the lake and after the war Bill acquired the adjoining site and established the Jolly Roger Sailing School, **boat-hire facilities and kiosk |14|**. A new generation of Hooper children grew up on the lake and became champion sailors.

Further along is **Albert Park Yacht Club |15|**, formed in 1871. The club organises the lake's sailing program; races are conducted on Saturdays and special events on Sundays. Beyond the club is **Parks Victoria Information Centre |16|** and The Point, an award-winning restaurant offering fine food and picturesque views. From here the track leads through a picnic area.

On your right is the former South Melbourne Cricket Ground, now the **Bob Jane Stadium |17|**. In 1878 the ground was shared by South Melbourne Cricket Club and South Melbourne Football Club. The residents of South Melbourne were loyal sporting fans, and as early as 1881, 10,000 spectators turned out to watch a football match between South Melbourne and Geelong. The red brick grandstand was constructed in 1926. In the club amalgamations of 1979 the South Melbourne players moved to Sydney and became known as the Sydney Swans.

With the demise of the 101-year-old football club, the South Melbourne Cricket Club soon found itself in financial difficulties and eventually, in the 1990s, the ground was sold. Bob Jane bought it for the South Melbourne Hellas Soccer Club.

Keep to the path and soon you will find yourself back at the point where you joined the lakeside track. Retrace your steps to the corner of Albert Road and Cecil Street.

Beacon Cove
Waterfront Place
Graham St
Stokes St
Bay St
Beach St
Rouse St
Port Melbourne Yacht Club
Lagoon Pier
Pickles St
Foote St
Graham St
Richardson St
BEACONSFIELD PDE
Kerferd Rd
FERRARS ST
ALBERT RD
ALBERT PARK LAKE
CANTERBURY RD
Mills St
Wright St
Harold St
Armstrong St
Fraser St
Cowderoy St
JACKA BLVD
Esplanade
Marine Parade
Kirby's Kiosk
S
F
1
2
3
4
5
6
7
8
9
10
11
12
13
14
15
16
17
N

Walk No. 20

Station Pier to St Kilda Pier

The sights of Port Phillip Bay

Start

Station Pier – tram 109.

Finish

St Kilda Pier – light rail 96; tram 12, 16, 69, 79.

Length/Time

4.6 km/2 hours

Walk key

1. Station Pier | **2.** Swallow & Ariell Steam Biscuit Manufactory | **3.** Wilbraham Liardet | **4.** Sandridge Bay Towers | **5.** Kilbride Centre | **6.** South Melbourne Lifesaving Club | **7.** Plum Garland Memorial Playground | **8.** Albert Park Yachting and Angling Club | **9.** Kerferd Road Pier | **10.** Our Lady of Mount Carmel | **11.** Le Kiosk on the Beach | **12.** Danish Club | **13.** Middle Park Lifesaving Club | **14.** Catani Gardens | **15.** West Beach natural history project | **16.** Royal Melbourne Yacht Squadron | **17.** St Kilda Pier

This is a walk for a fine day, when the sea breezes are gently blowing the fronds of the Canary Island palms that line the waterfront. In summer the bay is dotted with yachts and pleasure craft, while inshore waters play host to windsurfers and swimmers. Station Pier, the main overseas passenger terminal for Melbourne shipping, marks the start, and St Kilda Pier, where people promenade and take pleasure cruises, is the destination. The road changes its name four times: you begin in Waterfront Place, move on to Beach Street, continue on Beaconsfield Parade and finish on Jacka Boulevard. The walk leads through four suburbs (Port Melbourne, Albert Park, Middle Park and St Kilda), following the route constructed in the 1880s. The foreshore trail is a mecca for walkers, but watch out for the joggers, rollerbladers and cyclists who also frequent the trail.

Port Melbourne

The suburb, rimming Hobsons Bay, officially got its name in 1884, before which time it was known as Sandridge, the term applied by an early surveyor to the sandy stretch of foreshore by the river mouth, used as a landing place by small craft. The first permanent settler was Wilbraham Frederick Evelyn Liardet (1799–1878), who fell in love with the tea-tree-lined beach when he arrived there en route to Sydney in 1839. He set up camp with his wife and nine children. For the next five years Liardet was responsible for the development of the area, which later became known as Liardet's Beach.

Station Pier |1| was completed in 1854 and its 40-ship berthing capacity turned the little settlement into a thriving port. Costing £365,240, the pier was 532 metres long and was extended to 570 metres by 1858. The Hobson's Bay Railway Company built the rail link with the city the same year, the first railway in Victoria. Station Pier was reconstructed in 1930. The adjacent Princes Pier dates from 1912.

If you catch the light rail to Port Melbourne, get off at the restored Sandridge Railway Station terminus at Port Melbourne/Beacon Cove. Station Pier is directly ahead. The old wharves have been redeveloped, complete with several pre-First World War kiosks. This is where the passenger ship *Spirit of Tasmania* docks.

Cross the road, and you are now on the Port Melbourne Foreshore Trail. Looking at Station Pier, turn left and walk along the promenade. At Stokes Street make a detour away from the bay and walk the short distance to Rouse Street. The corner is the site of the **Swallow & Ariell Steam Biscuit Manufactory |2|** building. The company, founded by Thomas Swallow in 1854, manufactured ships' biscuits. The brick quadrangular factory complex was built in 1858 in the vicinity of the wharves, and additions were made over the following 30 years. Now converted to apartments, its Georgian and Classical features are still visible.

Retrace your steps to the foreshore walking trail. Large apartment blocks line this section of Beach Street, with sweeping views out over the bay. Just before the Port Melbourne Yacht Club is a small memorial to the suburb's founder, **Wilbraham Liardet |3|**.

After passing the end of Bay Street, where the main village of Port Melbourne is located several blocks from the beachfront, there is a large apartment complex, Station Pier Condominium and **Sandridge Bay Towers |4|**. This interesting development incorporates a high brick chimney, which was part of an old factory complex. Opposite is Lagoon Pier and a little further along is the Port Melbourne Lifesaving Club. On the left is a row of one-storey terrace cottages, somewhat dilapidated but typical of the 19th-century workers' cottages that dot the suburb of Port Melbourne.

Albert Park

Past the end of Pickles Street, the homes become larger, two-storey and many are Edwardian in style. On the south-eastern corner of Foote Street is a two-storey ecclesiastical building, the **Kilbride Centre |5|**, with large arcaded verandahs on both levels. Built in 1886 it was Melbourne's first Carmelite House. When the Carmelites moved out in the early 20th century, it became a convent for the Brigidine Sisters.

On the right you pass the **South Melbourne Lifesaving Club |6|**, just opposite the end of Withers Street. There are changing facilities here, for those who want to take to the water for a swim. Below on the foreshore is the oddly named **Plum Garland Memorial Playground |7|**. Past the Beach House Hotel is a long row of attractive double-storey terrace houses, replete with iron-lace verandahs.

At Kerferd Road, dominating the north corner is the Hotel Victoria, a once grand establishment dating from 1889. In the middle of the wide suburban street is Kerferds Restaurant & Bar. On the foreshore is the **Albert Park Yachting & Angling Club |8|** and running out from the beach is the **Kerferd Road Pier |9|**, built between 1887 and 1889 to a design by Sydney W. Smith, and restored in 1988. This stretch of sand has long been the summer haunt of the young and the beautiful, intent on achieving the ultimate sun tan.

At Nos. 141–150 is the dilapidated two-storey edifice of **Our Lady of Mount Carmel |10|**. The foundation stone of the convent was laid on 4 March 1892 and the building was opened in January 1893. By the end of the 19th century there were nearly 200 girls in care. In 1899 a Ladies Rest Home

Opening Times

Station Pier: The passenger ship *Spirit of Tasmania,* which plies between the mainland and Tasmania, also offers cruises of the bay. Sunset cruises depart Station Pier Sun 5.30pm throughout the year (132010). The steam tug *Wattle* departs for Williamstown on Sun and public holidays (9328 2739).

Catani Gardens: You can observe the friendly brushtail possums that live here; the best viewing time is one hour after dusk.

Royal Melbourne Yacht Squadron: Offers sailing on the bay, with your crew or theirs (9525 5221).

St Kilda Pier: On weekends and public holidays ferries run from the pier to Williamstown (9658 9949). Cruises to see the penguin colony depart at various times each day and evening (9645 0533).

Refreshments

There are numerous cafes and pubs for snacks, drinks and coffee. Try **Kerferds Restaurant Bar** (129 Beaconsfield Parade, 9696 6334) or **Le Kiosk on the Beach** (opposite Mills Street, Middle Park, 9696 6334). At the end of the walk **Kirby's Kiosk** is a restored turn-of-the-century tearooms on St Kilda Pier (9525 3198).

Renovated 19th-century kiosks offer enjoyable resting points along Beaconsfield Parade.

was established for boarders, which operated until 1938. Between 1898 and 1910, with a view to expansion, the convent acquired adjoining properties fronting Beaconsfield Parade and Ashworth Street. The building work was carried out from 1911 to 1920, often slowly due to high wages and the scarcity of labour. The convent continued to operate until the 1970s, and was sold to the state government in 1976. Most of the land has been sold to developers; all that remains is now much the worse for wear.

Middle Park

Opposite the end of Mills Street is **Le Kiosk on the Beach |11|**, a good place to stop for coffee or a light lunch – you can eat inside or alfresco on the beach. Just past the end of Mills Street is a splendid Victorian building, once called Hughenden and now housing the **Danish Club |12|**. It is an Italianate building designed in 1890 by Frederick de Garis for J.R. Buxton, the founder of the Buxton real estate firm. Next door, at 178–181 Beaconsfield Parade, is a group of grand Victorian terraces called The Elms. In the blocks between Wright and Armstrong streets is a mix of housing styles, although the majority are Edwardian residences; around McGregor Street the mix includes modern apartment blocks. Opposite the end of Armstrong Street is the **Middle Park Lifesaving Club |13|**, complete with public change rooms, and a small kiosk.

St Kilda

Near the corner of Cowderoy Street, at 335 Beaconsfield Parade, is Robinsons by the Sea, a highly acclaimed bed and breakfast establishment in a restored two-storey triple-fronted terrace. On the right is the Royal Melbourne Yacht Squadron Junior Training Centre, a long low building, its cement rendering painted cream, and the Surf Lifesaving Association of Australia. There is also a small kiosk. Follow the path round to the right, keeping the park – the **Catani Gardens |14|** – on your left. The gardens were designed by Carlo Catani (1852–1918), a Florentine trained engineer who arrived in Australia in 1876. He became Chief Engineer of the Public Works Department and a great advocate of St Kilda. The gardens were landscaped in 1910 on an area of reclaimed swamp.

On the right is the **West Beach natural history project |15|**, a local initiative to revegetate the dune environment and beautify the foreshore. Started in 1988, volunteers have constructed an artificial wetland to filter stormwater from the Cowderoy Street drain, which has provided an ideal habitat for local and migratory birds. The road curves around the grounds of the **Royal Melbourne Yacht Squadron |16|**, on your left, as the St Kilda Pier comes into full view. The yachts directly out from here belong to Squadron members. The organisation was founded in the 1880s and has been here since 1904. The present building was erected in 1926. In 1956 it was the administrative headquarters for yachting events during the Olympic Games.

At the start of the **St Kilda Pier |17|** is a small enclosure, a rotunda or shelter shed of sorts. The first jetty on the site, erected in 1853 by the St Kilda Pier & Jetty Company, was destroyed by storms three years later. A new pier was built in its place in 1859, with further extensions made in 1883. The kiosk and tearooms were erected at the end of the pier in 1904 and the kiosk pavilion underwent extensive restoration in 1988. Later additions to the pier included the concrete arm built at right angles from the end, which now serves as a shelter for yachts and small craft. During the 1956 Olympic Games a rock structure was created stretching westwards from the end of the pier. It has become home to a colony of little penguins and night tours take visitors out to the sanctuary.

Continue to Jacka Boulevard, named after Albert Jacka, the first Australian to win a VC in the First World War for his bravery at Gallipoli. He returned to live in St Kilda, was elected to the council, and was mayor of St Kilda in 1930. Turn left into Jacka Boulevard and head to Fitzroy Street.

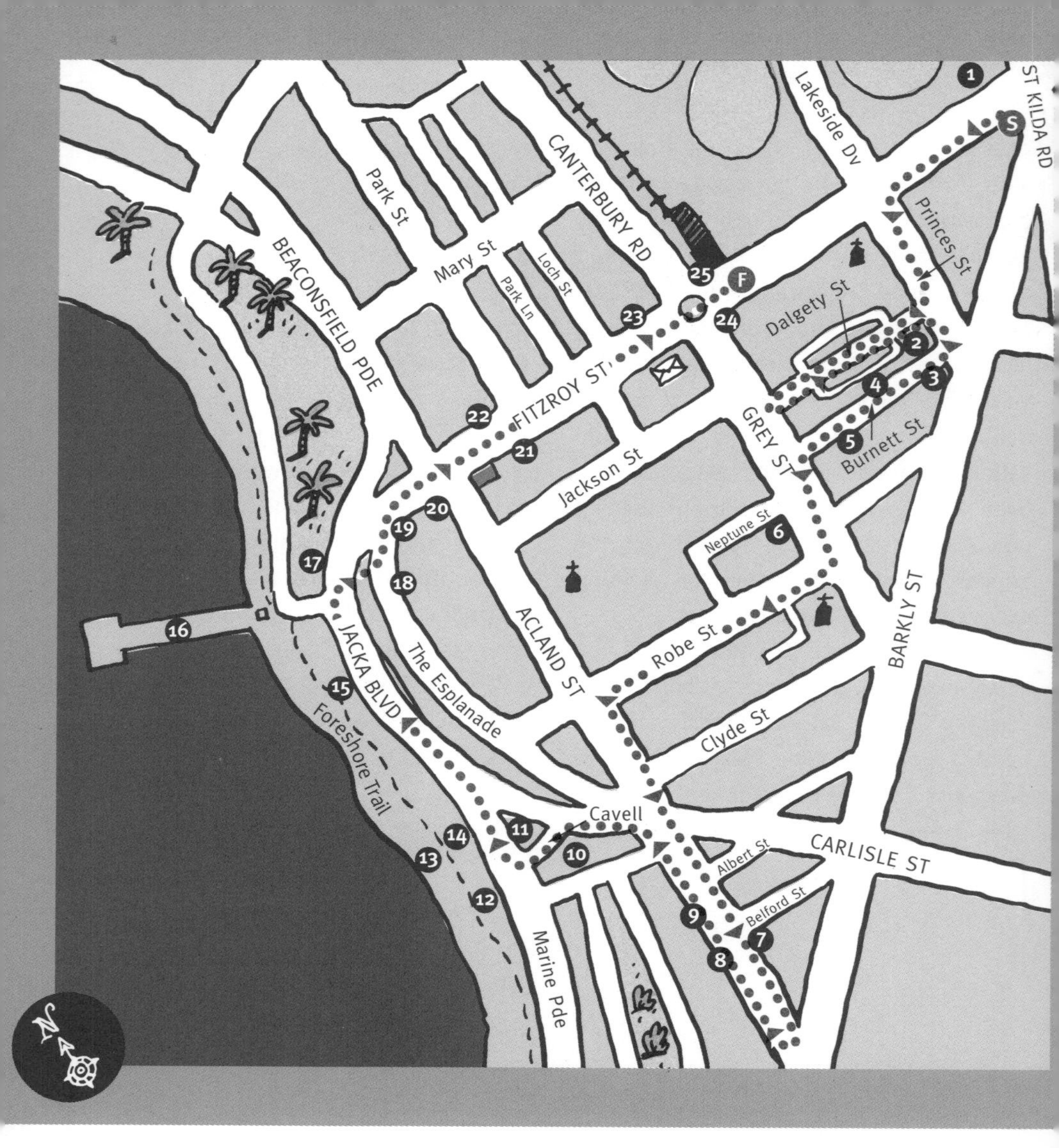

Walk key

1. Junction Oval | **2.** Berkeley Hall | **3.** Oberwyl | **4.** Marion Terrace | **5.** Fenagh Cottage | **6.** Church of the Sacred Heart | **7.** Cosmos Books & Music | **8.** Edelweiss Delicatessen | **9.** Scheherazade | **10.** Luna Park | **11.** Palais Theatre | **12.** Donovans Restaurant | **13.** St Kilda Lifesaving Club | **14.** Stokehouse Restaurant | **15.** St Kilda Sea Baths | **16.** St Kilda Pier | **17.** Captain Cook | **18.** Esplanade Hotel | **19.** Number One | **20.** Madam Joe Joe | **21.** Cafe Di Stasio | **22.** Bortolotto's | **23.** Tolarno Bar & Bistro | **24.** George Hotel | **25.** St Kilda Station

Walk No. 21

St Kilda Bayside Precinct

Faded glories, cafe society and entertainment by the sea

Start

St Kilda Junction – trams 3, 5, 64, 67; bus 246.

Finish

Old St Kilda station – tram 16; light rail 96.

Length/Time

3 km/2.5 hours

St Kilda has an eclectic mix of cultures and styles. Fashionable cafes, displaying lots of chrome and glass, sit beside seedy and run-down establishments, with peeling paint the result of years of neglect. The walk starts at St Kilda Junction and winds through some quiet back streets where mansions of a more glorious era have more often than not become boarding houses and hostels, their once luxurious interiors stripped bare. The route continues along Acland Street – you must do this walk on a Sunday morning to fully appreciate the Eastern European ambience – and then down to the sea, offering great foreshore views or a meander through the bustling Sunday art and craft market on the upper Esplanade. You finish back in the cafe precinct of Fitzroy Street, with the choice of a hundred places to lunch or snack.

Faded glories of Victorian streetscapes

Stand on the south-west corner of Fitzroy Street, where it forms a junction with St Kilda Road, and head south towards the sea. On the other side of the road is the southern extremity of Albert Park (see Walk No. 19, Albert Park). Beyond the lawns you can see the **Junction Oval |1|**. Once the base of the St Kilda Football Club, founded in 1873, this was the home ground of the Saints until they moved to Moorabbin in 1965. It remains the home of the St Kilda Cricket Club, which had its beginnings in 1855. On your left are a series of unremarkable office buildings. At No. 171 is an Art Deco style block of apartments, Ritz Mansions. On the corner of Princes Street is the Elephant & Wheelbarrow hotel – a side entrance in Fitzroy Street advertises backpacker accommodation.

Turn left into Princes Street and walk up the slight hill. There are some large old Victorian residences; No. 5, with its unpainted brickwork and cast-iron lacework gracing the verandahs of its two storeys, is typical of the area. Dating from 1889, it was built as the manse for the Wesleyan Methodist Church, which once occupied the Princes–Fitzroy Street corner but is now surrounded by apartment blocks and only accessible from Fitzroy Street. It was built in 1857–58.

It is worth a detour down Dalgety Street to look at the terraces at Nos. 4–18 (Eden Terrace, dating from 1858) on one side of the road and Nos. 5–17 (1860s) on the other.

Return to Princes Street and continue up the hill. You pass No. 11, **Berkeley Hall |2|**, a huge old residence. It was built in 1854 to a Georgian design by Albert Purchas for Melbourne's first town clerk, Henry Field Gurner. One of the oldest surviving St Kilda residences, the house was altered in the early 19th century, when the Classical colonnaded verandah was added. On the corner of Burnett Street is a grand High Victorian Classical style town house, Berkeley Court, built for lawyer John Barker in 1882. Opposite, on the other corner at No. 35 Burnett Street, is **Oberwyl |3|**, dating from 1856. An unusual timber-framed balcony runs the length of the upper floor, softening the austerity of the facade. Built for wealthy merchant John Gomes De Silva in the Classical Revival style, the house was dubbed 'De Silva's folly' due to the excessive amount of money spent on its construction. De Silva only lived here for three years. The louvred shutters are an unusual feature, apparently installed as a fortification against bushrangers. A highlight of the interior is a Baronial style dining room, complete with carved heraldic lions above the fireplace. Nineteenth-century additions include the colonnaded verandah, and a two-storey wing erected after 1878. Between 1898 and 1930 it housed a private girls' school, and its name, Oberwyl, dates from this period. Much of the house is now hidden by trees.

Walk along Burnett Street. The Victorian splendour here is frequently interrupted by the ugly 1960s apartment blocks, but you can well imagine the original streetscape. Halfway along is **Marion Terrace |4|**, dating from 1882. Comprising Nos. 14–24, the main structure is two storeys and the adjoining towers rise to three storeys. Next door, at No. 12, is a gracious dwelling set back from the road and, further down, No. 6 (1866) and No. 8 (1864) are almost carbon copies. Originally called Wilgah, the pair feature grand arcaded verandahs in the Classical style. No. 7, **Fenagh Cottage |5|**, on the other side of the street, is a timber pre-fabricated house dating from 1855.

At the end of the street, turn left into Grey Street. Walk along the left side of the road, which is largely apartment blocks, and you will get a better perspective of the former grandeur on the west side of the street. The ecclesiastical building on your right is the **Church of the Sacred Heart |6|** and next door is the Sacred Heart Mission.

Turn right into Robe Street, quite a wide suburban roadway, with landscaped round-abouts to slow the speed of the through traffic. Again you will notice the haphazard mix of styles: Victorian remnants sit cheek-by-jowl with the ubiquitous 1960s brick-box apartments, some Edwardian apartment blocks and the occasional Edwardian residence in a garden setting. The mansion at No. 73 dates from 1886. A terrace pair that looks to have been lovingly restored, its polychrome brickwork highlighted by the freshly painted iron lace adorning its verandahs, is Fareham and Figsby, Nos. 49 and 47 respectively. Fareham was once considered as a name for the suburb.

Opening Times

Linden Arts Centre and Gallery: Tue–Sun 1pm–6pm (12 noon–5pm during winter), free admission. (9209 6794, 9209 6560).
Luna Park: Admission is free if you merely want to wander in and look around. If you wish to try the rides you can purchase multiple-ticket booklets at discounted prices. Opening hours vary, recorded information, 1902 240 112.
St Kilda Esplanade Art and Craft Market: Sun 10am–5pm.

Refreshments

You can stop for breakfast, a snack or coffee at any one of the cafes in Acland or Fitzroy streets. If you want a great lunch with spectacular views, dine upstairs at the **Stokehouse**, lunch and dinner daily (9525 5555).

Gourmet delights

When you reach Acland Street turn left – this is part of the residential section. On the left you pass a row of old cottages, verandahs adorned with timber surrounds and fretwork on the gabled roofs. These extend down to the corner of Clyde Street. From here you can see the junction with Carlisle Street, where the 'real' Acland Street begins. Before you get there, however, you pass a series of cafes, some with dark interiors that show little attempt at sophistication – a window into St Kilda as it was 20 years ago. Here, too, is the popular Greasy Joe's cafe, its name doing nothing to deter the hordes of loyal patrons.

Cross Carlisle Street and a few shops down cross Albert Street. On the far corner, at No. 88, is the facade of the St Kilda Army and Navy Club. A few doors further is the Malaysian restaurant Chinta Ria, one of several eateries made famous for its recipes in a best-selling book, *Hot Food Cool Jazz.*

Cross Irwell and Belford streets and you come to the highly respected **Cosmos Books & Music |7|,** which has been in business for more than 40 years. The inner depths entice you to browse for hours through the marvellous mix of fiction, biography, reference, classical pop, jazz – everything from the mundane to the esoteric. Further down the street at No. 160 is its sister store, Metropolis, a much grander and more open modern space, in keeping with its offerings on design, art, photography, classics and computer books.

At Barkly Street cross to the other side of Acland Street and go back in the other direction. This is the best side of the street for food shops, often with various forms of street entertainment on offer. First shop of note is **Edelweiss Delicatessen |8|** at No. 143, which rubs shoulders with a great seafood place at No. 141. Passers-by block the pavements to stare at the window display. Deveroli's at No. 129 is a popular breakfast spot. Monarch Quality Cakes, established since 1934, stands at No. 103 and at No. 99 is the famous **Scheherazade |9|,** restaurant and coffee lounge. Next door is the Acland Street Cake Shop, and at No. 93 is the Bon Cake Shop. No. 81 is the irresistible Europa cake shop, again with window shoppers always gazing longingly at the exotic displays. Cross Shakespeare Grove and walk past the bluestone Vineyard Restaurant.

Bayside precinct

You are now passing streets that run up from the bay. An area of parkland, the O'Donnell Gardens, opens up on your left. On a Sunday you will find a few street stalls along here, stragglers from the nearby art and craft market, which is generally confined to the higher reaches of the upper Esplanade. On the west side of the park are the outer walls of **Luna Park |10|,** the fun and entertainment complex that has enthralled young Melburnians for generations. Opened in 1912, this old-fashioned fun park was built by four Americans, who modelled it on a Luna Park at Coney Island in New York. The entrance face, its adjacent towers and the elevated scenic railway around the perimeter date from this period.

At the entrance to Luna Park keep to the left and walk along Cavell Street. On the right, and stretching almost an entire block, looms the large white edifice of the **Palais Theatre |11|**. First opened in 1915, it burned to the ground in 1926, but was quickly rebuilt and opened again in 1927. With seating for around 3,000, it is one of the largest theatres in Australia. It has hosted a diverse range of entertainment from ballet, opera, ice shows, circus acts and movies. It was for many years the venue for the Melbourne International Film Festival. Harry Belafonte sang here in the 1960s, Bob Dylan in the 1980s and Kylie Minogue in 1998. The smaller building next door is the Palace, a live music venue, built on the site of the renowned Palais de Danse. The latter, built in 1913, hosted shows by national and international musicians; big bands played here in the 1920s, it was home to the first Australian amateur dancing championships, and in the 1940s it was a popular dance hall where the young would congregate on Friday nights. In 1962 it was extended to include the Stardust Room, a large space featuring a blue interior dotted with 'stars', which was used for functions such as balls and wedding receptions. The complex was destroyed by fire in 1968.

Cavell Street takes you down to Marine Parade, which rims the foreshore. Cross at the lights and, almost opposite the end of Cavell Street, hugging the beachfront, is a long low yellow building, **Donovans Restaurant |12|**. A path alongside leads to the beach. Watch out for the rollerbladers and cyclists. The views are spectacular here: in summer the water sparkles in the harsh Australian light and in the winter the tones are muted blues and pinks. To the left is an old jetty and beyond a lighthouse and the St Kilda Marina; to the right is the St Kilda pier, the city high rise, the port of Melbourne, Williamstown and, on a clear day, the pointed hills of the You Yangs are visible almost directly in front of you.

You can either walk along the foreshore path or return to the road, which is the route of this walk. From here you get a street perspective as well as generous glimpses of the bay. Past Donovans is a grassy space before you reach the **St Kilda Lifesaving Club |13|**. Next to this, in a turn-of-the-century teahouse, is the **Stokehouse Restaurant |14|**, an absolute 'must' for lunch. Eat upstairs for a more refined dining experience with great views, or downstairs for a less expensive nosh. Looking east you can see tall apartment blocks rising from the upper Esplanade, the site of the Sunday market. Next to the Stokehouse is the small Rotary playground for children and a kiosk with a curved corrugated tin roof painted red and white.

The long low building featuring two Moorish copper domed towers was the **St Kilda Sea Baths |15|**. The first baths on the site were constructed in the late 1840s, but were destroyed by fire in the 1920s and rebuilt. Decades later, sadly in need of repair, they closed for restoration in the early 1990s. Partially restored to their former glory, the project was halted by the complaints of locals worried about the extent of the refurbishment. Now a completion date is set for September 1999. On the other side of the road is the Catani Clock Tower, a well-known St Kilda landmark built in honour of Carlo Catani, who designed the nearby gardens.

Large signs proclaim the proximity of **St Kilda Pier |16|**, ferries to Williamstown and Southgate, penguin tours and fishing charters. Cross Pier Road and pass by another kiosk. A ramp leads to a pedestrian overpass that takes you to the Upper Esplanade. If you wish to have a browse at the market you should take this route. If not, we suggest walking halfway up the circular elevation to enjoy the view of the bay, the pier and the multitude of yachts moored out from the Royal Yacht Squadron, claiming to have been sailing since 1876. A statue of **Captain Cook |17|** gazes out over the water from the parkland below.

If you take the high road, you exit onto the upper Esplanade opposite the historic **Esplanade Hotel |18|**, just visible from Jacka Boulevard below. This historic pub, the Espy, much-loved by locals, was designed in 1877 by Smith & Johnson as a resort hotel. It numbers among its patrons a host of famous people, including actress Sarah Bernhardt in 1891, and arts patron and benefactor Alfred Felton, who took up residence in the 1890s. Over the years the hotel developed a reputation as one of the city's best live music venues and the centre of artistic counterculture, hosting non-mainstream music, comedy, theatre and poetry. Threatened on a number of occasions with demolition by latter-day developers, the preservation of the pub has become a cause celebre for St Kilda residents.

Built on the rim of the bay, the Stokehouse provides a great dining experience.

Near the corner of Jacka Boulevard and Fitzroy Street, overlooking Catani Gardens, is a sandstone monolith. Erected by the citizens of St Kilda in honour of residents who served and gave their lives in the First World War, it also carries a small plaque commemorating those who served in the Second World War. Walk further to the traffic lights, where you can cross Canterbury Road to the south end of Fitzroy Street.

Cafe society

Walk along the north side of Fitzroy Street so you can get a broader view of the bustling cafes on the other side. There must be over 100 in the strip and we will only mention a few. On the corner is the popular, stylish and simply named **Number One |19|**, with its upper level verandah a great place to eat in summer. At No. 9 is something of an institution, **Madam Joe Joe |20|**. At Acland Street you may like to detour right to visit Linden Arts Centre and Gallery (about a 5-minute walk). Built as the family home for Moritz Michaelis in 1870 to a Classical design by Alfred Kursteiner, Linden is one of the magnificent remnants of 19th-century St Kilda.

The Prince of Wales Hotel is on the north-east corner of Fitzroy and Acland streets, and further along, at No. 31, is **Cafe Di Stasio |21|** – a frenetic Italian eatery open seven days. On the north side of the road is **Bortolotto's |22|** at No. 16, a well-patronised Italian restaurant. On the east corner of Park Street is a grand old Victorian residence (18–20 Fitzroy Street), a somewhat shabby reminder of better days when there were three frontages. Built in 1881–82 in the Classical style, with arcaded verandahs, this was a one-time home of politician Sir Graham Berry, who arrived in Australia in 1852.

Cross Park Lane and Loch Street. Next to the terrace pair on the corner is Tolarno Boutique Hotel and **Tolarno Bar & Bistro |23|**, owned by television chef Iain Hewitson. This marvellous place was started in the 1960s by Frenchman Georges Mora and his artist wife, Mirka. She painted the murals that adorn the restaurant walls. There was an art gallery in the rear, Tolarno Galleries, which has long since moved to the northern suburb of Fitzroy. Next door at No. 50 is a beautifully restored terrace. Continue on to the corner of Canterbury Road, a good place from which to survey the **George Hotel |24|**, diagonally opposite and housing some of Melbourne's smartest eating and drinking venues. Another grand old dame of St Kilda, this was originally Bennett's Terminus Hotel dating from 1857, with later additions in 1885 and 1925. Bennett's, opposite the terminus of the Melbourne–St Kilda railway, which also opened in 1857, welcomed the first train passengers from the city. It was a favourite destination of honeymooners in the 19th century, and of wealthy squatters down from the bush. During a brief period in the 1880s it was owned by the mayor of St Kilda, Frederick Wimpole. Writer Hal Porter was assistant manager in the 1940s. A rock venue in the 1970s and a punk music place in the 1980s, the 1990s has seen it largely made over to apartments.

Over Canterbury Road is the Victory Cafe, in the restored **St Kilda Station |25|**, another St Kilda structure to suffer the ravages of fire. If you have managed to resist the delights of the cafe strip, this is a good place to end your journey. From here you can catch the light rail back to the city or walk to the St Kilda Junction and catch a tram or bus from there.

Walk key

1. Capitol Bakeries | **2.** Caffe e Cucina | **3.** Jam Factory | **4.** Old Baptist Church | **5.** Conway's Buildings | **6.** Love & Lewis building | **7.** Rechabite Hall | **8.** Maclellan & Co's Big Store | **9.** Dan Murphy's Cellar | **10.** Corder's Buildings | **11.** Colosseum Building | **12.** Holt's Chambers | **13.** Osment Buildings | **14.** Maples Furniture Emporium | **15.** Prahran Town Hall | **16.** Former court house and police station | **17.** Leggett Building | **18.** Ann Terrace | **19.** Finney Display | **20.** Prahran Market

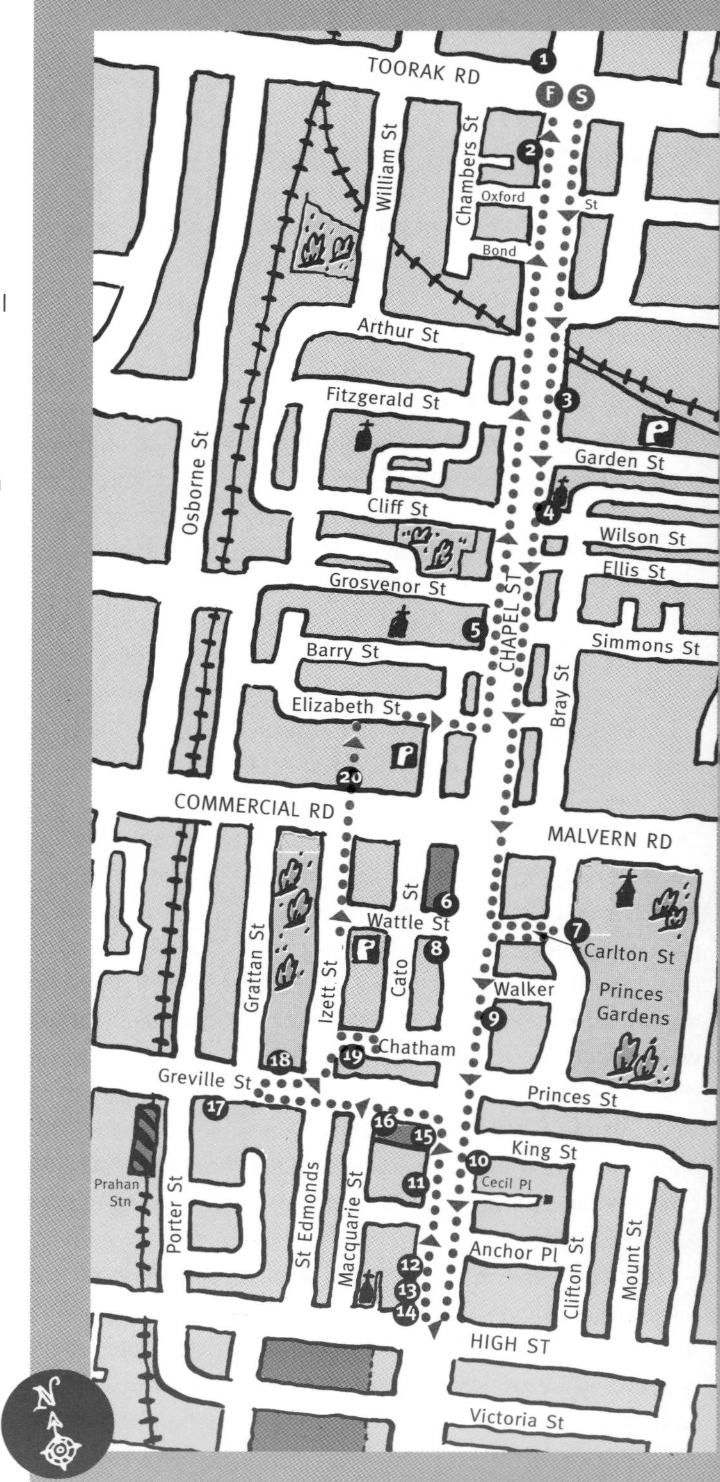

Walk No. 22

Chapel Street Precinct

Cosmopolitan sophistication amid down-at-heel facades

Start & Finish

Corner of Toorak Road and Chapel Street – train stations at South Yarra and Prahran are nearby; trams 8, 78, 79.

Length/Time

4 km/2 hours

Chapel Street has always been the centre of the city of Prahran, a microcosm of the community with its people from all walks of life. The first dwelling in Prahran is considered to have been Waterloo Cottage, built for Lieutenant Charles Forrest in 1841 on Forrest Hill at the north end of Chapel Street. It seems the street itself took its name from the first church in the area, the Congregational Chapel. In the 1850s the swampy bushland beside the Yarra became dotted with clay pits, brick-making factories and sawmills. Returned diggers from the goldfields settled in the area and small hamlets spread out from the river bank. The first Prahran Council was elected in 1856 and met in the Mechanics' Institute until the erection of the town hall in 1861. By 1858 Chapel Street was a well-used roadway.

Prahran was proclaimed a city in 1879 and in 1888 divided into four wards: Prahran, Windsor, Toorak and South Yarra. This structure remained for over 100 years, until 1994 when the city was amalgamated with Malvern to create the City of Stonnington.

Chapel Street is an extraordinary mix of cosmopolitan sophistication, high fashion boutiques, trend-setting youth and not-so-hip bargain seekers. Summer is the time to see the area and the people and you could spend a pleasurable hour or so sitting in a pavement cafe watching the world go by.

The northern end

The first section of the walk, starting at the Toorak Road corner, gives an idea of the industrial nature of the 19th-century streetscape. On the north-west corner is a large cream building occupied by an assortment of fast food outlets and a fun parlour. High on the facade is the name **Capitol Bakeries |1|**. The building was originally constructed as the Toorak Engine House to house the machinery that powered the cable for the cable trams, introduced in Melbourne in 1886. Betty Malone in her history of the street recounts how children delighted in being taken there to see the engines spinning. The introduction of electric trams in the 1920s made the machinery redundant and the building has changed hands many times, including a period when J.B. Stockdale converted it into a bakery.

On the south-west corner of Toorak Road is a Country Road store, built on the site of the South Yarra Arms Hotel. Until its demolition in the early 1990s, a hotel had stood on this spot since the 1850s; first the Ayres Arms, then the New Bridge and finally the South Yarra Arms. Further along on the right at No. 581 is the quintessential Melbourne Italian cafe, **Caffe e Cucina |2|**, so tiny you could miss it. From here to the Jam Factory, which hugs the south side of the railway line further along on the left, there are many young high fashion designers, including Collette Dinnigan at No. 553. There are some interesting specialty shops as well – Made in Japan is worth a browse. On the left on the corner of Palermo Street is the old Imperial Hotel, opened in 1876.

Over the railway line is the **Jam Factory |3|**, which was given a complete makeover in the mid-1990s. Originally built as a brewery, the structure was bought in 1876 by the Victoria Jam Company. Later trading as the Victoria Preserving Company, the firm produced jams, pickles and sauces, and canned fruits and vegetables. A change of ownership in 1885 brought a change of name, to the Australasian Jam Company (AJC), known locally as Peacock's Jam Factory after its owner George Peacock. When he retired in 1891 the factory was taken over by the firm of Henry Jones and Company. The Jam Factory now houses an entertainment and cinema complex, and Melbourne's first book and music superstore, Borders.

19th-century retail sector

One block past the Jam Factory on the north corner of Wilson Street is the **old Baptist Church |4|**. Not much seems to be known about the building, but it could have been erected as early as 1855, one year after the establishment of the church in Prahran. The building has taken on many guises in past decades, including that of clothing store and restaurant, and is now occupied by the Irish pub chain of Bridie O'Reilly. On the opposite side of the road, on the corner of Cliff Street, is the Black Prince Hotel dating from the 1850s. Called the Prince of Wales Hotel until 1988, this was built by W. Clifford, an early landowner, after whom the street probably takes its name. This is the oldest surviving hotel in Chapel Street.

On the right at Nos. 411–425 is **Conway's Buildings |5|**, a two-storey terrace of eight shops dating from 1890, still retaining its old iron-lace verandah. Francis Conway was a prosperous bootmaker who owned at least four large buildings in Chapel Street, all of which are still in use. (Another two, located just south of High Street, date from 1880 and 1881.) Following his death in 1914, the executors of his estate completed a final building just south of the town hall.

The little building on the corner of Barry Street was erected in 1910. On the left on the north-east corner of Simmons Street, opposite Conway's, is an old hotel, still with its tiled facade. Subject to many name changes over the years, it was built in about 1862 as the Morning Star Hotel.

Cross Malvern Road (on the west side of Chapel Street it becomes Commercial Road). On the south-west corner is Chapel Street's best known commercial landmark,

Opening Times

Prahran Market: Open Tue, Thur, Fri, dawn to 5pm, Sat, dawn to noon.

Refreshments

There are cafes and restaurants all along the walk, but if we had to recommend one it would be the **Greville Bar**, 143 Greville Street (9529 4800). Also wonderful is **Caffe e Cucina**, 581 Chapel Street (9827 4139), a 'living legend [that] plays host to the rich and famous as well as the impoverished and unknown with equal pleasure'.

Old Baptist Church, dating from the 1850s and now a popular pub venue.

formerly Read's and then Moore's store. In the 1880s a hotel occupied the site and George Read and his son had several small clothing shops nearby. By 1903 Charles Moore opened an emporium, which he named Charles Read Co. The store specialised in women's wear and imported the latest fashions from Paris. The attractive building features twin domes, which were used during the Second World War as lookout posts for spotting potential enemy aircraft. After extensive renovation in the early 1980s the building was transformed into Pran Central shopping centre.

On the north-west corner of Wattle Street is the **Love & Lewis building |6|**, established in 1913. Smaller than the neighbouring Read's store and concentrating on cheaper products, it sold drapery of all kinds. Make a short detour along Carlton Street, off to the left. At Nos. 2–4 Carlton Street, in an old brick building, is Grant's Old and Rare Books. The inside of the building retains a number of original features. At the far end, facing up Carlton Street, is the **Rechabite Hall |7|**, which is actually located at No.10 Little Chapel Street. This was built in 1888.

Walk back to Chapel Street and ahead of you, on the south-west corner of Wattle Street, is **Maclellan & Co's Big Store |8|** building. It was completed in 1902 and is now occupied by the Coles supermarket chain. Later in the walk you pass the back of the building, where the old signs remain: Drapery, Clothing, Ironmongery, Hosiery, Bedding, Mercury, Grocery, etc. Here shoppers could purchase practically anything until the store closed its doors in 1967. John Maclellan became a business partner with his uncle, Scottish-born William Gibson. After surviving the 1890s depression the firm established hosiery and woollen mills to supply their stores with manufactured products, including Gibsonia blankets – renowned at the time. Maclellan was later to merge his business interests with Foy's to become Foy & Gibson's, for long a well-known Melbourne department store.

Continue south and just past Walker Street you will see the old Centreway Arcade, occupied by **Dan Murphy's Cellar |9|**. This business arrived in Chapel Street in 1930, apparently trading from No.280, which had large cellars. The arcade was next door and when it failed as a shopping complex Dan Murphy's took over the premises. The Centreway Arcade, dating from about 1890, has a wonderful facade including among its features a moulded pair of eagles. Designed by George McMullen in 1889, it once housed about 30 shops, a bakehouse, large cellars and Turkish baths. Inside you can see rooms that would have been part of the baths, with low vaulted ceilings and interconnecting arched openings between them. In 1998 Dan Murphy's was bought by Coles, who plan to retain the name and the business.

Nos. 259–261, on the west side just before Greville Street, is the site of the building which first housed the Prahran Mechanics' Institute. These institutes were established from the 1850s for 'moral and mental improvement' and became meeting places for the local community. The Prahran institute was founded in about 1854 when some residents met to set up a committee, and by 1856 they had completed the Chapel Street building. The organisation declined in the latter part of the 19th century until an Act passed by the Victorian government incorporated the institute, thereby ensuring it had a committee made up of the mayor and council representatives. It again flourished as a community organisation. In the early 1900s the institute ran cooking classes and a technical art school at 140 High Street (just west of the Chapel Street corner). The organisation conceived, planned and financed the idea of a technical art school for Prahran and to this end they handed over the High Street building to the Education Department in 1915. This is now the central part of Swinburne University of Technology's Prahran Campus, and the Prahran Mechanics' Institute occupies the front of the building. By 1915 the Chapel Street premises had been reconstructed and since then has been let to retail firms, providing the institute with an income. Since 1920 it has concentrated its resources on providing an alternative library service to the community.

To the right is the imposing Prahran Town Hall building (now Stonnington City Hall), on the corner of Greville Street – a precinct included on the return journey. Opposite, on the left at No. 262, is a bookshop and newsagent that was formerly Hall's Book Store, a favourite with schoolchildren of the 1950s and 1960s. The timber staircase to the upstairs showroom is still intact.

Past the town hall on the right side are the Conway's Buildings referred to earlier. This building, as mentioned before, dates from 1914. On your left, at No. 242, is **Corder's Buildings |10|** with distinctive Art Deco features. Take a short walk down Cecil Place, off to the left, and have a look at the old Protestant Hall at the end of the street.

Back in Chapel Street at No. 234 you will find the building erected for Raybould's Funeral Parlours, established in 1852. On the right next to Conway's is a four-storey facade with massive Corinthian pillars rising the height of the first and second floors – this is the appropriately named **Colosseum Building |11|**, once a vast department store selling all sorts of elaborate soft furnishings and household furniture. Its founder was John Treadway who came to Australia in the 1860s. Walton's took over in 1963 and the large Colosseum store was closed in 1982. Opposite at Nos. 218–220 on the north-east corner of Anchor Place is the Olde Court building dating from 1895. On the south-east corner is Rudduck's Buildings, a four-fronted two-storey Victorian facade with a balustrade, once home to the estate agent firm of Arnold & Scott.

At No. 211 is **Holt's Chambers |12|**, now the Prahran Mission, which is part of the Uniting Church. The building was constructed just before the First World War. It has been occupied by knitting mills, dressmakers, jewellers and, during the Second World War, G.J. Coles and the RAAF. In 1944 the building was purchased by the Methodist Mission, which in 1977 became part of the Uniting Church. The building now houses offices, counselling rooms, a library, lounge and cafeteria.

The adjacent **Osment Buildings |13|** date from 1910, on the site of the original office of the *Telegraph* newspaper. William H. Osment bought the newspaper in 1861 and after his death in 1875 his son Henry, a partner in the business, sold the paper to Crabb & Brotherton in 1882. He repurchased it in 1895 when his son Arthur turned twenty-one. Brotherton later regained control of then-named Osment & Son.

Opposite is McPhee's Fine Antiques, in Holt's Chambers, Holywells Terrace, in a building dating from 1886. The business is one of the oldest traders in Chapel Street.

On the left, one building from the corner of High Street, is an Art Deco building, which has been occupied by a range of businesses. On the north-west corner is the old **Maples Furniture Emporium |14|**. This building was erected in 1906 by its owner Benjamin Nathan and originally featured a corner tower, demolished later during extensive renovations. The Maples Store dealt exclusively in furniture and fittings. A 1922 account quoted by Anthony Harvey described it as 'four storeys of green and oxblood art nouveau tiling surmounted by a small turret'.

On the south-west corner of High Street is the Duke of Windsor Hotel, which first operated as the Albion and was opened in 1859 by Richard and Charles Langridge. It was apparently one of the most popular of the early hotels. Retrace your steps to the town hall and Greville Street.

Greville Street precinct

This small street has a unique character. It is a fascinating enclave of funky cafes, memorabilia, bookshops and a Sunday market (12 noon–5pm). The railway station complex in Porter Street dates from 1895.

The Prahran Town Hall |15| stretches some way down Greville Street. It was constructed in three stages from 1860: first the hall, offices and reading room in 1861; second the clock tower in 1863; and third the post office and enlarged reading room in 1878 (a lending library followed in 1914). These buildings were constructed to a design by Crouch & Wilson in Classical Revival style and more ornate features were added in 1888 to a design by Charles D'Ebro. Built of brick which was later stuccoed, the interior of the building was severely damaged by fire in 1914, but essentially it has been the municipal centre of Prahran since 1860.

Behind the town hall and dating from 1886 are the **former court house and police station |16|** on the corner of Greville and Macquarie streets. Designed by Public Works architect C.R. Gilchrist in the Gothic Revival style, the two-storey court building, although constructed of brick, features a facade of sandstone and Waurn Ponds (near Geelong) limestone, along with ornamental ironwork and stained glass windows. Part of the police station is a large brick observation tower, tucked away in Macquarie Street.

There are some good bookshops in the street – one not far from the Court House is Elizabeth Campbell Old and Rare Books. At No. 142 is Cafe Blu Poles. A little further along is the **Leggett Building |17|**, built by Harry Leggett in 1919. In the 1920s dance era it claimed space for 4,000 dancers. On the north side of Greville Street, between Izett and Grattan streets, is **Ann Terrace |18|** dating from 1886. A worthwhile stop for lunch or a coffee is the Greville Bar, with its warm timber panelling and Italian food. The gates at the Izett Street entrance to the Grattan Street Gardens, and the fountain in the park, were both donated in 1910 by John Maclellan, one of the partners who operated the Big Store.

Retrace your steps and walk along Izett Street. In Chatham Street, at Nos. 20–30, you will find **Finney Display |19|**, a gallery and picture framing business. Next door to Finney is Beads and Buttons Galore, which has a great array of ribbons as well. Continue down Izett Street, past the back of the Big Store where you will see the signage mentioned earlier. Continue along until you reach Commercial Road.

Opposite the end of Izett Street is **Prahran Market |20|**, established in 1864. If it is a market day take a little time to browse among the stalls. The market is renowned for its fresh produce. The meat and fish hall, located on the west side, is a shopper's delight. The main market hall houses the fruit and vegetable stalls at one end and clothing and non-food items at the east end. The delicatessen section is at the front of the building facing Commercial Road. You can exit at the back of the market, then turn right into Elizabeth Street to make your way back onto Chapel Street. Retrace your steps to Toorak Road.

Bibliography

Among the Terraces. Carlton Forest Project/Carlton Association Historical Group, Melbourne, 1987.

Annear, Robyn. ***Bearbrass: Imagining Early Melbourne***. Reed Books, Melbourne, 1995.

Apperly, Richard, Irving, Robert & Reynolds, Peter. ***A Pictorial Guide to Identifying Australian Architecture***. Angus & Robertson, Sydney, 1989.

Armstrong, Mark. ***Melbourne: A Lonely Planet City Guide***. Lonely Planet, Melbourne, 1997.

Arnold, John (ed.). ***The Imagined City: Melbourne in the Mind of its Writers***. George Allen & Unwin, Sydney, 1983.

Australia's Yesterdays. A look at our recent past. Readers Digest, Sydney, 1974.

Australian Dictionary of Biography. Vols 1–11. Melbourne University Press, Melbourne, 1966–1988.

Barnard, Jill & Keating, Jenny. ***People's Playground: A History of Albert Park***. Chandos, Melbourne, 1996.

Bertram, Alexandra & Trumble, Angus. ***Edwardian Melbourne in Picture Postcards***. Miegunyah/Melbourne University Press, Melbourne, 1995.

Blainey, Geoffrey. ***A Game of Our Own***. Information Australia, Melbourne, 1990.

Blair's Guide to Victoria & Melbourne. 6th edn. Universal Press, Melbourne, 1994.

Book of Historic Towns. Readers Digest, Sydney, 1982.

Brodie, Bill & Marks, Stan. ***St Kilda Heritage Sketchbook***. Cosmos Books & Music, Melbourne, 1995.

Brookes, Graham & D'Byrd, Anna. ***Alive in Melbourne Victoria Australia***. Norline Enterprises, Melbourne, 1996.

Buckrich, Judith R. ***Melbourne's Grand Boulevard: The Story of St Kilda Road***. State Library of Victoria, Melbourne, 1996.

Burchett, Winston H. ***East Melbourne Walkabout***. Cypress Books, Melbourne, 1975.

Cafe Melbourne. A Guide to Inner City Eating. Shayne Farquhar, Melbourne, n.d.

Cannon, Michael (ed.). ***Historical Records of Victoria***. Vols 1–3. Victorian Government Printing Office, Melbourne, 1981–1984.

Cannon, Michael. ***Australia in the Victorian Age: 3: Life in the Cities***. Nelson, Melbourne, 1975.

Cannon, Michael. ***Australia: The Spirit of a Nation*** Currey O'Neil Ross, Melbourne, 1985.

Cannon, Michael. ***Melbourne After The Goldrush***. Loch Haven Books, Main Ridge, 1993.

Cannon, Michael. ***The Exploration of Australia***. Readers Digest, Sydney, 1987.

Carroll, Brian. ***Melbourne Sketchbook***. Loch Haven Books, Main Ridge, 1990.

Casey, Maie, *et al.* ***Early Melbourne Architecture: 1840 to 1888***. Oxford University Press, Melbourne, 1963.

Change and Tradition: A Portrait of the University of Melbourne. University of Melbourne, 1993.

Copping It Sweet: Shared Memories of Richmond. City of Richmond, Melbourne, 1988.

de Lacy Lowe, Marion. ***Walking Around Melbourne***. Leisure Press, Melbourne, Victoria, 1989.

Eidelson, Meyer. ***The Melbourne Dreaming: A Guide to the Aboriginal Places of Melbourne***. Aboriginal Studies Press, Canberra, 1997.

Ferguson, George. ***Some Early Australian Bookmen***. Australian National University Press, Canberra, 1978.

Fiddian, Marc. ***Civic Places: A Tableau of Australian Town Halls***. Pakenham Gazette, Pakenham, 1986.

Fitzroy: Melbourne's First Suburb. Cutten History Committee of the Fitzroy History Society, Hyland House, Melbourne, 1989.

Flower, Cedric. ***Treasures of Australia***. Currey O'Neil Ross, Melbourne, 1983.

Forell, Claude & Erlich, Rita. ***The Age Good Food Guide***. Anne O'Donovan, Melbourne, 1993–1999 (various editions).

Grant, James & Serle, Geoffrey. ***The Melbourne Scene 1803–1956***. Melbourne University Press, Melbourne, 1957.

Gray, Les. ***Carlton***. Sun Books, Melbourne, 1973.

Harvey, Anthony. ***The Melbourne Book***. Hutchinson, Melbourne, 1982.

Heritage Walk. (Series 1–7). City of Melbourne, Melbourne. n.d.

Hetherington, John. ***Portrait of Melbourne***. Ure Smith, Sydney, n.d.

Hewitt, Sue. ***Discovering Victoria's Bike Paths***. Sabey & Assoc, Melbourne, 1998.

Historic Buildings Council Register 1993. Historic Buildings Council Victoria, Melbourne, 1993.

Jones, Shar. ***J.W. Lindt Master Photographer***. Currey O'Neil Ross, Melbourne, Victoria, 1985.

Keating, John D. ***Mind the Curve!: A History of the Cable Tram***. Transit Australia Publishing, Sydney, 1996.

Lamattina, Jennifer. ***Beautiful B&Bs & Small Hotels: The discerning guide to charming accommodation in Victoria, Australia***. What Next? Productions, Melbourne, 1997.

Lewis, Hilary. ***South Parkville***. The Parkville Association, Melbourne, 1996.

Lewis, Miles (ed.). ***Victorian Churches: Their Origins, their Story, and their Architecture***. National Trust of Australia (Victoria), Melbourne, 1991.

Lewis, Miles. ***Melbourne: The City's History and Development***. City of Melbourne, Melbourne, 1992.

Lord, John (ed.). ***The Gardens of the City of Melbourne***. City of Melbourne, Melbourne, 1993.

Malone, Betty, *et al.* ***Prahran Historical Series.*** Vols 1–9. Prahran Historical Society, Melbourne, 1982–1988.

Martin, John S. ***The Danish Club Dannebrog In Melbourne Australia 1889–1989***. The Danish Club, Melbourne, 1989.

McConville, Chris. ***Aird's Guide to Melbourne***. Aird Books, Melbourne, 1989.

McCoy, Lisa. ***The Vic Venue Guide***. Hyland House, Melbourne, 1998.

Melbourne City of Charm. Axiom Publishers, Melbourne, 1997.

Mietta's Eating & Drinking in Melbourne. Hardie Grant, Melbourne, 1998.

Molony, John. ***The Penguin Bicentennial History of Australia***. Viking O'Neil, Melbourne, 1987.

Newnham, W.H. ***Melbourne Sketchbook***. Rigby, Adelaide, 1967.

Newnham, W.H. ***Melbourne: The Biography Of A City***. Cheshire, Melbourne, 1956.

Paine, Cameron & Shaw, Kate. ***The Esplanade Hotel 1878–***. The Esplanade Alliance, Melbourne, 1998.

Peachey, A.F. (ed.). ***Australian National Trust Properties Guide Book***. Australian Council of National Trusts, Canberra, 1995.

Peter, Graeme & Wilson, Drysdale. ***Melbourne Australia: Premier Attractions & Activities Within Melbourne & Victoria***. Handy Books, Melbourne, 1994.

Picturesque Atlas of Australasia. Facsimile edition. Ure Smith, Sydney, 1974.

Pierce, Peter. ***The Oxford Literary Guide to Australia***. Oxford University Press, Melbourne, 1987.

Priestly, Susan. ***The Victorians: Making Their Mark***. Fairfax Syme & Weldon, Sydney, 1984.

Reilly, Dianne & Carew, Jennifer. ***Sun Pictures of Victoria: the Fauchery–Daintree Collection 1858***. Currey O'Neil Ross, Melbourne, 1983.

Ridley, Ronald T. ***Melbourne's Monuments***. Melbourne University Press, Melbourne, 1996.

Robertson, E. Graeme. ***Decorative Cast Iron in Australia***. Currey O'Neil Ross, Melbourne, 1984.

Sagazio, Celestina. ***A Walk Through Italian Carlton***. National Trust (Victoria), 1988.

Sagazio, Celestina. ***Tour of the Melbourne General Cemetery***. National Trust of Australia (Victoria), Melbourne, 1998.

Scott, Ernest. ***Historical Memoir of the Melbourne Club***. Specialty Press, Melbourne, 1936.

Sendy, John. ***Melbourne's Radical Bookshops***. International Bookshop, Melbourne, 1983.

Slattery, Marshall. ***Historic Monuments: Melbourne General Cemetery***. Melbourne General Cemetery Trustees, Melbourne, 1978.

Smith, James. ***Historical Sketch of Victoria***. Lansdowne, Sydney, 1980.

South Melbourne's Heritage. City of South Melbourne, 1988.

Starke, Monica. ***The Alexandra Club. A N arrative 1903–1983***. Elm Grove Press, Melbourne, 1986.

The Gardens of the City of Melbourne. City of Melbourne, Melbourne, 1993.

The Heritage of Australia: The Illustrated Register of the National Estate. Macmillan, Melbourne, 1981.

The Royal Exhibition Building. Royal Exhibition Building Trustees, Melbourne, 1993.

Truslove, Colin. ***Fitzroy: Images of a Suburb***. Redpoint Books, Melbourne, 1991.

Turnbull, Clive (ed.). ***The Melbourne Album***. Georgian House, Melbourne, 1961.

U'Ren, Nancy & Turnbull, Noel. ***A History of Port Melbourne***. Oxford University Press, Melbourne, 1983.

Vellacott, Helen (ed.). ***A Girl at Government House***. Currey O'Neil, Melbourne, 1982.

Vellacott, Helen (ed.). ***Some Recollections of a Happy Life***. ***Marianne North in Australia & New Zealand.*** Edward Arnold, Melbourne, 1986.

Victoria Illustrated 1857 & 1862. Engravings from the original editions by S.T. Gill & N . Chevalier. Introduction by W.H. Newnham. Landsdowne Press, Melbourne, 1971.

Walking Melbourne. National Trust of Australia (Victoria), Melbourne, 1991.

Wilde, Sally. ***The History of Prahran Volume II 1925–1990***. Melbourne University Press, Melbourne, 1993.

CENTRAL MELBOURNE

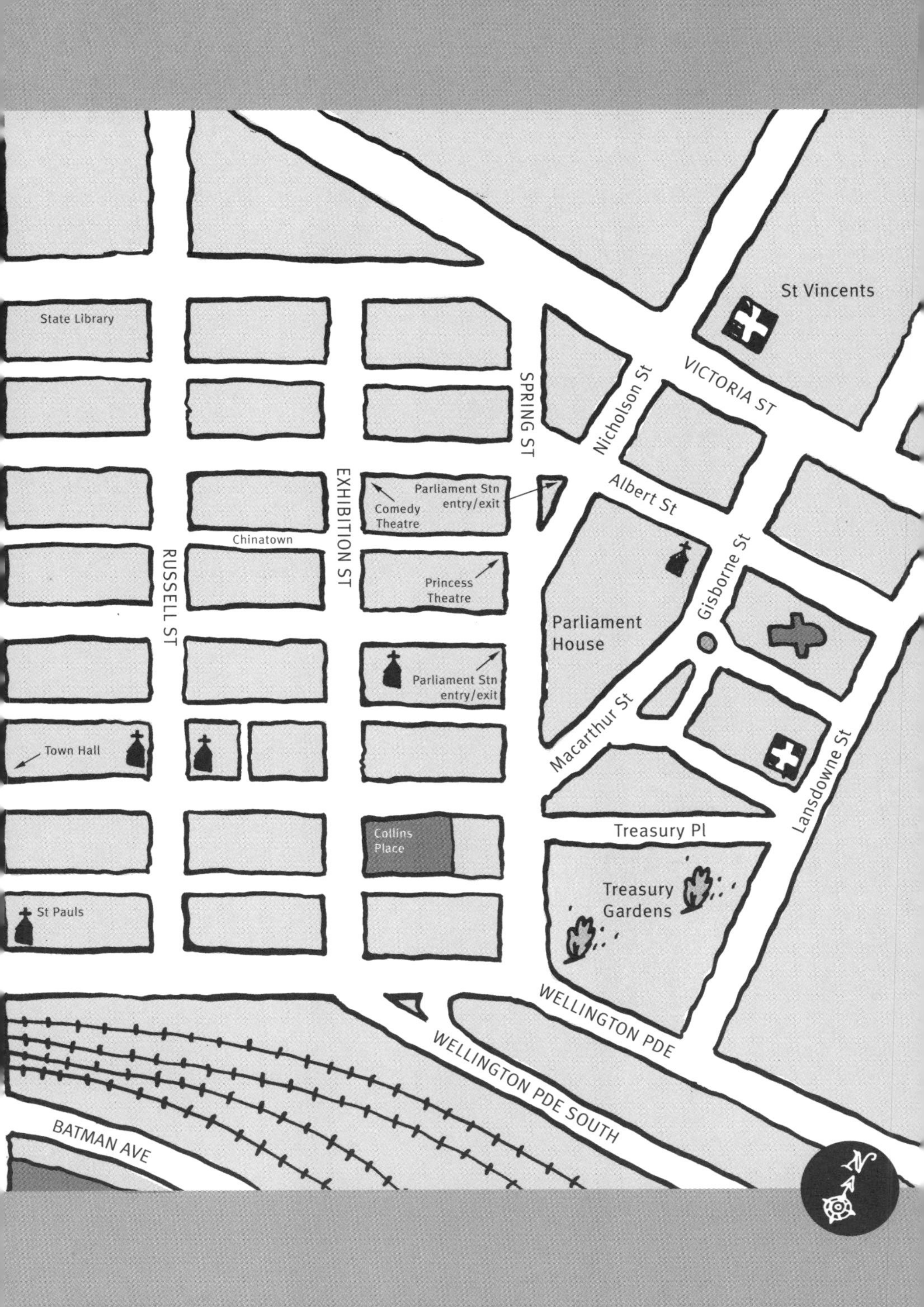

St Vincents
State Library
VICTORIA ST
SPRING ST
Nicholson St
Albert St
EXHIBITION ST
Parliament Stn entry/exit
Comedy Theatre
Chinatown
RUSSELL ST
Princess Theatre
Gisborne St
Parliament House
Parliament Stn entry/exit
Macarthur St
Town Hall
Lansdowne St
Treasury Pl
Collins Place
Treasury Gardens
St Pauls
WELLINGTON PDE
WELLINGTON PDE SOUTH
BATMAN AVE
N